D1418641

DOCAT

What to do?

DOCAT

What to do?

The Social Teaching
of the Catholic Church

With a Foreword by
Pope Francis

CATHOLIC TRUTH SOCIETY

Published by the Austrian Bishops' Conference. Approved by the Pontifical Council for Promoting the New Evangelization on 7th April 2016.

Revision of the translation: Reverend George Schultze, SJ
Nihil Obstat and Imprimatur for English translation:
+ Most Reverend Salvatore J. Cordileone, Archbishop of San Francisco 7th April 2016.

DOCAT was produced by Arnd Kuppers and Peter Schallenberg
in co-operation with Stefan Ahrens, Nils Baer, Thomas Berenz, Christoph Bohr, Marco Bonacker, Luisa Fischer, Julia Horstmann, Joachim Hupkes, Christoph Kraus, Markus Krienke, Gerhard Kruip, Hermann von Laer, Anton Losinger, Bertram Meier, Bernhard Meuser, Elmar Nass, Ursula Nothelle-Wildfeuer, Martin Schlag, Walter Schweidler, Christian Stoll, Cornelius Sturm, Markus Vogt, Anno Zilkens and Elisabeth Zschiedrich.

Original German edition: DOCAT - Was tun? Die Soziallehre der katholischen Kirche
© 2016 YOUCAT Foundation GmbH, a division of the international papal charity Aid to the Church in Need with headquarters in Königstein in Taunus, Germany

Cover, Layout, Design, Illustrations by Alexander von Lengerke, Cologne, Germany

Published by the Incorporated Catholic Truth Society,
40-46 Harleyford Road
London
SE11 5AY
Tel: 020 7640 0042
Fax: 020 7640 0046
© 2016 The Incorporated Catholic Truth Society
ISBN: 978-1-78469-131-8

From the proceeds of its publications and from donations, the not-for-profit YOUCAT Foundation gGmbH supports worldwide projects of New Evangelization which encourage young people to discover the Christian faith as a foundation for their lives.

You can help further the work of the YOUCAT Foundation with your donations, which can be made through:

Deutsche Bank AG
BLZ: 720 700 24
Account No.: 031 888 100
IBAN: DE13 7207 0024

About this book

DOCAT is a popular adaptation of the social doctrine of the Catholic Church, as it has been developed in important documents since Pope Leo XIII. Young people especially ought to take an interest in reading the major documents of the Church in the original text and in guiding their actions by the maxims of truth, justice, and charity that are contained in them. Again and again Pope Francis challenges Christians to become actively involved in working for greater justice in the world: "A Christian who in these times is not a revolutionary is not a Christian."

The Symbols and Their Meaning

 Here a passage from a book of the Bible is quoted that helps you to understand more deeply the passage you are reading right now.

 This signals a quotation. Sometimes it underscores the meaning of the text; other times it creates a tension with the text. The point is always to foster a living confrontation with the truth.

 The quotations that are marked with the symbol of St Peter's Basilica contain the current magisterial teaching of the pope, but also important statements by his immediate predecessors.

 Here terms are defined or explained.

The coloured squares followed by numbers at the end of each Q&A refer to thematically related passages in the Compendium of Social Doctrine (→), the Catechism (→) or YOUCAT ( ).

Contents

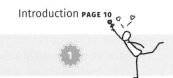

God's Master Plan: Love

Together We Are Strong: The Church's Social Mission

Unique and Infinitely Valuable: The Human Person

4

The Common Good, Personhood, Solidarity, Subsidiarity: The Principles of the Church's Social Teaching

QUESTIONS 84 TO 111

with the collaboration of Christoph Krauss and Joachim Hüpkes

Why we speak about four major principles of social doctrine; how they are ethically justified and put into practice. And why they are especially well qualified to analyze and improve societal conditions. **PAGE 90**

5

The Foundation of Society: The Family

QUESTIONS 112 TO 133

with the collaboration of Ursula Nothelle-Wildfeuer and Elisabeth Zschiedrich

Why the family is the germ cell of society, what the family accomplishes for society, why the family life-style is particularly exposed to dangers (and not just today), and why it must therefore be especially protected. **PAGE 114**

6

Occupation and Vocation: Human Work

QUESTIONS 134 TO 157

with the collaboration of Arnd Küppers

Why work is not a curse but an expression of human self-realization. Why work makes us collaborators with God. Why work is for man and not man for work. **PAGE 134**

Welfare and Justice for All: Economic Life

QUESTIONS 158 TO 194

with the collaboration of Hermann von Laer and Martin Schlag

Why economic life has its own laws. Why economic activity is humanly just only if all who are involved gain something from it. Why the market, too, has limits and how we can respond to globalization. **PAGE 156**

From important Church documents **PAGE 180**

Power and Morality: The Political Community

QUESTIONS 195 TO 228

with the collaboration of Markus Krienke and Christoph Böhr

Why politics needs foundations, legitimacy, and an ethical framework in order to be humane and useful. Why Christians cannot stay out of politics. Why Christians stand up for freedom and justice for all. And why it is in their best interests to be good citizens. **PAGE 184**

From important Church documents **PAGE 206**

One World, One Humanity:
The International Community

QUESTIONS 229 TO 255

with the collaboration of Gerhard Kruip, Julia Horstmann and Luisa Fischer

Why Christians must respond with new methods to a radically changing world. Why the Church has a special option for the poor and how we can organize solidarity and global co-operation. **PAGE 208**

From important Church documents **PAGE 234**

10 Safeguarding Creation: The Environment

11 Living in Freedom from Violence: Peace

12 Personal and Societal Commitment: Love in Action

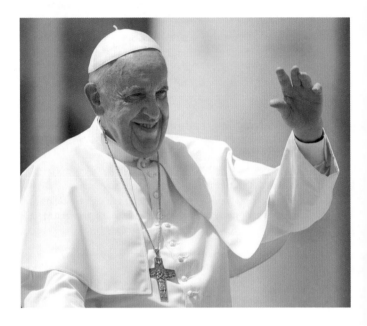

Dear Young People!

My predecessor, Pope Benedict XVI, put into your hands a Youth Catechism, YOUCAT. Today I would like to commend to you another book, DOCAT, which contains the social doctrine of the Church.

The English verb "to do" is part of the title. DOCAT answers the question: "What should we do?"; it is like a user's manual that helps us to change ourselves with the Gospel first, and then our closest surroundings, and finally the whole world. For with the power of the Gospel, we can truly change the world.

Jesus says: "As you did it to one of the least of these my brethren, you did to me." Many saints were shaken to the core by this passage from the Bible. On account of it, St Francis of Assisi changed his whole life. Mother Teresa converted because of this saying. And Charles de Foucauld acknowledges: "In all of the Gospel, there is no saying that had greater influence on me and changed my life more deeply than this: 'Whatsoever you did for one of the least of my brethren, you did for me.' When I reflect that these words come from the mouth of Jesus, the Eternal Word of God, and that it is the same mouth that says, 'This is my Body, ... this is my Blood ...', then I see that I am called to seek and to love Jesus above all in these little ones, in the least."

Dear young friends! Only conversion of heart can make our world, which is full of terror and violence, more humane. And that means patience, justice, prudence, dialogue, integrity, solidarity with victims, the needy, and the poorest, limitless dedication, love even unto death for the sake of the other. When you have understood that quite deeply, then you can change the world as committed Christians. The world cannot continue down the path that it is taking now. If a Christian in these days looks away from the need of the poorest of the poor, then in reality he is not a Christian!

Can we not do more to make this revolution of love and justice a reality in many parts of this tormented planet? The social doctrine of the Church can help so many people! Under the experienced direction of Cardinals Christoph Schönborn and Reinhard Marx, a team set to work to bring the liberating message of Catholic social doctrine to the attention of the youth of the world. They collaborated with famous scholars and also with young people on this project. Young Catholic women and men from all over the world sent in their best photos. Other young people discussed the text, offered their questions and suggestions, and made sure that the text is readily comprehensible. Social doctrine calls that "participation"! The team itself applied an important principle of the social doctrine from the start. Thus DOCAT became a magnificent introduction to Christian action.

What we call Catholic social teaching today came about in the nineteenth century. With industrialization, a brutal form of capitalism arose: a sort of economy that destroyed human beings. Unscrupulous industrialists reduced the impoverished rural population to the point where they toiled in mines or in rusty factories for starvation wages. Children no longer saw the light of day. They were sent underground like slaves to pull coal carts. With great commitment, Christians offered aid to those in need, but they noticed that that was not enough. So they developed ideas for counteracting the injustice socially and politically as well. Actually the fundamental proclamation of Catholic social doctrine was and is the 1891 encyclical letter by Pope Leo XIII, *Rerum novarum,* "On Capital and Labour." The Pope wrote clearly and unmistakably: "To defraud any one of wages that are his due is a great crime which cries to the avenging anger of heaven." With the full weight of her authority, the Church fought for the rights of the workers.

Because the needs of the time demanded it, Catholic social teaching was increasingly enriched and refined over the years. Many people debated about community, justice, peace, and the common good. They found the principles of personhood, solidarity, and subsidiarity, which DOCAT, too, explains. But actually this social doctrine does not come from any particular pope or from any particular scholar. It comes from the heart of the Gospel. It comes from Jesus himself. Jesus is the social teaching of God.

"This economy kills", I wrote in my apostolic exhortation *Evangelii Gaudium,* for today that economy of exclusion and disparity of incomes still exists. There are countries in which 40 or 50 percent of the young people are unemployed. In many societies, older people are marginalized because they seemingly have no "value" and are no longer "productive". Great stretches of land are depopulated because the poor of the earth flee to the slums of the major cities in the hope of finding something left there on which to survive. The production methods of a globalized economy have destroyed the modest economic and agricultural structures of their native regions. By now, approximately 1 percent of the world's population owns 40 percent of the entire wealth of the world, and 10 percent of the world's population owns 85 percent of the wealth. On the other hand, just about 1 percent of this world "belongs" to half of the world's population. About 1.4 billion human beings live on less than one euro [approximately 75p] per day.

When I invite you all now really to get to know the social doctrine of the Church, I am dreaming not just about groups that sit under trees and discuss it. That is good! Do that! My dream is of something greater: I wish I had a million young Christians or, even better, a whole generation who are for their contemporaries "walking, talking social doctrine". Nothing else will change the world but people who with Jesus devote themselves to it, who with him go to the margins and right into the middle of the dirt. Go into politics, too, and fight for justice and human dignity, especially for the poorest of the poor. All of you are the Church. Make sure, then, that this Church is transformed, that she is alive, because she allows herself to be challenged by the cries of the dispossessed, by the pleading of the destitute, and by those for whom nobody cares.

Become active yourselves, also. When many do that together, then there will be improvements in this world and people will sense that the Spirit of God is working through you. And maybe then you will be like torches that make the path to God brighter for these people.

And so I give you this magnificent little book, hoping that it might kindle a fire in you. I pray every day for you. Pray for me, too!

Yours truly,

Franciscus

Francis

6th November 2015

1

QUESTIONS
1–21

God's
Master Plan

LOVE

"

The world is created for the honour of God.

Vatican Council I

" I am created to do something or to be something for which no one else is created; I have a place in God's counsels, in God's world, which no one else has; whether I be rich or poor, despised or esteemed by man, God knows me and calls me by my name.

BL. JOHN HENRY NEWMAN (1801–1890), English cardinal and philosopher

1 *Did God act according to a plan when he created the world and us?*

Yes, God created the whole world according to his idea and plan. Just as a human being can devise a game, for instance draughts or chess, and with the rules for playing it creates the entire logic of the game, so God created the world and mankind. The red thread running through God's creation is love. God's plan, therefore, is that human beings should love and respond to God's love and thus think, speak, and act in love themselves. (Cf. Eph 3:9)

→ 20 → 2062 → 1, 2

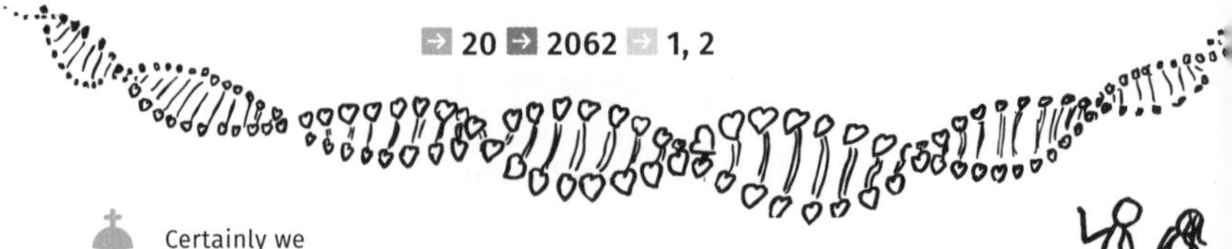

Certainly we come from our parents and we are their children, but we also come from God who has created us in his image and called us to be his children. Consequently, at the origin of every human being there is not something haphazard or chance, but a loving plan of God.

POPE BENEDICT XVI, 9th July 2006

2 *Who is God in the first place?*

God, we can say, is the origin of all that exists. He is the final reason for and the ultimate cause of all things, who also keeps them in existence. With reference to contemporary science, we can say: He is before the Big Bang and is the origin of all the laws of nature. Without God, everything that exists would collapse. God is also the goal of everything that exists.

→ 34, 279 ff. → 33

3   *What significance does God have for our actions?*

If God is the originator of the whole cosmos, then he is also the standard for everything that ought to be. All actions are measured against him and his plan. This is how we can recognize what good actions are. To put it intuitively: God wrote the DNA of our lives; it is in freely choosing to follow the instructions he has made part of us that we fulfill our God-given potential. What God wants for us and of us is the norm and the rule of a good, righteous life. Christians act with solidarity because God first treated them lovingly.

➡ **20, 25, 26** ➡ **1694**

> For you created all things, and by your will they existed and were created.
> **REV 4:11**

> O Lord, how manifold are your works! In wisdom you have made them all.
> **PS 104:24**

> " What was not part of my plan was part of God's plan. And the more often something like this happens to me, the more convinced I become in faith that—from God's perspective—there is no chance.
> **ST EDITH STEIN** (1891–1942), German-Jewish philosopher, concentration camp victim, *Finite and Eternal Being* (1935/1936)

> " Three things are necessary to man for salvation: to know what he should believe, to know what he should desire, and to know what he should do.
> **ST THOMAS AQUINAS** (1225–1274), a great Christian thinker of the Middle Ages, *On the Ten Commandments* (Prologue)

4   *Can we experience God?*

If you reflect on yourself, you soon recognize that you did not make yourself. No one asked you whether you actually wanted to exist or would rather not. You were suddenly there. The next thing that you recognize is that you are finite. Today, tomorrow, or the day

To say "I love you"
is to say "You shall
not die."

GABRIEL MARCEL (1889–1973) French philosopher

All created things show the goodness and generosity of the Creator; the sun sheds light, the fire heat, every tree extends its arms, which are its boughs, and yields us the fruit which it produces, and the water and the air, and all nature shows forth the liberality of the Creator. It is because of avarice, I say, that we who are His living image do not represent Him, but by our unloving selfishness deny Him in our actions, although with our mouth we confess Him.

ST PHILIP NERI (1515–1595)

after tomorrow your life will be over. And everything around you will no longer exist someday. Nevertheless, you can think about the infinite: something that exists but will not pass away. Therefore, although you are surrounded exclusively by transitory things, you long for what is infinite and does not pass away. You would like something of yourself to last. How sad it would be, too, if the whole beautiful world were only a snapshot, a meaningless flash that sinks again into nothingness. Only if God really exists are you in safekeeping with him. And all of creation is kept in being, too. Having an idea of God and longing for him are part of being human. Yearning for the infinite and absolute is found in all cultures.

➡ **20** ➡ **1147** ➡ **20**

5   *Why did God create man and the world?*

God created the world out of his overflowing love. He would like us to love him as he loves us. He wants to gather us into the great family of his Church.

➡ **49, 68, 142** ➡ **2**

6   *If God created the world out of love, then why is it full of injustice, oppression, and suffering?*

God created the world as something good in itself. But man fell away from God, deciding against God's love and bringing evil into the world. The Bible tells about this in the story of the first sin and fall of Adam and Eve. Human beings—the story about the Tower

You love all things that exist, and you loathe none of the things which you have made, for you would not have made anything if you had hated it.
WIS 11:24

I have seen the affliction of my people who are in Egypt, and have heard their cry because of their taskmasters; I know their sufferings, and I have come down to deliver them out of the hand of the Egyptians.
EX 3:7–8

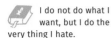

Sin is the prison in which we are all born.

ST IGNATIUS OF LOYOLA
(1491–1556), Founder of the Jesuits

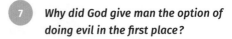

I do not do what I want, but I do the very thing I hate.

The Apostle Paul in
ROM 7:15

Full power to sin is not the key to freedom. Free will is not the independence of the creature, but rather his self-realization in perfect dependence.

ST CATHERINE OF SIENA
(1786–1859), Third Order Dominican, mystic, and theologian

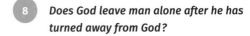

There are those who say: "I have committed too many sins, the Good Lord cannot forgive me." This is a gross blasphemy. It is the same as putting a limit on God's mercy, which has none: it is infinite. Nothing offends the Good Lord as much as doubting his mercy.

ST JOHN VIANNEY (1786–1859), the Curé of Ars

of Babel explains—wanted to be like God. Since then there has been a flaw in the fabric of the world, a destructive principle. Since then nothing is quite as God planned it to be. Our present decisions also contribute to the fact that there is injustice, oppression, and suffering in this world. Many wrong decisions can sometimes coalesce into structures of evil and sin. The individual must therefore live within a system that on the whole is evil and unjust, and it is not at all easy to distance oneself from it, for example, when a soldier is obliged to participate in an unjust war.

→ 27 → 365 ff., 415 → 66, 68

7 *Why did God give man the option of doing evil in the first place?*

God created man to love. One cannot be forced to love, however; love is always voluntary. If a human being is really to be able to love, he must therefore be free. If there is genuine freedom, however, there is always the possibility also of deciding in a way that is fundamentally wrong. We human beings can even destroy freedom itself.

→ 311 ff. → 286

8 *Does God leave man alone after he has turned away from God?*

No. God's "love never ends" (1 Cor 13:8). He goes after us, looks for us in our caves and hiding places, wishes to come into contact with us. He wishes to show us who he is.

→ 27, 773

9 *How can God be found?*

God can be found only if he *shows* himself to us or (to say the same thing with another word) reveals himself to us. We do have by nature an intuition of

God and can also recognize through reflection the fact *that* God exists. But it is beyond our understanding exactly *what* God is like, what his thoughts and plans are. God himself, therefore, must communicate to us what he is like. He does not do that by sending us an idea, a book, or a political system; he did so by becoming man. In Jesus Christ God revealed himself completely and definitively: God became man so that man might understand who God is. Jesus is God's language.

➡ 20, 21 ➡ 36–38 ➡ 7–10

10 How did God reveal himself to mankind before Jesus?

The existence of God was never beyond the knowledge of human reason. Over the history of Israel's faith, God revealed something of his interior life and spoke to Abraham, Isaac, and Jacob. He commanded Moses to free his people from slavery in Egypt. Again and again he called prophets to speak and act publicly in his name.

➡ 54 ff. ➡ 7–8

11 How do the People of Israel respond to God's communication of himself?

When God shows himself, man must set everything else aside and reflect on how his life is changed in the sight of the living God. Once God is known, nothing can remain as it was. The People of Israel make this clear through their response to the covenant God makes with them. God gave the Ten Commandments to Moses on Mount Sinai (Ex 19–24). If we obey the Commandments and so try to act justly, then that is our response to God's loving gift. In that way we have the opportunity to collaborate in God's master plan for the world and for history.

➡ 22 ➡ 34

For as the heavens are higher than the earth, so are my ways higher than your ways and my thoughts than your thoughts. For my thoughts are not your thoughts, neither are your ways my ways, says the LORD.
IS 55:8–9

God so loved the world that he gave his only-begotten Son, that whoever believes in him should not perish but have eternal life.
JN 3:16

MASTER PLAN 1

In all cultures there are examples of ethical convergence, some isolated, some interrelated, as an expression of the one human nature, willed by the Creator; the tradition of ethical wisdom knows this as the natural law.

POPE BENEDICT XVI, from the Encyclical CARITAS IN VERITATE (CiV 59)

ENCYCLICAL
Papal teaching document

12 *What significance do the Ten Commandments have for our life together?*

In the Ten Commandments, God supplies us with the everlasting principles of the good life. We can rely on them as a guide. And this brings about a world as God designed it to be. In them we learn what our duties are—for example, we must not steal from anyone—and at the same time, our rights become clear: no one may steal from us, either. The content of the Ten Commandments is similar to that of natural law, in other words, what is written on the heart of every human being as a notion of good action. In them universal ways of acting are described that are binding for all human beings and cultures. Hence the Ten Commandments are also the basic rules of life together in society.

➡ **22** ➡ **434** ➡ **335, 348 ff.**

❝❞ Again and again I wonder about this: There are more than thirty million laws worldwide to enforce the Ten Commandments.

ALBERT SCHWEITZER (1875–1965), missionary doctor and Nobel Peace Prize winner

13 *How does God reveal himself in Jesus of Nazareth?*

❝❞ To me Jesus is my God, Jesus is my life, Jesus is my only Love, Jesus is my All in all, Jesus my everything. Jesus, I love you with my whole heart, with my whole being.

ST TERESA OF CALCUTTA (1910–1997), Nobel Peace Prize winner

In Jesus Christ, God's self-revelation reaches its highest point. In his person, as true man and true God, the love of God manifests itself in an absolute and unsurpassable way. In him the Word of God became flesh, as the beginning of the Gospel of John reports. Who God is and how he encounters man becomes visible and even physically tangible in Jesus Christ. So he can say: "He who has seen me has seen

the Father" (Jn 14:9). Christ became like to us human beings in everything except sin: consequently, Jesus is the ideal human being, man according to God's master plan. Jesus lived out the will of God: love. To be a Christian means to come as near to Jesus as possible. Through

the sacraments we even enter into Jesus; we become "the Body of Christ".

➡ 28–29 ➡ 456 ff. ➡ 9–10

The weakness of human means is a source of strength. Jesus is the Master of the Impossible.

BL. CHARLES DE FOUCAULD (1858–1916)

As you did it to one of the least of these my brethren, you did it to me.

MT 25:40

14 *What is the new commandment of love in the New Testament?*

The Golden Rule ("Treat others as you would have them treat you") is recognized in many cultures as a norm of the good life. The commandment of love in the Old Testament is even more forceful: "You shall love your neighbour as yourself" (Lev 19:18). Jesus intensifies the commandment of mutual love and makes it more specific by attaching it to himself and the sacrifice of his life: "This is my commandment, that you love one another as I have loved you" (Jn 15:12). This love is oriented toward *community* and the *individual* in equal measure: everyone matters, as a unique, unrepeatable person loved by God—and through love everyone relies on others. Divine love is the beginning of a "civilization of love" (Popes Paul VI and John Paul II), to which all human beings can contribute.

➡ 54 ➡ 2055 ➡ 322

Love begins today. Today somebody is suffering, today somebody is in the street, today somebody is hungry. Our work is for today, yesterday has gone, tomorrow has not yet come. We have only today to make Jesus known, loved, served, fed, clothed, sheltered. Do not wait for tomorrow. Tomorrow we will not have them if we do not feed them today.

ST TERESA OF CALCUTTA

VIRTUE
(from Latin *virtus*, power) is an acquired, habitual disposition that helps a person do good more readily.

 Is man called to love?

Yes, it is profoundly in keeping with human nature to be loved and to offer love. In this, God himself serves as our ideal. Jesus showed us that the very being of God is love. Between the Father, the Son, and the Holy Spirit, an eternal exchange of love takes place. A loving human being, too, has a share in this communion of love. Our life can succeed only if we do not shut ourselves off from the stream of divine love but rather open our hearts to it. Love causes us to be open to the needs of our neighbour and makes us capable of going beyond ourselves. Jesus Christ, who out of love for mankind freely sacrificed himself on the Cross, accomplished the greatest deed of love precisely by going beyond his own human life.

➡ **34–37** ➡ **1, 260** ➡ **309**

16   Is loving your neighbour something you can practise and learn?

Yes. Indeed, it is very important. Love is not only a feeling. Love is also a → VIRTUE, a power than can be trained. Becoming braver and bolder, as well as more just and more loving is a true challenge for every Christian. We must learn to look at the world from the other person's perspective. People whom we meet with sincere goodwill sense that they are being taken seriously as persons and can express themselves freely. If we practise love when it is easy to do so, we will become, with God's help, increasingly capable of loving even when it is painful and when we are not "loved in return". This is the case in caring for the poorest of the poor, and it is even more true when we have to deal in a new way with our opponents: renouncing revenge, retaliation, and violence.

➡ **105, 160, 184, 193** ➡ **2052, 2055, 2069, 2443–2446** ➡ **321, 328**

17   *Is there meaning and progress in history?*

Salvation, the definitive wholeness and perfect happiness that is granted to us through Jesus Christ, is not something that only a few people can attain. God wants the salvation of all mankind. This salvation liberates man in all his dimensions: as body and spirit, personally and socially, in his earthly history and forever in heaven. In history, and therefore in the time in which we find ourselves, this salvation is already dawning; however, it will be perfect only in eternity. Hence we must reject all political ideologies that promise salvation already on earth. The fact that we will find paradise only in heaven is not a consolation prize, nor is it disdain for the world. Rather, because of our hope for eternal life, we can shape the here and now in justice and love. Nothing good that we do here on earth is in vain; rather, it is taken up into the perfection of eternity.

> There is no intelligible history without a religion.
> **G.K. CHESTERTON** (1874–1936), English author and journalist

> Christians remain people of hope even amidst recurrent disappointments.
> **AL KRESTA,** broadcaster, journalist, and author

→ 40–58 → 450 → 110

> It seems to me that we cannot accomplish any good while we indulge in self-seeking.
> **ST THÉRÈSE OF LISIEUX** (1873–1897), Carmelite and Doctor of the Church

18   *How does a change of society come about?*

The Good News of the Bible, God's self-revelation, changes us in every respect. We acquire a new way of looking at the world and our society. All change starts in the human heart: first, the person himself must change interiorly and think and live according to God's command; then, he can work outwardly, too. Conversion of heart, for which we must strive ever anew, is the real beginning of a better world. Only through that conversion do we recognize how institutions and systems must be changed and improved.

> Someone who has no love, not even for one human being, cannot please God. Let us love all people, as Jesus loved them, by wanting for them all the good things that He wanted for them, by doing for them as much good as we can, by committing ourselves to their salvation, ready and willing to give our blood for each one of them.
> **BL. CHARLES DE FOUCAULD**

→ 42 → 1889

> If you do not love your brother who is right before your eyes, you cannot love God whom you do not see.

ST AUGUSTINE
(354–430), Doctor of the Church, the greatest thinker in the early Church

> For those who love God, He turns all things into good; God even allows their wanderings and errors to be for their good.

ST AUGUSTINE (354–430)

19 Why is man's selfishness the core of every human sin?

As long as man looks at himself egotistically, he wastes away. We are made in such a way that we are not enough for ourselves. We need human community and a liberating orientation toward the meaning and source of our being, ultimately toward God. We must go out of ourselves, because we are created for love. By loving, we go beyond ourselves, toward another person and ultimately toward God. Being turned in on oneself is synonymous with sinning. Someone who does not (or cannot) love is living in self-imposed alienation. This is true also for whole societies. Where production and consumption and prolonging life come first, there will be a lack of solidarity and real humanity.

→ 47–48 → 400 → 315

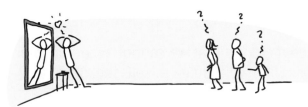

20 What is the Church's task in God's master plan?

> What good would it do if a man gained and owned the whole world and then sat there with stomach cancer, heartburn, and a swollen prostate?

JOHN STEINBECK
(1902–1968), American writer

The master plan of God's love is the salvation and redemption of all men through his Son, Jesus Christ. The Church exists because Jesus invited us to enter into deep, saving communion with him. This communion, the "Body of Christ", is the Church. Through baptism and the other sacraments, we belong to Christ and, through him, are endowed with a new, everlasting life. Through heeding the word of God, we obey his will. The Church is the place where we can develop in God's love. The Church is not an end in herself.

She bears responsibility for mankind and society and must by her work contribute to the peace and development of the human family.

➔ **49–51** ➔ **122, 123**

21   *Is the Kingdom of God already visible in the Church?*

The Church exists "in order that space may be made in the world for God, so that he may dwell therein and the world may thus become his 'Kingdom'" (Joseph Ratzinger). With Jesus Christ, the Kingdom of God has really started in the world. Wherever the sacraments are administered, the old world of sin and death is conquered at its root and transformed. A new creation begins; the Kingdom of God becomes visible. The sacraments are only empty signs, however, if Christians do not translate the new life that has been granted them into authentic action. One cannot go to Communion and at the same time deny others their daily bread. The sacraments call us to a love that is willing "to go out of [itself] and to go to the peripheries, not only geographically, but also to the existential peripheries: the mystery of sin, of suffering, of injustice, of ignorance and indifference to religion, of intellectual currents, and of all sorts of poverty" (speech by Cardinal Bergoglio in the pre-conclave, 2013).

➔ **49–51** ➔ **123, 124**

> " The Church serves those in need not because they are Catholic but because we are.
>
> **BISHOP FULTON J. SHEEN** (1895–1979),
> American bishop, radio, and television preacher

> " The Church is called to go out of herself and to go to the peripheries, not only geographically, but also to the existential peripheries: the mystery of sin, of suffering, of injustice, of ignorance and indifference to religion, of intellectual currents, and of all sorts of poverty.
>
> **CARDINAL BERGOGLIO (POPE FRANCIS)**
> before the 2013 conclave

Jesus opened the book and found the place where it was written, "The Spirit of the Lord is upon me, because he has anointed me to preach good news to the poor. He has sent me to proclaim release to the captives and recovering of sight to the blind, to set at liberty those who are oppressed, to proclaim the acceptable year of the Lord." And he closed the book, and gave it back to the attendant, and sat down; and the eyes of all in the synagogue were fixed on him. And he began to say to them, "Today this Scripture has been fulfilled in your hearing.

LK 4:18–21

From important Church documents

LOVE

Christian Love

Mater et Magistra

Animated, too, by the charity of Christ, [a Christian] finds it impossible not to love his fellow men. He makes his own their needs, their sufferings, and their joys. There is a sureness of touch in all his activity in every field. It is energetic, generous, and considerate. For "charity is patient, is kind; charity envieth not, dealeth not perversely, is not puffed up, is not ambitious, seeketh not her own, is not provoked to anger, thinketh no evil; rejoiceth not in iniquity, but rejoiceth with the truth; beareth all things, believeth all things, hopeth all things, endureth all things" (1 Cor 13:4–7).

Pope St John XXIII, Encyclical Mater et Magistra (1961), 257

Love Has a Name

Redemptor Hominis

The God of creation is revealed as the God of redemption, as the God who is "faithful to himself" and faithful to his love for man and the world, which he revealed on the day of creation. His is a love that does not draw back before anything that justice requires in him. Therefore "for our sake (God) made him (the Son) to be sin who knew no sin." If he "made to be sin" him who was without any sin whatever, it was to reveal the love that is always greater than the whole of creation, the love that is he himself, since "God is love." Above all, love is greater than sin, than weakness, than the "futility of creation", it is stronger than death; it is a love always ready to raise up and forgive, always ready to go to meet the prodigal son, always looking for "the revealing of the sons of God", who are called to the glory that is to be revealed. This revelation of love is also described as mercy, and in man's history this revelation of love and mercy has taken a form and a name: that of Jesus Christ.

Pope St John Paul II, Encyclical Redemptor Hominis (1979), 9

Man Cannot Live without Love

Redemptor Hominis

Man cannot live without love. He remains a being that is incomprehensible for himself, his life is senseless if love is not revealed to him, if he does not encounter love, if he does not experience it and make it his own, if he does not participate intimately in it. This, as has already been said, is why Christ the Redeemer "fully reveals man to himself". If we may use the expression, this is the human dimension of the mystery of the Redemption. In this dimension man finds again the greatness, dignity, and value that belong to his humanity. In the mystery of the Redemption man becomes newly "expressed" and, in a way, is newly created. He is newly created! "There is neither Jew nor Greek, there is neither slave nor free, there is neither male nor female; for you are all one in Christ Jesus" (Gal 3:28). The man who wishes to understand himself thoroughly—and not just in accordance with immediate, partial, often superficial, and even illusory standards and measures of his being—he must with his unrest, uncertainty, and even his weakness and sinfulness, with his life and death, draw near to Christ. He must, so to speak, enter into him with all his own self, he must "appropriate" and assimilate the whole of the reality of the Incarnation and Redemption in order to find himself. If this profound process takes place within him, he then bears fruit not only of adoration of God but also of deep wonder at himself. How precious must man be in the eyes of the Creator, if he "gained so great a Redeemer".

Pope St John Paul II, Encyclical Redemptor Hominis (1979), 10

The Sense of God and the Sense of man

Evangelium Vitae

When the sense of God is lost, there is also a tendency to lose the sense of man, of his dignity and his life; in turn, the systematic violation of the moral law, especially in the serious matter of respect for human life and its dignity, produces a kind of progressive darkening of the capacity to discern God's living and saving presence.

Pope St John Paul II, Encyclical Evangelium Vitae (1995), 21

The Basis for Being a Christian

Deus Caritas est

Being Christian is not the result of an ethical choice or a lofty idea, but the encounter with an event, a person, which gives life a new horizon and a decisive direction. St John's Gospel describes that event in these words: "God so loved the world that he gave his only Son, that whoever believes in him should … have eternal life" (3:16).

Pope Benedict XVI, Encyclical Deus Caritas est (2005), 1

Love Forever

Deus Caritas est

It is part of love's growth towards higher levels and inward purification that it now seeks to become definitive, and it does so in a twofold sense: both in the sense of exclusivity (this particular person alone) and in the sense of being "forever". Love embraces the whole of existence in each of its dimensions, including the dimension of time. It could hardly be otherwise, since its promise looks towards its definitive goal: love looks to the eternal.

Pope Benedict XVI, Encyclical Deus Caritas est (2005), 6

Love as Service to the Church

Deus Caritas est

The entire activity of the Church is an expression of a love that seeks the integral good of man: it seeks his evangelization through Word and Sacrament, an undertaking that is often heroic in the way it is acted out in history; and it seeks to promote man in the various arenas of life and human activity. Love is therefore the service that the Church carries out in order to attend constantly to man's sufferings and his needs, including material needs.

Pope Benedict XVI, Encyclical Deus Caritas (2005), 19

Society without Love?

Deus Caritas est

Love—*caritas*—will always prove necessary, even in the most just society. There is no ordering of the State so just that it can eliminate the need for a service of love. Whoever wants to eliminate love is preparing to eliminate man as such. There will always be suffering which cries out for consolation and help. There will always be loneliness. There will always be situations of material need where help in the form of concrete love of neighbour is indispensable. The State which would provide everything, absorbing everything into itself, would ultimately become a mere bureaucracy incapable of guaranteeing the very thing which the suffering person—every person—needs: namely, loving personal concern.

Pope Benedict XVI, Encyclical Deus Caritas est (2005), 28b

Love: The Central Value

Caritas in Veritate

Charity is at the heart of the Church's social doctrine. Every responsibility and every commitment spelled out by that doctrine is derived from charity, which, according to the teaching of Jesus, is the synthesis of the entire Law (cf. Mt 22:36–40). It gives real substance to the personal relationship with God and with neighbour; it is the principle not only of micro-relationships (with friends, with family members or within small groups) but also of macro-relationships (social, economic, and political ones)… . *Everything has its origin in God's love, everything is shaped by it, everything is directed towards it.* Love is God's greatest gift to humanity, it is his promise and our hope.

Pope Benedict XVI, Encyclical Caritas in Veritate (2009), 2

Love Redeems and Liberates

Evangelii Gaudium

Thanks solely to this encounter—or renewed encounter—with God's love, which blossoms into an enriching friendship, we are liberated from our narrowness and self-absorption. We become fully human when we become more than human, when we let God bring us beyond ourselves in order to attain the fullest truth of our being. Here we find the source and inspiration of all our efforts at evangelization. For if we have received the love which restores meaning to our lives, how can we fail to share that love with others?

Pope Francis, Apostolic Exhortation Evangelii Gaudium (2013), 8

The Great Plan of Love

Evangelii Gaudium

Being Church means being God's people, in accordance with the great plan of his fatherly love. This means that we are to be God's leaven in the midst of humanity. It means proclaiming and bringing God's salvation into our world, which often goes astray and needs to be encouraged, given hope and strengthened on the way. The Church must be a place of mercy freely given, where everyone can feel welcomed, loved, forgiven, and encouraged to live the good life of the Gospel.

Pope Francis, Apostolic Exhortation Evangelii Gaudium (2013), 114

The Final Synthesis

Evangelii Gaudium

Clearly, whenever the New Testament authors want to present the heart of the Christian moral message, they present the essential requirement of love for one's neighbour: "The one who loves his neighbour has fulfilled the whole law... therefore love of neighbour is the fulfilling of the law" (Rom 13:8, 10). These are the words of St Paul, for whom the commandment of love not only sums up the law but constitutes its very heart and purpose: "For the whole law is fulfilled in one word, 'you shall love your neighbour as yourself'" (Gal 5:14). To his communities Paul presents the Christian life as a journey of growth in love: "May the Lord make you increase and abound in love for one another and for all" (1 Th 3:12). St James likewise exhorts Christians to fulfill "the royal law according to the Scripture: You shall love your neighbour as yourself" (2:8), in order not to fall short of any commandment.

Pope Francis, Apostolic Exhortation Evangelii Gaudium (2013), 161

Love welcomes a challenge

Laudato Si

The urgent challenge to protect our common home includes a concern to bring the whole human family together to seek a sustainable and integral development, for we know that things can change. The Creator does not abandon us; he never forsakes his loving plan or repents of having created us. Humanity still has the ability to work together in building our common home.

Pope Francis, Encyclical Laudato Sì (2015), 13

Together
We Are
Strong

THE CHURCH'S
SOCIAL MISSION

"

Do all the good you can, by all the means you can, in all the ways you can, in all the places you can, at all the times you can, to all the people you can, as long as ever you can.

JOHN WESLEY (1703–1791),
Known as "John Wesley's Rule"

 SOCIAL
(from Latin *socialis*, having to do with allies or partners): concerning the (regulated) coexistence of human beings in a state or society; related to human society or belonging to it.

All Christians, their pastors included, are called to show concern for the building of a better world. ... The Church's social thought is primarily positive: it offers proposals, it works for change, and in this sense it constantly points to the hope born of the loving heart of Jesus Christ.
POPE FRANCIS, Evangelii Gaudium (EG 183)

22 *Why does the Church have a social doctrine?*

Human beings are profoundly → SOCIAL creatures. Both in heaven and on earth man is dependent on community. Back in the Old Testament, God gave his people humane regulations and commandments by which they could lead a life that is just and good. Human reason can distinguish unjust actions from the just deeds that are necessary to build a just social order. In Jesus we see that justice is fulfilled only in love. Our present-day notions of solidarity are inspired by Christian love of neighbour.

➡ **62 ff.** ➡ **2419–2420, 2422–2423** ➡ **45, 438**

23 *What are the purposes of social doctrine?*

Social doctrine has two purposes:

1. To set forth the requirements of just social action as they appear in the Gospel.
2. In the name of justice to denounce social, economic, or political actions and structures whenever they contradict the Gospel message.

The Christian faith has a clear concept of the dignity of man, and from this concept it

derives certain principles, norms, and value judgements that make a free and just social order possible. As clear as the principles of social doctrine are, they still must be applied again and again to current social questions. In applying her social doctrine, the Church becomes the advocate of all people who for very different reasons cannot raise their voices and not infrequently are the ones most affected by unjust actions and structures.

➡ **81, 82** ➡ **2423**

24 *Who determines what the social doctrine of the Church is?*

All members of the Church, according to their particular tasks and charisms, participate in the development of social doctrine. The principles of social doctrine have been spelled out in important Church documents. Social doctrine is an official "teaching" of the Church. The Magisterium of the Church—meaning the pope and the bishops in communion with him—repeatedly instructs the Church and mankind about the requirements for just, peaceful, and social communities.

➡ **70, 90** ➡ **344**

The living teaching office of the Church [i.e., the Magisterium] … is not above the word of God, but serves it, teaching only what has been handed on, since, listening to it devoutly, guarding it scrupulously, and explaining it faithfully in accord with a divine commission and with the help of the Holy Spirit, it draws from this one deposit of faith everything which it presents for belief as divinely revealed.

Vatican Council II,
Dei Verbum 10

The blind receive their sight and the lame walk, lepers are cleansed and the deaf hear, and the dead are raised up, and the poor have good news preached to them.
MT 11:5

Charity is at the heart of the Church's social doctrine.
BENEDICT XVI, CiV 2

" How can it be that it is not a news item when an elderly homeless person dies of exposure, but it is news when the stock market loses two points? This is a case of exclusion. Can we continue to stand by when food is thrown away while people are starving? This is a case of inequality.

POPE FRANCIS, EG 53

25 How did the Church's social doctrine come into being?

No one can listen to the Gospel without being challenged socially. The term "social doctrine", however, refers to those statements on social questions that the Church's Magisterium has issued since the Encyclical RERUM NOVARUM, by Pope Leo XIII. With industrialization in the nineteenth century, an entirely new "social question" emerged. Most people were no longer employed in agriculture but worked in industry, instead. There was no worker protection, no health insurance, no guaranteed vacation time, and very often there was even child labour. Unions were formed to stand up for the workers' interests. It was clear to Pope Leo XIII that he had to respond with an extraordinary measure. In his Encyclical RERUM NOVARUM, he sketched the outline of a just social order. Since then, the popes have responded again and again to the "signs of the times" and have addressed especially urgent social questions in the tradition of RERUM NOVARUM. The statements that accumulated in this way over time are called the Church's *social doctrine*. Besides the documents of the Universal Church (i.e., statements by the pope, a council, or the Roman Curia), regional statements, too, for instance the pastoral letters of a bishops' conference on social questions, can be part of the Church's social doctrine.

➡ **87, 88, 104** ➡ **4395**

26 Why is the Church interested not only in the individual?

It used to be that the Church was accused of being interested only in the salvation of the individual soul. In fact, every individual human being counts in God's sight. We are all irreplaceable and unique. Nevertheless, from our mother's womb we are dependent on communion with other human beings. We can be

 Then the LORD said to Cain, "Where is Abel your brother?" He said, "I do not know; am I my brother's keeper?"

GEN 4:9

It is no longer possible to claim that religion should be restricted to the private sphere and that it exists only to prepare souls for heaven.

POPE FRANCIS, EG 182

happy only in good relationships with others. Therefore it says in the account of creation: "Then the LORD God said, 'It is not good that the man should be alone; I will make him a helper fit for him'" (Gen 2:18). God is interested in the total welfare of a person and, therefore, also in his development of community, in which people participate in manifold ways.

→ 61 → 210, 321

27 *Why does the Church practise solidarity?*

A Church that showed no solidarity would be a contradiction in terms. The Church is the place in which God's lasting solidarity with mankind comes about. In the communion of the Church, God's love is supposed to have its human continuation and finally reach all mankind. The Church is the place where God wants to gather all men: "Behold, the dwelling of God is with men" (Rev 21:3). The Church is the "sign and instrument of a very closely knit union with God and of the unity of the whole human race" (LG 1). Through his Church, which follows the example of her Lord and shows solidarity with the helpless, the victims of injustice, and the poor of her times, God tries to reach the people of all nations and cultures and to help them. Whenever people try to shape a more human

 Can a woman forget her sucking child, that she should have no compassion on the son of her womb? Even these may forget, yet I will not forget you.
IS 49:15

" We men and women are all in the same boat upon a stormy sea. We owe to each other a terrible and tragic loyalty.
G.K. CHESTERTON
(1874–1936)

Mercy and faithfulness will meet; righteousness and peace will kiss each other. Faithfulness will spring up from the ground, and righteousness will look down from heaven.
PS 85:11

Milestones
of Social Doctrine

Year	Name	Central themes and statements
1891	Leo XIII: Encyclical RERUM NOVARUM (RN)	First social encyclical: on the right to property, the rejection of class warfare, the rights of the weak and the dignity of the poor; on the right of workers to form trade unions.
1931	Pius XI: Encyclical QUADRAGESIMO ANNO (QA)	Encyclical on the 40th anniversary of RERUM NOVARUM: demands a "living wage" that can feed a family; rejects unlimited free enterprise; develops the principle of subsidiarity.
1961	John XXIII: Encyclical MATER ET MAGISTRA (MM)	The goal of social doctrine is to create a genuine community in which needs are satisfied and the dignity of each individual is promoted.
1963	John XXIII: Encyclical PACEM IN TERRIS (PT)	Promotes freedom and the propagation of human rights as central concerns of the Church.
1965	Pastoral Constitution GAUDIUM ET SPES (GS) of Vatican Council II	A comprehensive dialogue with modern culture, economy, and society begins; society and its structures should be ordered to the "progress of the human person" (GS 25).
1965	Declaration DIGNITATIS HUMANAE (DH) of Vatican Council II	Ecclesiastical recognition of religious liberty as a right that is founded on the dignity of the person; a goal is to establish a foothold for freedom of religion in national constitutions worldwide.

1967	Paul VI: Encyclical POPULORUM PROGRESSIO (PP)	Reflections on a worldwide common effort for the development of all peoples and world peace.
1968	Paul VI: ENCYCLICAL HUMANAE VITAE (HV)	On the transmission of human life and the dignity of marriage.
1971	Paul VI: Apostolic Exhortation OCTOGESIMA ADVENIENS (OA)	On the 80th anniversary of RERUM NOVARUM a series of special issues are addressed, for instance: unemployment, environmental problems, and population growth.
1981	John Paul II: Encyclical LABOREM EXERCENS (LE)	Human work not only earns a living but also has a special dignity. It shares in the dignity of the person and of his Christian vocation.
1987	John Paul II: Encyclical SOLLICITUDO REI SOCIALIS (SRS)	20 years after POPULORUM PROGRESSIO the development of the so-called Third World is again addressed; development must be understood not just economically, but comprehensively, including moral development.
1991	John Paul II: Encyclical CENTESIMUS ANNUS (CA)	On the 100th anniversary of RERUM NOVARUM and after the collapse of Communism, the value of democracy and the free market economy is emphasized; the market must nevertheless remain within the framework of solidarity.
2009	Benedict XVI: Encyclical CARITAS IN VERITATE (CIV)	Citing POPULORUM PROGRESSIO, this document deals at great length with the various facets of globalization.
2015	Francis: Encyclical LAUDATO SÌ (LS)	The second encyclical by Pope Francis discusses questions of preserving the environment in the larger context of the right of all human beings to life and comprehensive, dignified development.

world, God is on their side. The Church is therefore in solidarity with all who want to give God's salvation a visible face in the world.

→ **60** → **122**

28 *How are social doctrine and faith connected?*

Not everyone who is socially or politically involved is a Christian. But someone can hardly call himself a Christian if he is not socially involved. The Gospel very emphatically leads people to commit themselves to love, justice, freedom, and peace. When Jesus proclaims the coming of the Kingdom of God, he does not just heal and save individual human beings; rather, he starts a new form of community—a kingdom of peace and justice. Now God alone can bring about this kingdom definitively. Christians, however, should work for a better society. They should build a city of man "that is more human because it is in greater conformity with the Kingdom of God" (*Compendium of Social Doctrine* 63). When Jesus compares the Kingdom of God to yeast that gradually leavens a large measure of dough (Mt 13:33), he shows the way in which Christians should work in society.

→ **63** → **123**

29 *Can social justice be the final goal of the Church?*

No. The Church would not have reached all her desired goals if there were a just society. The salvation that the Church proclaims begins on earth; it saves the individual person, transforms human relations, and heals the wounds of society. Redemption begins as a sign of hope in just social structures here on earth. Nevertheless, the "new city" is not the result of human struggles and efforts. Although we may have done everything in our power, still the "holy city" comes down "out of heaven" (Rev 21:10) into our situation. Real peace is a gift from God.

→ **64, 65, 67** → **769**

30   *Is the Gospel synonymous with development aid?*

Development aid and the proclamation of the faith must go hand in hand. Along with Liturgy and proclamation, there is charity—active love of neighbour,

The aid given by the West to developing countries, based purely on technical-material principles, which has not only left God to the side but has also distanced people from God with the pride of its presumed superior wisdom, has made the Third World into the "Third World" in the modern sense.
POPE BENEDICT XVI,
19th March 2009

God alone is the redemption of man. And we can see in the history of the last century that in the States where God was abolished, not only was the economy destroyed, but above all the souls.

BENEDICT XVI, 05.02.2006

one of the three fundamental activities of the Church. If the Church were only to proclaim the faith while ignoring the miserable living conditions of the people, she would betray Jesus, who accepted and healed men and women, body and soul, in their personal uniqueness and with their social needs. But if the Church were to promote only the social development of people, she would betray the destiny of the individual human being, who is called to eternal communion with God, and she would also fail to do justice to the social destiny of man as a member of Christ's Body. To separate the social message of the Gospel from its faith message would be to divide the Good News in half.

How in fact can one proclaim the new commandment [of love] without promoting in justice and in peace the true, authentic advancement of man?
POPE PAUL VI (1897–1978),
Evangelii Nuntiandi, (EN 31)

→ **66**

"" The joys and the hopes, the griefs and the
anxieties of the men of this age, especially
those who are poor or in any way afflicted,
these are the joys and hopes, the griefs and
anxieties of the followers of Christ. Vatican Council II, GS 1

31 *How deeply can the Church become
involved in social questions?*

It is not the Church's responsibility to replace
the State and politics. That is why she offers no
technical solutions for individual social problems. She herself does not make policies but,
rather, inspires policies that are in keeping with
the Gospel. In their social encyclicals, the popes

have developed central themes such as wages, property, and unions, which are supposed to help in building a just society. The only ones who should intervene concretely in politics, however, are Christian laymen who become involved in that field. Moreover, many Christians put their Christian commitment and thinking into practice in unions, groups, and associations that campaign for particular social causes, e.g., aid for refugees or worker protection.

→ 68 → 440

32 *Does the Church favour a particular societal and political model?*

The Church can approve a wide range of political forms, provided the dignity and rights of every person and the common good are respected and

> When they came to take away the Communists, I said nothing, because I was not a Communist. When they came for the Social Democrats, I said nothing, because I was not a Social Democrat. When they came for the trade unionists, I said nothing, because I was not a trade unionist. When they came for me, there was no one left who could protest.

MARTIN NIEMÖLLER (1892–1984), German Evangelical Lutheran theologian and member of the anti-Nazi resistance

"Lord, when did we see you hungry or thirsty or a stranger or naked or sick or in prison, and did not minister to you?" Then he will answer them, "Truly, I say to you, as you did it not to one of the least of these, you did it not to me."

MT 25:44–45

 If I can help at least one person to have a better life, that already justifies the offering of my life. It is a wonderful thing to be God's faithful people. We achieve fulfillment when we break down walls and our heart is filled with faces and names!

POPE FRANCIS, EG 274

POLITICS

ECONOMY

ENVIRONMENT

TECHNOLOGY

SOCIAL SERVICES

protected. She supports a free, democratic social order to the extent that this offers the best guarantee for the social participation of all and safeguards human rights. On this topic Pope St John Paul II writes: "The Church values the democratic system inasmuch as it ensures the participation of citizens in making political choices, guarantees to the governed the possibility both of electing and holding accountable those who govern them, and of replacing them through peaceful means when appropriate. Thus she cannot encourage the formation of narrow ruling groups which usurp the power of the State for individual interests or for ideological ends. Authentic democracy is possible only in a State ruled by law and on the basis of a correct conception of the human person" (Pope St John Paul II, CENTESIMUS ANNUS 46)

➡ 72, 73

33 *Does the Church not exceed her competence when she speaks out on social questions?*

When the Church speaks out on social questions, she is not meddling in "other people's" business. The individual does not belong to the State, just as the family, being the essential cell of society, does not belong to the State. Inspired by the Gospel, the Church makes herself the advocate of the most primordial rights of human persons and of human communities. The Church does not want to gain power and external influence thereby. It is her right and duty to speak out whenever injustice endangers social life.

➡ 69–71 ➡ 1913–1917 ➡ 322, 328

34 *Is Catholic social doctrine a complete system?*

No, the Church's social doctrine is not a fully articulated branch of theology with which to judge complex societal, economic, and political situations from outside, so to speak. Rather, this social doctrine makes a point of constantly conducting a dialogue with political science, economics, the natural sciences, technology, and sociology. In this way the social doctrine can better understand, reflect on, and interpret man and his connections in social life.

➡ **76, 77, 78**

35 *Was the Church's social doctrine intended exclusively for Christians?*

The social doctrine of the Church contains nothing that cannot be understood and confirmed by human reason. The popes have always emphasized, however, that the Church's social doctrine has special significance for Catholics. Since the social doctrine is essentially inspired by faith in a loving, just God, every act of love and justice should be viewed in light of God and his promises. This obliges Christians even more to accomplish good in practice, too. Furthermore, however, *all people of goodwill* should feel that this social teaching is addressed to them.

➡ **75, 83, 84** ➡ **328**

36 *Will this social doctrine ever be finished?*

Life in society has always been and is especially now characterized by a constant development and incredible dynamism on all its levels. Hence the social doctrine of the Church has never regarded itself as being a complete and self-contained teaching. It does stand on the firm foundation of the Gospel, with definite principles and concepts. From that starting point, however, it must always seek anew the answers to the social questions and challenges of the present.

➡ **85, 86**

 For believers, the world derives neither from blind chance nor from strict necessity, but from God's plan. This is what gives rise to the duty of believers to unite their efforts with those of all men and women of good will, with the followers of other religions, and with non-believers, so that this world of ours may effectively correspond to the divine plan: living as a family under the Creator's watchful eye.
POPE BENEDICT XVI, CiV 57

" To love someone is to wish him good things.
ST THOMAS AQUINAS,
Summa Theologiae II–II, q. 26, art. 6, obj. 3

 We do not live better when we flee, hide, refuse to share, stop giving, and lock ourselves up in our own comforts. Such a life is nothing less than slow suicide.
POPE FRANCIS, EG 272

DIGRESSION

NEW MEDIA

37 *What are the media for?*

When *direct* communication is not possible, we use the media as *indirect* providers of information and as platforms for exchange and discussion. The media serve to educate, inform, and entertain, with the entertainment aspect often outweighing the others. Without the media, we could organize neither our private life nor the complexity of our modern society. The media are like the communicative cement that holds society together—the larger and more complex the society, the more urgently we need the media. A democracy, especially, cannot function without the free exchange of opinions and information and without the participation of all.

➡ 414, 415 ➡ 2993, 2994

38 *How does the Church see the media?*

The media are necessary building blocks of modern societies. They are not ends in themselves; rather, as *social means of communication,* they serve people and help them to understand one another. The media—and those who make them available and distribute them—have an ethical responsibility. They must direct their activity toward the goal of *mutual understanding*: what fosters this understanding, what impedes it? How can man and his social relations be promoted? What developments serve the common good, for example, the free exchange of news and opinions? The Pontifical Council for Social Communications, which was founded in 1948, deals intensively with the questions: 1) How can the faith be proclaimed in an appropriate way in the media? and 2) How are the media to be used "correctly"?

➡ **166, 414, 415** ➡ **2494, 2495** ➡ **459**

39 *What is the Church's attitude toward the social networks?*

The Internet and above all the social networks are regarded as an important extension of the possibilities for communication. Pope Benedict XVI repeatedly took up this theme; thus he says: "The new technologies allow people to meet each other beyond the confines of space and of their own culture, creating in this

> One cannot *not* communicate.
>
> **PAUL WATZLAWICK**
> (1921–2007),
> communications theorist

> In my opinion, part of it is the right to privacy, the right not to be spied on and not to be impeded or blocked from having access. Free access to the commercial marketplaces is important too. Political websites should be freely accessible—even the ones that, we agree, convey illegal, horrible content. And then of course there is the fundamental right to access: Still today less than half of humanity can use the Web.
>
> **TIM BERNERS-LEE** in response to the question: What should an Internet Charter establish?

> The digital space is said to be open, free and peer-to-peer—it does not automatically recognize or privilege the contributions of established authorities or institutions. In this environment, authority has to be earned, it is not an entitlement.
>
> **CLAUDIO MARIA CELLI** (b. 1941), President of the Pontifical Council for Social Communications

way an entirely new world of potential friendships. This is a great opportunity, but it also requires greater attention to and awareness of possible risks" (Benedict XVI, Message for the 45th World Communications Day, 2011). Just like all the media, however, the social

It is not acceptable that the exercise of the freedom of communication should depend upon wealth, education, or political power. The right to communicate is the right of all.

PONTIFICAL COUNCIL FOR SOCIAL COMMUNICATIONS, Pastoral Instruction on Social Communications Aetatis Novae (1992), (AN) 15

networks, too, should serve the common good and human development. Pope Benedict calls for "serious reflection on the significance of communication in the digital age". As a matter of principle, communication on social networks takes the form of a dialogue; this is a great opportunity for the Church to realize her potential as a *communio,* or fellowship. Pope Francis has a Twitter account (@pontifex), which Pope Benedict started. In early 2016 he had 26 million followers.

➡ **415** ➡ **2494, 2496**

> Social networks, as well as being a means of evangelization, can also be a factor in human development.
> **POPE BENEDICT XVI,** Message for the 47th World Communications Day, 2013

You wake up one morning to discover that your handwriting's gone. You can't sign your name. Your business has lost its letterhead, envelopes, checks, logos, and even the ink in your pens has disappeared. You open your mouth, and no sounds come out. You can no longer shake hands, frown, snicker, or laugh out loud. Oh, you can still communicate, using the same uniform style imposed on everyone: ASCII text. The only difference between your messages and another's is their contents.

CLIFFORD STOLL (b. 1950), American astrophysicist and computer pioneer

 40   *What is the "digital divide"?*

The noblest goal of all social media is *universal participation in shaping public affairs.* On the Internet and in the social networks some people are excluded from the start, if for structural, financial, or personal reasons they have no access to the Internet or if they cannot use it competently. In order to avoid the exclusion of individuals or groups (the "digital divide"), the Church repeatedly calls for universal access to the means of social communication and a prohibition of monopolies and ideological supervision. If the exclusion affects the elderly, the unemployed, and people with less formal education, it is more correct to talk about a *social divide,* which absolutely must be overcome. Therefore this is a question not only about communicating but also about overcoming unjust structures that exclude individuals or groups from information and thus from education and development.

➡ **414, 416, 557, 561** ➡ **2495, 2498, 2499**

41   *What is the right way to use the media?*

Using the media sensibly is a challenge for every individual. Even with the classic mass media (newspaper, radio, television), one must *decide* what to be concerned about. Merely passive consumption often leaves the "user" feeling sad and spiritually empty. In this regard, parents, teachers, or youth group leaders have a particular responsibility. They must model for children and young people a disciplined way of using the media and acquaint them with media that are enriching. In the case of the digital media, a new level of responsibility is added: especially in social networks, one is no longer just a *passive* recipient, who receives what others have produced, printed, or sent. One can at any time be active also as a *producer*, "like" or comment on something or else post a message, a blog entry, a video, or a photo online. Thus one has a responsibility comparable to that of any other media producer.

➡ 376, 560, 563 ➡ 2496

> He had 1,000 Facebook Friends but not one single friend.
>
> unknown

> The Internet is a place for searching, copying and browsing. At worst it is a place for executions, sexual abuse, a place for data mining and privacy groups. More trivially, it is a world of escapist nonsense.
>
> **BRUCE WILLIS** (b. 1955). American film actor, 2007

Real life is fellowship.

MARTIN BUBER (1878–1965), jewish religious philosopher

The digital media make people fat, stupid, aggressive, lonely, sick, and unhappy.

MANFRED SPITZER (1958), German psychiatrist who coined the expression *digital dementia*

In the digital world, transmitting information … means making it known within a social network where knowledge is shared in the context of personal exchanges. The clear distinction between the producer and consumer of information is relativized and communication appears not only as an exchange of data, but also as a form of sharing.

POPE BENEDICT XVI, Message for the 45th World Communications Day, 2011

42   *What responsibility do I have in using the media?*

The social media can bring people together or lead them into isolation. They can help people be better informed, enrich and inspire them, or seduce them to evil. What we do and permit in the media and the social networks ought to serve the purpose of all human communication: overcoming the confusion of languages at Babel (Gen 11:4–8) and coming to an understanding of all by the Spirit of God (Acts 2:5–11). The central ethical concept here is "responsibility": responsibility to God, who wants us to help truth prevail and to seek one another in love; responsibility to our neighbour, who should be integrated, involved, and enriched through the social media; responsibility to myself, since I should enter into true community with others through the media instead of shutting myself off in self-centred "virtual" isolation from other people and their real needs.

➡ 198, 416, 562 ➡ 2494, 2495, 2497 ➡ 459, 460

43   *What does ideal communication on the Internet look like?*

As desirable as it is for Christians to conquer the "digital continent" and to fill it with the light of the Gospel, the way in which they communicate must be set apart from the usual approaches. It makes sense for Christians to post messages and run blogs dealing with Christian topics. But if they denounce other people in them, if they slander, belittle, and condemn others, if they cause or support divisions, then they are doing the opposite of what Pope Francis calls for in *Evangelii gaudium:* "The joy of the Gospel is for all people: no one can be excluded." This applies also to the presence of Christians in the social media: "It is vitally important for the Church today to go forth and preach the Gospel to all: to all places, on all occasions, without hesitation, reluctance, or fear" (EG 23).

44   *Are there good media and bad media?*

Media as such are good, but they can be used badly; some are more useful, others less so. It always depends on one's purpose and how one uses them. One can employ media in such a way that the result

> " The right to information is inseparable from freedom of communication. Social life depends on a continual interchange, both individual and collective, between people.
>
> Pastoral Instruction *Communio et progressio* 44

> " All who, of their own free choice, make use of these media of communications ... [should] avoid those that may be a cause or occasion of spiritual harm to themselves, or that can lead others into danger through base example, or that hinder desirable presentations and promote those that are evil. To patronize such presentations, in most instances, would merely reward those who use these media only for profit.
>
> Vatican Council II, Decree *Inter mirifica* (IM) 9

" Disinformation means telling half-truths, the part that is most convenient to me, and not saying the other half. Therefore, those who watch the television or listen to the radio are not able to arrive at a perfect judgement, because they do not have all the elements necessary to do so, and the media do not give them. Please, shun these sins.

POPE FRANCIS to journalists, 23rd March 2014

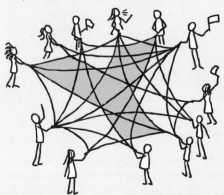

" Google is not a medium; Google is a business model.

FRANK A. MEYER (b. 1944), Swiss publicist

" A continuous stream of advertising on television loses its effect when it is interrupted every few minutes by an incomprehensible part of a film.

LORIOT (Vicco von Bülow, 1923–2011), German humorist

is nothing but meaningless entertainment and useless information; thereby one can keep people away from real life. Media owners can exploit the media by deliberately inducing addictive behaviours in media users. The media are becoming more and more commercialized. They often degenerate into cheap stimulants that distract from a dreary world without hope. People often go on the Internet for content that glorifies violence, and even more often for pornography. Providers, therefore, are always developing new forms of presenting media content (for instance, computer games) and marketing strategies so as to generate dependent (and often addicted) "users". All this is an abuse of the media. Christians must therefore consistently avoid certain sorts of content and lovingly help individuals who are dependent on the Internet (especially young people) out of their misery.

 2498–2499

45 *How can we protect the media from being misused?*

Misuse of the media should be decisively counteracted. Markets need freedom, but they also need to set moral goals. Those who offer access, services, and platforms are required more than ever to accept the ethical standard of the common good and human development. The devaluation of human sexuality, especially the distribution of child pornography, is a much too serious abuse for those responsible to keep ignoring it. Just as unacceptable are all forms of cyber-mobbing and disturbances that are becoming widespread based on the ability to use the Internet anonymously. With regard to the danger of the possible misuse of data by companies like Google, Facebook etc. (or even by governments), it is important not to reveal online everything about oneself and not to use a smartphone for pictures (selfies) of an intimate sort.

 235, 349 **459**

46 *Must the Church go along with every technological development?*

Science and technology are a "magnificent product of God-given creativity". Yet progress is not an end in itself, and just because something is new does not automatically make it good. Every development has to be tested to determine whether it serves man (and thus the common good) or whether instead it disregards human dignity because it touts deceptive values and/or causes dependency.

457, 458 **2493, 2294**

> Cold words freeze people, and hot words scorch them, and bitter words make them bitter, and wrathful words make them wrathful. Kind words produce their own image on men's souls. They smooth and quiet and comfort the hearer.
> **BLAISE PASCAL** (1623–1662) French mathematician and philosopher

> The ability to employ the new means of communication is required, not just to keep up with the times, but precisely in order to enable the infinite richness of the Gospel to find forms of expression capable of reaching the minds and hearts of all.
> **BENEDICT XVI,** Message for the 47th World Communications Day, 2013

> Do not be afraid to become citizens of the digital world around us.
> **POPE FRANCIS,** 23rd January 2014

From important Church documents

THE CHURCH'S SOCIAL MISSION

Rerum Novarum

The Social Task of the Church

The elements of the conflict now raging are unmistakable, in the vast expansion of industrial pursuits and the marvellous discoveries of science; in the changed relations between masters and workmen; in the enormous fortunes of some few individuals, and the utter poverty of the masses; the increased self-reliance and closer mutual co-operation of the working classes; as also, finally, in the prevailing moral degeneracy.
Pope Leo XIII, Encyclical Rerum Novarum (1891), 1

Rerum Novarum

Man Needs Community

The consciousness of his own weakness urges man to call in aid from without... It is this natural impulse which binds men together in civil society; and it is likewise this which leads them to join together in associations which are, it is true, lesser and not independent societies, but, nevertheless, real societies.
Pope Leo XIII, Encyclical Rerum Novarum (1891), 37

Gaudium et Spes

The Equality of All Men and Social Justice

Since all men possess a rational soul and are created in God's likeness, since they have the same nature and origin, have been redeemed by Christ and enjoy the same divine calling and destiny, the basic equality of all must receive increasingly greater recognition. True, all men are not alike from the point of view of varying physical power and the diversity of intellectual and moral resources. Nevertheless, with respect to the fundamental rights of the person, every type of discrimination, whether social or cultural, whether based on sex, race, colour, social condition, language, or religion, is to be overcome and eradicated as contrary to God's intent. For in truth it must still be regretted that fundamental personal rights are still not being universally honoured. Such is the case of a woman who is denied the right to choose a husband freely, to embrace a state of life, or to acquire an education or cultural benefits equal to those recognized for men.

Therefore, although rightful differences exist between men, the equal dignity of persons demands that a more humane and just condition of life be brought about. For excessive economic and social differences between the members of the one human family or population groups cause scandal and militate against social justice, equity, the dignity of the human person, as well as social and international peace. Human institutions, both private and public, must labour to minister to the dignity and purpose of man. At the same time let them put up a stubborn fight against any kind of slavery, whether social or political, and

safeguard the basic rights of man under every political system. Indeed human institutions themselves must conform by degrees to the highest of all realities, spiritual ones, even if, meanwhile, a rather long time is required before they arrive at the desired goal.
Vatican Council II, Pastoral Constitution Gaudium et spes (1965), 29

The Roots of Social Conflict

Centesimus Annus

As far as the Church is concerned, the social message of the Gospel must not be considered a theory, but above all else a basis and a motivation for action. Inspired by this message, some of the first Christians distributed their goods to the poor, bearing witness to the fact that, despite different social origins, it was possible for people to live together in peace and harmony. Through the power of the Gospel, down the centuries monks tilled the land, men and women Religious founded hospitals and shelters for the poor, Confraternities as well as individual men and women of all states of life devoted themselves to the needy and to those on the margins of society, convinced as they were that Christ's words "as you did it to one of the least of these my brethren, you did it to me" (Mt 25:40) were not intended to remain a pious wish, but were meant to become a concrete life commitment.
Pope St John Paul II, Encyclical Centesimus Annus (1991), 57

The New Significance of the Social Media

Caritas in Veritate

For better or for worse, they [i.e., *the means of social communication*] are so integral a part of life today that it seems quite absurd to maintain that they are neutral—and hence unaffected by any moral considerations concerning people. Often such views, stressing the strictly technical nature of the media, effectively support their subordination to economic interests intent on dominating the market and, not least, to attempts to impose cultural models that serve ideological and political agendas. Given the media's fundamental importance in engineering changes in attitude towards reality and the human person, we must reflect carefully on their influence, especially in regard to the ethical-cultural dimension of globalization and the development of peoples in solidarity... This means that they can have a *civilizing effect* not only when, thanks to technological development, they increase the possibilities of communicating information, but above all when they are geared towards a vision of the person and the common good that reflects truly universal values. Just because social communications increase the possibilities of interconnection and the dissemination of ideas, it does not follow that they promote freedom or internationalize development and democracy for all. To achieve goals of this kind, they need to focus on promoting the dignity of persons and peoples, they need to be clearly inspired by charity and placed at the service of truth, of the good, and of natural and supernatural fraternity. In fact, human freedom is intrinsically linked with these higher values. The media can make an important contribution towards the growth in communion of the human family and the *ethos* of society when they are used to promote universal participation in the common search for what is just.
Pope Benedict XVI, Encyclical Caritas in Veritate (2009), 73

The Laws of the New Media

We must recognize that today the digital arena is a reality in the lives of many persons, more so in the Western world, but growing also among the young people in the developing world. We must not consider it a "virtual" space, somehow less important than the "real" world. If the Church is not present in this space, if the Good News is not also proclaimed "digitally", we run the risk of abandoning many persons, for whom this is the world in which they live; this is the forum where they acquire news and information, develop and express their opinions, engage in debate and dialogue, and seek answers to their questions. The Church is already a presence in the digital space, but the next challenge is to change our style of communicating to make this presence effective... The digital space is said to be open, free, and peer-to-peer—it does not automatically recognize or privilege the contributions of established authorities or institutions. In this environment, authority has to be earned; it is not an entitlement. This means that the ecclesiastical hierarchy, like the political and society hierarchy, must find new forms in which to elaborate its own communication, so that its contribution to this forum receives adequate attention.

Claudio M. Celli, President of the Pontifical Council for Social Communications, at the 13th Ordinary Synod of Bishops (2012) on *The Importance of Social Networks for Ecclesiastical Communication*

Evangelii Gaudium

The Greater Possibilities of Communication

Today, when the networks and means of human communication have made unprecedented advances, we sense the challenge of finding and sharing a "mystique" of living together, of mingling and encounter, of embracing and supporting one another, of stepping into this flood tide which, while chaotic, can become a genuine experience of fraternity, a caravan of solidarity, a sacred pilgrimage. Greater possibilities for communication thus turn into greater possibilities for encounter and solidarity for everyone. If we were able to take this route, it would be so good, so soothing, so liberating and hope-filled! To go out of ourselves and to join others is healthy for us. To be self-enclosed is to taste the bitter poison of immanence, and humanity will be worse for every selfish choice we make.

Pope Francis, Apostolic Exhortation Evangelii Gaudium (2013), 87

The Good Sides of Communication

Good communication helps us to grow closer, to know one another better, and ultimately, to grow in unity. The walls which divide us can be broken down only if we are prepared to listen and learn from one another. We need to resolve our differences through forms of dialogue which help us grow in understanding and mutual respect. A culture of encounter demands that we be ready not only to give, but also to receive. Media can help us greatly in this, especially nowadays, when the networks of human communication have made unprecedented advances. The internet, in particular, offers immense possibilities for encounter and solidarity. This is something truly good, a gift from God... By means of the internet, the Christian message can reach "to the ends of the earth" (Acts 1:8). Keeping the doors of our churches open also means keeping them open in the digital environment so that people, whatever their situation in life, can enter and so that the Gospel can go out to reach everyone. We are called to show that the Church is the home of all. Are we capable of communicating the image of such a Church? Communication is a means of expressing the missionary vocation of the entire Church; today the social networks are one way to experience this call to discover the beauty of faith, the beauty of encountering Christ. In the area of communications too, we need a Church capable of bringing warmth and of stirring hearts.

Pope Francis, Message for the 48th World Communication Day, 24th January 2014

3

QUESTIONS
47–83

Unique
and Infinitely
Valuable

THE HUMAN
PERSON

Then God said, "Let us make man in our image, after our likeness... So God created man in his own image, in the image of God he created him; male and female he created them.

GEN 1:26–27

IMAGO DEI
(Latin for "image of God"): the doctrine which describes biblically (Gen 1:26–27) the outstanding place of man among all creatures: he is the being that can communicate with God.

By his innermost nature, man is a social being.
Vatican Council II, GS 12

The human being develops when he grows in the spirit, when his soul comes to know itself and the truths that God has implanted deep within, when he enters into dialogue with himself and his Creator. When he is far away from God, man is unsettled and ill at ease.
POPE BENEDICT XVI, CiV 11

47 *What do we mean when we speak about a person?*

With the word "person" we express the fact that every human being has an inviolable dignity. Man was created in God's image (→ IMAGO DEI) (Gen 1:27). So he is the one creature of God that represents the Creator himself in creation. He is "the only creature on earth that God willed for its own sake" (GS 24). As a person created by God, a human being is not *something*, but rather *someone* and hence uniquely valuable. As a person, a human being is capable of self-knowledge and reflection on himself, of making free decisions and entering into community with others. And he is called to respond to God in faith. The fact that he is made in God's image and likeness therefore means also that a human being always remains related to God and can develop his full personal potential only in God.

 108, 109 **356–361, 1702, 1704** **56, 58, 63**

48 *Why is every person a social being?*

A human person can survive and develop only with the help of other human beings. Being human entails not only living in a good relationship with God; one must also be very careful to live in good relationships with other people. This begins in the family; it affects one's circle of friends and finally society as a whole. Fundamental for the *social dimension of the human person* is the fact that we are created as man and woman (Gen 2:23). From the very beginning, man and woman possess the same dignity. In mutual help and complementarity, they cope with their lives. God makes the loving union of man and woman fruitful when it results in a child. This is why the family is the primordial cell of every society.

> We hold these truths to be self-evident, that all *men* are created equal, that they are endowed by their Creator with certain unalienable Rights, that among these are Life, Liberty, and the pursuit of Happiness.
>
> Declaration of Independence (1776) of the thirteen colonies that formed the United States of America

➡ 110, 111 ➡ 360–361 ➡ 61, 64

49 *What does it mean to live in society?*

Social life is originally experienced in the family. The family thrives when its members regularly talk to one another, when it develops a culture of mutual consideration, and when individual interests are repeatedly subordinated to the community and welfare of all. The family is creative as God is creative not only because it brings forth children. As social beings in relation, we human beings have a share in God's creative power. Hence we are also responsible for creation and for every other personal living being. Each one of these human persons is *sacred* and *inviolable*, always and everywhere. Our social responsibility pertains also to animals, which we should treat kindly. And it pertains also to nature, which must not be exploited but used sustainably and responsibly. Central to Catholic social teaching, however,

> In the realm of ends, everything has either a price or a dignity. What has a price can be replaced by something else as its equivalent; what on the other hand is raised above all price and therefore admits of no equivalent has a dignity.
>
> **IMMANUEL KANT** (1724–1804), German philosopher, *Groundwork of the Metaphysics of Morals II* (1785)

is the human person. The human person is the real foundation of society; therefore, the person has priority in everything that is done socially.

→ 105–107, 110–114 → 1877–1885 → 321–323

50 *What are the burdens on the human person?*

The human person with his dignity is exposed to many sorts of harm and danger. The crucial element of disturbance and destruction we call sin. Adam, who in the "original sin" disobeyed God's command, is, so to speak, the prototype of the human being, yields to the temptation to sin and harm others. We are all human beings, and we are all sinners. We harm others through our sinful way of living. Because this is so, the earth is no longer a paradise. Actually, we could say no to sin at every moment, but the power of sin reaches into our inmost being, to the place where freedom dwells. And so we deliberately do evil: in freedom we turn against God's will and thus separate ourselves from the source of life, from God.

→ 117, 120, 576, 578 → 390, 396–406, 415
→ 66–70, 287–288, 315

51 *Does sin have a social dimension, too?*

Sin is always the free, conscious act of a person, but it has its effects also in the realm of relationships, indeed in society as a whole. Hence every sin has at the same time a personal and a social dimension: sins are bad for the sinner himself, but at the same time they harm society, too, and injure others. "And thus they grow stronger, spread, and become the source of other sins, and so influence people's behaviour" (John Paul II, SRS 36). Think, for example, of political systems that perform acts of violence or do not protect minorities. Sin is never destiny, and even sinful structures can be changed. To recognize and to name the sin is the first step in freeing oneself from it.

> We must love our neighbour, either because he is good or in order that he might become good.
>
> **ST AUGUSTINE**

> Evil is the lack of good.
>
> **ST THOMAS AQUINAS** (1225–1274)

> If we say we have no sin, we deceive ourselves, and the truth is not in us.
>
> **1 JN 1:8**

> They took infants from their mothers' breasts, snatching them by the legs and pitching them headfirst against the crags or snatched them by the arms and threw them into the rivers, roaring with laughter and saying as the babies fell into the water, "Boil there, you offspring of the devil!"
>
> **BARTOLOMÉ DE LAS CASAS** (1484–1565), Dominican friar and "Apostle to the Indians", in his 1552 indictment against the *conquistadores*.

> Every sin hurts someone—including you.
>
> **BILLY GRAHAM** (b. 1918), Christian evangelist

Jesus Christ came in order to bring us out of our imprisonment in sin. Creation, which had become entangled in sin, is liberated by Christ for love and justice. The "civilization of love" begins with the conversion of the individual and his reconciliation with God.

→ 115–119, 193, 566
→ 1868–1869 → 320

52 *Of what does the unity of the human person consist?*

A human being has a body and a soul, but these are not separate realities. The human person always consists of a *unity*

 The victims of poverty

If we examine the situation more closely, we find that this poverty is not an accident, but rather the result of economic, social, political, and other realities and structures... This situation of pervasive extreme poverty takes on very concrete faces in real life. In these faces we ought to recognize the suffering features of Christ the Lord, who questions and challenges us. They include:

→ the faces of young children, struck down by poverty before they are born ...

→ the faces of young people, who are disoriented because they cannot find their place in society ...

→ the faces of labourers, who frequently are ill-paid, ...

→ the faces of marginalized and overcrowded urban dwellers ...

Puebla Document *On the Evangelization of Latin America in the Present and Future*, §§29–30

of body and soul. Materialism regards the soul as a mere function of the material body; *spiritualism,* in contrast, overvalues the soul at the expense of the body. The Church rejects both errors. Our body is not the prison of the soul, and the soul is an essential part of a living human being. Through his body, man is connected with the earth and is thus a part of nature. In his spiritual soul, a human being not only finds his personal identity (his "I"); his soul also contemplates God and is forever contemplated by him. The soul is immortal. But the body, too, must never be despised, because it is created by God as something good, and it is destined for the resurrection of the body on the Last Day. Jesus recognized the bodily sufferings of human beings and healed them. Man is at the same time a *material* and a *spiritual* being.

➡ **127–129** ➡ **355–357, 380** ➡ **58**

53 *Why does man think of things beyond himself?*

In all of material creation, only man is open to the infinite; he alone can have a concept of God and hunger for ultimate answers. Philosophy says that man is capable of → TRANSCENDENCE, that he can surpass himself. He fully comes into his own only by recognizing and understanding what is other, greater, and more important than himself: God, the source of all life. Because man is open to God, he can also be open for other people and show them respect. Community, dialogue, and the recognition of the other lead him closer to himself.

TRANSCENDENCE
(from Latin *transcendere* = to climb over): by his very existence man points beyond himself and cannot be understood without his relation to God.

→ **130** → **27–30, 1718–1719, 1725, 2548–2250, 2257**
→ **3–4, 281, 468, 470**

> Being human means that no one can ever be used as a means to an end.
> **ALBERT SCHWEITZER**

54 *What makes every human being unique?*

Every human being is unique because he or she was willed by God as an unrepeatable person, created out of love, and redeemed with even greater love. This shows us what dignity the human person has and how important it is to take everyone quite seriously as a person and to treat him with the greatest respect. This requirement applies also to political systems and institutions. They must not only respect the freedom and dignity of the human person. They should contribute to the comprehensive development of every person. A community cannot exclude individuals or entire groups from development.

> To recognize the Other is to recognize a hunger. To recognize the Other is to give. ... I can recognize the gaze of the stranger, the widow, and the orphan only in giving or in refusing.
> **EMMANUEL LEVINAS** (1905–1995), French-Jewish philosopher, *Totality and Infinity* (1961)

→ **131** → **2419–2420, 2422–2423** → **438**

55 *What does society owe the individual person?*

A just society must respect and promote the dignity of the human person. The social order exists for the sake of human beings and must be guided by what a human being needs for a dignified life. This rules

> We are not some casual and meaningless product of evolution. Each of us is the result of a thought of God. Each of us is willed, each of us is loved, each of us is necessary.
> **POPE BENEDICT XVI,** Homily at the Mass for the Inauguration of his Pontificate on 24th April 2005

" The most important hour is always the present one. The most important human being is always the one whom you face right now. The most important deed is always love.

MEISTER ECKHART (1260–1328), German mystic

out all forms of exploitation and instrumentalization for economic, political, or social ends. A human being should never be merely a means of reaching certain goals; he is, rather, an end in himself.

➡ 132–133 ➡ 1886–1887 ➡ 324

> **FREEDOM CAN MEAN:**
> **FREEDOM FROM...** = to have external freedom from constraint
> **FREEDOM TO...** = to be able to make a choice
> **FREEDOM FOR...** = to have the inner freedom to choose what is truly good

" The order of things must be subordinate to the order of persons and not the other way around.

Vatican Council II, GS 26

" Freedom is the freedom to say that two plus two equals four. Once that is granted, all else follows.

GEORGE ORWELL (1903–1950), English writer

" Freedom means responsibility. That is why most men dread it.

GEORGE BERNHARD SHAW (1856–1950), Irish dramatist

Then you will know the truth, and the truth will make you free.

JN 8:32

56 How much freedom does a human being need?

Freedom is a fundamental value. To be free and to act freely is a primordial right of human beings. Only when I decide freely do I also bear the full responsibility for my action. Only a free human being can turn to God in love and respond to him. Only in freedom can people shape their social and personal lives. Human freedom is restricted again and again by political, social, financial, legal, or even cultural circumstances. It is a great injustice to deprive a human being of freedom or to restrict that freedom unjustly; this injures his dignity and impedes him from developing personally.

➡ 135–137 ➡ 1705–1706, 1733 ➡ 286–287

57 How free is man?

Man is free, but his freedom has a goal. Ultimately freedom exists so that we might do what is truly good with understanding and free will. In this regard, freedom takes its orientation from the natural law and the order of creation (= the way in which God meaningfully designed the world). We can know the truth about good and evil through our conscience. Conscience is rather like the voice of truth in a human being, the natural law that is written on the hearts of all men (Rom 2:15). Through our reason we perceive in our conscience the values that are good at all times. It can never be right to deceive, to steal, to murder. Yet conscience can be wrong. Freedom is not always inclined toward what is truly good, but often selfishly wants what is only apparently good. That is why we must always train our conscience and allow ourselves to be instructed about true values. Freedom, too, needs to be liberated by Christ, so as to be able to accomplish what is truly good.

 Conscience without God is a terrifying thing.

FYODOR M. DOSTOEVSKY
(1821–1881), Russian author

 There is no greater freedom than that of allowing oneself to be guided by the Holy Spirit, renouncing the attempt to plan and control everything to the last detail, and instead letting him enlighten, guide, and direct us, leading us wherever he wills.

POPE FRANCIS, EG 280

➡ 16, 138–143 ➡ 1705–1706, 1730–1733, 1738, 1740–1744 ➡ 288–289

 All animals are equal, but some animals are more equal than others.

GEORGE ORWELL, *Animal Farm*

58 *Are there fundamental differences between human beings?*

No. God created all human persons in his image, and consequently all are endowed with the same inalienable dignity, regardless of sex, nationality, religion, or skin colour. Because this is true, injustices between

To love someone means to see him as God intended him.
FYODOR DOSTOEVSKY

The Church acknowledges the indispensable contribution which women make to society through the sensitivity, intuition, and other distinctive skill sets which they, more than men, tend to possess. … But we need to create still broader opportunities for a more incisive female presence in the Church. … The reservation of the priesthood to males, as a sign of Christ the Spouse who gives himself in the Eucharist, is not a question open to discussion, but it can prove especially divisive if sacramental power is too closely identified with power in general. … In the Church, functions "do not favour the superiority of some vis-à-vis the others". Indeed, a woman, Mary, is more important than the bishops.
POPE FRANCIS, EG 103–104

the sexes or between entire peoples must be overcome, in order to assure the personal growth, equal opportunity, and thus the dignity of everyone.

→ 144–145 → 1934–1935 → 330–331

59 *How are man and woman the same, and how are they different?*

Man and woman are the same in God's sight in their *dignity* as persons. God creates a human being, not in the abstract, but as either a man or a woman. And he creates human beings in such a way that men and women are fundamentally meant for each other and need one another, without one sex dominating or marginalizing the other (machismo, radical feminism). Therefore, to be a man or a woman means more than to assume a particular role. From the Christian perspective, man and woman in a loving relationship manifest the communion of persons in God.

→ 146–147 → 2331–2336 → 330–331

60 *What does the Church say about discrimination against handicapped persons?*

As Catholic social doctrine understands it, social justice is achieved when all people in society can participate in the central social, economic, political, and cultural activities in life. Forms of discrimination that exclude people from such participation are an injustice. It is therefore the task of the State and society to create the conditions for ensuring the participation of handicapped persons, also. Ultimately the dignity of the human person does not depend on bodily and intellectual abilities, and the respect due to a person cannot be defined in terms of achievements or efficiency.

→ 148 → 1936–1937 → 331

61 *What does it mean for the human person to belong to a community?*

Animals flock together; they form packs or stay in herds—human beings, in contrast, enter into *communion*. God, who in the depths of his inner life is communion and relationship itself, created them as a special kind of beings-in-relation: deliberately, by free choice, human beings form communities, take responsibility in them, and leave their distinctive mark on them. Human beings rely on all sorts of relationships; they are embedded in a network of other human beings and recognize the necessity of collaboration. In all communities, human beings are united by a principle of unity (family, nation, sports league, church, etc.); in them, they cultivate their history and shape their future.

→ 149 → 1879–1880 → 321–322

> I cried because I had no shoes until I met a man who had no feet.

HELEN ADAMS KELLER (1880–1968), U.S. social reformer and author, deaf and blind since early childhood

> We do not hold animals responsible for what they do, but persons can take responsibility, and they can be held responsible for their actions. Creatures of this sort possess dignity. And this dignity is not something assigned to them by others, but something that they possess merely by belonging to the species *homo sapiens*.

ROBERT SPAEMANN (b. 1927), German philosopher, in a radio interview on 14th September 2007

COMMON GOOD
The common good is the welfare of all. It "embraces the sum of those conditions of the social life whereby men, families, and associations more adequately and readily may attain their own perfection." (Vatican Council II, GS 74)

 I disapprove of what you say, but I will defend to the death your right to say it.
EVELYN BEATRICE HALL
(1868–1939), English writer

62 *Why do people often act in ways that undermine community?*

Although a human being is social, he often acts asocially: driven by selfishness, greed, or egotism, he leads other people astray, exploits and oppresses them, or else leaves them defenceless. True community, however, is a free association of human beings who want what is good for themselves and for others. An individual cannot bring about this → COMMON GOOD; it can be attained only through combined efforts. It may be, for example, a sports stadium that can only be financed jointly or an orchestra that performs music only when many people contribute their talents.

➡ **150–151** ➡ **1882, 1931** ➡ **327–328**

 All human beings are born free and equal in dignity and rights. They are endowed with reason and conscience and should act towards one another in a spirit of brotherhood.

Article 1 of the *Universal Declaration of Human Rights*

63 *What are human rights?*

A human right is a claim on something that is owed us because of our nature as human persons. There can be no rights unless others are bound to respect them, and what binds them is law. So rights, duties, and law are interrelated. The *Universal Declaration of Human Rights* (United Nations, 1948) is, Pope St John Paul II says, "a real milestone on the path of the moral progress of humanity" (2nd October 1979).

➡ **152** ➡ **1930** ➡ **136**

 There will be more, not less respect for human rights if they can be treated as divine rights
G.K. CHESTERTON
(1874–1936) English writer

64 *Where do human rights come from?*

Human rights are not an invention of legal scholars, nor are they an arbitrary agreement of well-meaning statesmen. Human rights, rather, are the primordial rights inscribed in human nature. Today they are recognized worldwide as a fundamental basis for agreement concerning a life of freedom, dignity, and equality. They can be recognized by means of reason, and they are ultimately rooted in the dignity that man possesses because he is made in God's image and likeness. Therefore, these rights are universal; they are also independent of place and time. They are *inviolable,* because the dignity of the human being on which they are founded is also inviolable. And they are *inalienable*, which means that no one can take these rights away from someone else (or has the power to grant or deny them). Human rights must therefore be acknowledged in their totality and be protected against ideological falsifications. All people, but especially Christians, must speak up when human rights violations become known or when certain human rights are (still) not recognized in some countries.

→ 153–154 → 1701–1709 → 280

65 *What are human rights about specifically?*

The fundamental human right is the right to life; this right exists from conception onward, since from that point in time the new human being already has the status of a separate person. Another human right is the right to freedom of opinion. Next, no human being can be denied the right to earn a living for himself and his family by his own work. The right to marry and start a family, to have children and raise them personally, is also a human right. The human right to choose and practise a religion freely is very important; there must be no compulsion in religious matters.

→ 155

Frequently, as a way of ridiculing the Church's effort to defend [the] lives [of the unborn], attempts are made to present her position as ideological, obscurantist, and conservative. Yet this defence of unborn life is closely linked to the defence of each and every other human right. It involves the conviction that a human being is always sacred and inviolable, in any situation and at every stage of development. Human beings are ends in themselves and never a means of resolving other problems.

POPE FRANCIS, EG 213

The conviction that there is a Creator God is what gave rise to the idea of human rights, the idea of the equality of all people before the law, the recognition of the inviolability of human dignity in every single person and the awareness of people's responsibility for their actions.

POPE BENEDICT XVI, 22nd September 2011

> We, the peoples of the United Nations, determined to save succeeding generations from the scourge of war, which twice in our lifetime has brought untold sorrow to mankind, … and to establish conditions under which justice and respect for the obligations arising from treaties and other sources of international law can be maintained, … have resolved to combine our efforts to accomplish these aims. Article 1. The Purposes of the United Nations are: 1. To maintain international peace and security, and to that end: to take effective collective measures for the prevention and removal of threats to the peace, and for the suppression of acts of aggression or other breaches of the peace, and to bring about by peaceful means, and in conformity with the principles of justice and international law, adjustment or settlement of international disputes or situations which might lead to a breach of the peace.

From the Charter of the United Nations dated 26th June 1945

> There is neither Jew nor Greek, there is neither slave nor free, there is neither male or female; for you are all one in Christ Jesus.

GAL 3:28

66 What is the connection between rights and duties?

A person who exercises a human right at the same time also assumes duties and thus responsibilities toward others. Pope St John XXIII comments in *Pacem in terris* (30): "To claim one's rights and ignore one's duties, or only half fulfill them, is like building a house with one hand and tearing it down with the other."

➡ 156 ➡ 2235–2243 ➡ 376

67 How can justice prevail between nations?

Not only individual human beings, but peoples and nations, too, have a right to justice. There is injustice when entire states are conquered, divided up, reduced to satellite states, plundered, or even become the object of exploitation by stronger states. Every nation is in principle naturally endowed with the right to existence and independence, to its own language and culture, to free self-determination and to the free choice of the states with which the nation would like to co-operate peacefully. Human rights must be applied on the higher level of states. In this way peace, respect, and solidarity can be made possible among all peoples. Sovereignty under international law must

of course not be taken as a pretext for denying human rights domestically or oppressing minorities.

➡ 157 ➡ 446–447

68 How can human rights and the rights of peoples and nations be promoted?

Every day we see all sorts of violence: genocide, war and exile, hunger and exploitation. Children are recruited as soldiers and forced to kill. New forms of slavery have developed. Human trafficking, prostitution, and drugs have become an illegal billion-dollar business in which political forces and even governments are also involved. Christians must not insist on human rights only when it is a question of protecting their own; they must realize that they also have the task of defending and strengthening the fundamental rights of all people. This is why the Church has made it her duty in all places and on every occasion to see to it that human rights are universally accepted and upheld and, above all, to respect them within the Church herself.

➡ 158–159 ➡ 1913–1917 ➡ 329

In the field of a new order founded on moral principles, there is no room for violation of freedom, integrity, and security of other nations, no matter what may be their territorial extension or their capacity for defence. It is inevitable that the powerful States, by reason of their greater potential and their power, should pave the way in the establishment of economic groups comprising not only themselves but also smaller and weaker States as well. It is nevertheless indispensable that in the interests of the common good they, as all others, should respect the rights of those smaller states to political freedom, to economic development, and to the adequate protection, in the case of conflicts between nations, of that neutrality which is theirs according to the natural, as well as international, law. In this way, and in this way only, will they be able to obtain a fitting share of the common good and assure the material and spiritual welfare of their people.

POPE PIUS XII, Christmas Message, 1941

You shall not wrong a stranger or oppress him, for you were strangers in the land of Egypt.

EX 22:21

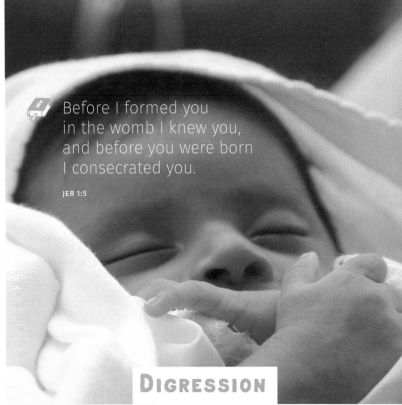

> Before I formed you
> in the womb I knew you,
> and before you were born
> I consecrated you.
>
> **JER 1:5**

DIGRESSION

THE PERSON IN BIOETHICS

 God's love does not differentiate between the newly conceived infant still in his or her mother's womb and the child or young person, or the adult and the elderly person. God does not distinguish between them because he sees an impression of his own image and likeness in each one. ... Therefore, the Magisterium of the Church has constantly proclaimed the sacred and inviolable character of every human life from its conception until its natural end.

POPE BENEDICT XVI,
27th February 2006

69 *What is bioethics about?*

The word "bioethics" is formed from the Greek words *bios* (= life) and *ethos* (= custom, usage, good habit); it is a set of teachings about how to deal fairly with all living things. Bioethics, therefore, is not just environmental ethics, research into how to preserve species and protect habitats. Good bioethics must also be ethics about the life of human beings, for the dignity of the human person is at stake, and not only in genetic research or the question of euthanasia (= May someone kill himself or another human being who is suffering badly?). National Socialism coined the expression "life not worth living", and thereby the Nazis sought in a criminal way to make themselves masters of life and death. A human being, however, is a person from the moment of conception; as a human being, he has a claim on all other human beings. No one has the right to deprive him of his God-given personal dignity. No one may violate the integrity of another human being: not for research purposes, not because someone is old, sick, demented, unborn, or disabled. The dignity of the person is the true foundation of human rights and the justification of the political order.

➡ 472–475 ➡ 2318–2330, 2274–2278, 2280–2283
➡ 435

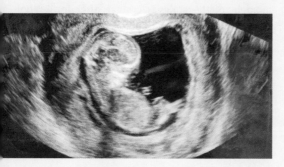

In fact, from the time that the ovum is fertilized, a life is begun which is that of neither the father nor the mother; it is rather the life of a new human being with his own growth. It would never be made human if it were not human already. ... [M]odern genetic science ... has demonstrated that from the first instant there is established the programme of what this living being will be: a person, this individual person with his characteristic aspects already well determined.

POPE ST JOHN PAUL II (1920–2005), Evangelium Vitae (EV 60)

70 *Why must we take responsibility in bioethics?*

In many questions of bioethics—for example: what value do sick, unborn, or elderly human beings have?—it is no longer merely a matter of private decisions by individuals. Many things are determined at the political level. New technologies—for instance, human embryo research and stem cell research—raise urgent new questions. Christians must become highly qualified in order to exercise their social responsibility and take an active part in shaping the humanitarian and social parameters in society. (Cf. DP 1.)

➡ 472–480 ➡ 2274–2278, 2280–2283, 2318–2330

Whatever the word "dignity" may mean in particular and whatever connotations it may have, in any case it means one thing primarily: everything that is done with such a being must be not only in the interests of the parents, but above all in its own interests. The human embryo is already an "end in itself", *propter seipsum existens*, something that exists for its own sake, as Thomas Aquinas says, and Kant agrees with him.

ROBERT SPAEMANN, radio interview, 27th January 2011

Men and women risk being reduced to mere cogs in a machine that treats them as items of consumption to be exploited, with the result that … whenever a human life no longer proves useful for that machine, it is discarded with few qualms, as in the case of the sick,… the elderly who are abandoned and uncared for, and children who are killed in the womb… It is the inevitable consequence of a "throwaway culture" and an uncontrolled consumerism. Upholding the dignity of the person means instead acknowledging the value of human life, which is freely given us and hence cannot be an object of trade or commerce.

POPE FRANCIS,
25th November 2014

71   *When does a human being start to be a person?*

Some say that we can talk about a human person only after he is born. Others even dispute that and say: someone is truly human only when he can think and decide. Still others define the beginning of the human person as the moment when the brain stem is formed or the moment when there is no more possibility of identical twinning. The Church rejects all these interpretations and says: human life begins with the fusion of an ovum and a sperm cell. At the earliest moment of the embryonic stage after fertilization, the Church in accord with both science and common sense regards the life that has resulted as a complete human being already and as such endowed with the dignity that belongs to every human person. Respect for this dignity must also be shown to the unborn and to the weakest members of society. (Cf. DP 5.)

→ 2319, 2322–2323 → 56, 58, 62–63

72   *When is the human person especially endangered?*

Especially at the beginning of life and at the end of life, human beings cannot or can hardly defend their right to life, their human dignity, and their personal integrity by themselves. They need another person who recognizes the inviolable dignity and sanctity of another living human being, who loves this life and accepts it, who helps and cares for, protects, nourishes, and supports it. The life of a handicapped or sick person has inalienable dignity, too; it is inconceivable that it should in any case be considered less valuable or worthless. (Cf. EV 11–12.)

→ 160, 458 → 2276, 2322

73 Can one select from among embryos conceived outside the body?

Discarding an embryo because of a diagnosis that it has a genetic disorder, for instance, trisomy 21 (= Down syndrome), violates the precept of respect for human dignity and the fundamental right to life and bodily integrity. At the same time, it violates the prohibition in the constitutional law of many nations against discrimination based on a handicap, which protects an embryo with a probable gene defect just as much as a handicapped human being who is born.

74 Why does the Church reject abortion in principle?

Every human being, from the moment of conception, has absolute rights and inviolable personal dignity. Therefore, the killing of an embryo is always morally objectionable—regardless of the circumstances in which the child was conceived, the stage of development in which this new human being happens to be, or the health problems with which he will come into the world. An embryo does not develop *into* a human being, rather he develops *as* a human being. Therefore, an abortion is in every case the deliberate killing of an innocent human being. However, as long as Christians do not do everything possible to assist pregnant women who are in difficulty and to make it easier for them to decide in favour of their child, their commitment against abortion and laws that condone it will not seem very credible. The mother's right to freedom, which is often weighed against the child's right to life, is situated on another level and must not be pitted against the right to life.

→ 2270–2275, 2322 → 292, 379, 383–384

> God, the Lord of life, has conferred on men the surpassing ministry of safeguarding life in a manner which is worthy of man. Therefore, from the moment of its conception, life must be guarded with the greatest care, while abortion and infanticide are unspeakable crimes.
>
> Vatican Council II, GS 51

> I will give no deadly medicine to anyone if asked, nor suggest any such counsel; and in like manner I will not give to a woman a pessary to produce abortion.
>
> From the Oath of **HIPPOCRATES** (around 460 – around 370 BC)

> There is a tendency to justify transgressing all boundaries when experimentation is carried out on living human embryos. We forget that the inalienable worth of a human being transcends his or her degree of development.
>
> **POPE FRANCIS,** LS 136

> I have noticed that everyone who is for abortion has already been born.
>
> **RONALD REAGAN** (1911–2004), American President

Puh...

What can a woman do in an unplanned pregnancy?

In crisis situations, and also in the case of an unplanned pregnancy, one can turn to any priest or directly to Catholic counselling centres. All of them are instructed to welcome people lovingly and not to judge them. No one should be left alone in such a situation, and various kinds of help and support are available.

Our relationship with the environment can never be isolated from our relationship with others and with God ....Since everything is interrelated, concern for the protection of nature is also incompatible with the justification of abortion.

POPE FRANCIS, LS 119–120

"Is a black baby a legal injury? Because of her child's skin colour a white lesbian American is suing a sperm bank for damages. By mistake the sperm of an African-American man was sent to the woman instead of that belonging to another white donor whom she had deliberately decided on. →

75   *What can be done to help a woman who has become pregnant after a rape?*

In the case of a rape we must distinguish between two sets of facts. In the first place, a terrible crime has been committed against a woman; it must be prosecuted and viewed as morally reprehensible. Help must be made available to the victim, both by government agencies and by those who provide pastoral care. A priest or (in some countries) specially trained co-workers at Church-owned hospitals and Catholic counselling centres can help the victim. They can offer her consolation and show her ways of coping. Secondly, the human being that resulted from the rape is a child willed and loved by God. Regardless of the biological father, God has a plan for this child. However serious the emotional harm done to the woman may be, the child can become a consolation and give new hope to the woman. Or the child can be adopted. Whatever happens, God cares for all involved and wants what is good. Because of human free will, God cannot prevent crimes, but he can make sure that new hope and new life come of them. The resulting child needs a mother's care and love. But those in the mother's social circle must also take care that the pregnant woman feels safe and accepted.

→ 2270–2275, 2284–2287, 2322
292, 379, 383–384, 386, 392

76 *What about pre-implantation diagnosis (PID)?*

New medical procedures are not always advantageous for a pregnant women and her unborn child. With → PRE-IMPLANTATION DIAGNOSIS (PID) there is an obvious danger of setting an arbitrary value on human life and being selective. Thus children with genetic anomalies or suspected of being handicapped are screened and not allowed to live. More and more often, PID is used even to end the life of a child who is not of the sex desired by the parents. Critics warn that we are going down the path toward "designer babies". No physicians and

not even the parents of an unborn child have the right to decide whether or not the life of a human being is worth living. Many disabled people perceive the debate itself over PID as blatant discrimination: they would not be alive today if PID had already existed when they were conceived. Christians can never approve of selecting among human embryos.

→ 472–473 → 2274–2275, 2323

→ The plaintiff has a good chance of a ruling in her favour: the complaint maintains that the donor numbers were noted by the sperm bank in handwriting only. It argues that this was a violation of duty by the sperm bank.

As reported by Legal Tribune Online, 9th October 2014

PID
Abbreviation for pre-implantation diagnosis. A procedure for the prenatal diagnosis of diseases. Through this procedure, embryos at a very early stage are examined for signs of congenital diseases, such as Trisomy 21 (Down syndrome).

Before I formed you in the womb I knew you, and before you were born I consecrated you.
JER 1:5

PALLIATIVE MEDICINE
(from Latin *pallium* = cloak). When a human being is terminally ill and all medical options have been exhausted, one can finally still accompany the dying process and make sure that the patient does not suffer needlessly. This palliative care alleviates suffering when healing is no longer possible; the use of painkillers makes it possible for the patient to endure his illness better.

Suicide and euthanasia are never morally acceptable options. The task of medicine is to care even when it cannot cure. Physicians and their patients must evaluate the use of technology at their disposal. Reflection on the innate dignity of human life in all its dimensions and on the purpose of medical care is indispensable for formulating a true moral judgement about the use of technology to maintain life... In this way two extremes are avoided: on the one hand, an insistence on useless or burdensome technology even when a patient may legitimately wish to forgo it and, on the other hand, the withdrawal of technology with the intention of causing death.

United States Conference of Catholic Bishops, *Ethical and Religious Directives for Catholic Health Care Services* (Fifth Edition, 2009)

77 *Is euthanasia morally permissible?*

The direct killing of a human being, even if he is terminally ill, is always against the Fifth Commandment (Ex 20:13): *You shall not kill.* That applies to my own life, too. Only God is the master of life and death. On the other hand, to support a dying person and supply him with all possible medical and human care so as to alleviate his sufferings is to practise love of neighbour and perform a work of mercy. The hospice movement and → PALLIATIVE MEDICINE provide important services in this regard. The principle must be: We help the dying person (and not: "We help the person to die"). Accordingly, from a medical and moral perspective, it may even be imperative to discontinue procedures that offer no hope of improvement and also to use palliative means, even if they shorten the patient's life. In all this, however, the patient's will must be taken into consideration. If no directives have been made and the patient himself can no longer state his wishes, they can be expressed by an authorized representative, but they must, however, be consistent with the moral law.

→ 2276–2779, 2324 → 379, 382

78 *Do I have the right to determine for myself the moment of my death?*

No. Christians believe that "life" is not personal property with which you can do whatever you want. Because God is the one who gave us life, there is no absolute freedom in dealing with this gift that is entrusted to us for a time. "You shall not kill" applies to my own life, too. The desire to live and to have life is the deepest desire of a human being. Physicians

report that even the request to be killed because of unbearable suffering is often a last desperate cry for help. Moreover, we should ask how free the call for euthanasia really is. Where euthanasia is already possible today, suffering patients often ask for it so as not to be a burden to others. Thus the supposed *right* to "death on one's own terms" suddenly seems to become a *duty* to one's relatives.

 2280–2283, 2325 379

79 How should commercial euthanasia organizations be viewed?

Any sort of commercialized euthanasia is absolutely objectionable. Human life has no price, and death must not become a profitable business, either. It is in no way ethically defensible for associations and companies to perform euthanasia for a fee. Physician-assisted suicide must also be rejected. A physician must not become the instrument of a patient's subjective desire for death. Every act of euthanasia by a doctor or a nurse turns a healer into a killer. That does not mean that we ignore the suffering that is no doubt present. Improved methods of palliative medicine

> The request for active euthanasia is an attempt to take the final process of life completely into one's own hands. This is incompatible with the commending of oneself into God's loving hand, as the Church's sacramental liturgy puts it. … Euthanasia does not solve suffering, but rather snuffs out the suffering person.
>
> Pastoral Assistance of the Dutch Bishops Conference, 2005

> God took from us authority not only over the life of another but also over our own life.
>
> **ST THOMAS MORE** (1478–1535), Lord Chancellor of Henry VIII, and martyr.

Progress becomes true progress only if it serves the human person and if the human person grows: not only in terms of his or her technical power, but also in his or her moral awareness.

POPE BENEDICT XVI,
Interview in Castelgandolfo on 5th August 2006

As far as the right to life is concerned, we must denounce its widespread violation in our society: alongside the victims of armed conflicts, terrorism, and the different forms of violence, there are the silent deaths caused by hunger, abortion, experimentation on human embryos, and euthanasia. How can we fail to see in all this an attack on peace? Abortion and embryonic experimentation constitute a direct denial of that attitude of acceptance of others which is indispensable for establishing lasting relationships of peace.

POPE BENEDICT XVI,
Message for the World Day of Peace 2007

and hospice care for the dying are important ways of dealing with it.

→ 2277–2279 → 382

80 *Why does the Church get involved in the bioethics debate?*

The Church welcomes all genuine scientific progress, for it is in keeping with God's command to be stewards of creation. Advances in medical technology in particular are very beneficial for mankind. Through them, however, human beings acquire more and more decision-making power over others. Suddenly it seems "useful" to cultivate human embryos in a Petri dish, it seems "feasible" to kill handicapped infants in their mother's womb, and it seems "humane" to put sick people out of their suffering. Whenever there is a misuse of human power, the Church must always stand on the side of the victims. Research must not be exploited and suddenly turned against human beings, especially the weakest members of society. The Church is not interested in making narrow-minded prohibitions; rather, she wishes to promote the dignity of the human person at all stages of life and in all circumstances.

→ 1699–1715, 2292–2295 → 393, 154–155

81 *Why do so many people want the option of assisted suicide?*

People are afraid of serious pain. Moreover, they have a fear of becoming incapacitated. We can address such fears very well today, however, through proper care, comprehensive support of the dying, palliative medicine, and hospice care. Experience shows that the great majority of patients stop asking for death once they learn about the possibilities of pain management and end-of-life care. To help dying persons (instead of "helping people to die") may mean discontinuing or refusing some treatments or else relieving intolerable suffering through painkillers and sedatives. This is true even if administering them shortens the patient's remaining lifetime.

→ 2278–2279 382

82 *Why are people afraid of becoming incapacitated?*

There is a concern about being at the mercy of others. People fear dependency or loneliness. The legitimate hospice movement addresses all these concerns. Precisely in the final phase of life, we must give the dying the opportunity to approach their own death with the loving care of other people. In addition to that, they especially need spiritual assistance in the last weeks and days of their life.

→ 1506–1510 242

83 *What is the significance of dying from the Christian perspective?*

Today dying often appears to be nothing more than bodily deterioration. Dying, however, is a decisive part of life, and for many people—the step to final maturity. For a Christian, life is a gift. This thought inspires trust even in one's difficult last hours. We know that we are in the hand of a loving God and have hope that death is not the end but a transition to eternal life. This puts the experience of suffering into a completely different perspective. Again and again those in pastoral ministry find that this hope gives consolation even to seemingly irreligious people who are facing their actual death. In the suffering and dying person, Christ is especially close to us.

→ 1010–1014, 2299 393, 154–155

Respect for the right to life at every stage firmly establishes a principle of decisive importance: *life is a gift which is not completely at the disposal of the subject.*

POPE BENEDICT XVI, Message for the World Day of Peace 2007

Where are we going, then? Always homeward.

NOVALIS (1772–1801, pen-name for Friedrich Baron von Hardenberg), German author

From important Church documents

THE HUMAN PERSON

Rerum Novarum

The Freedom of the Human Person

For man, fathoming by his faculty of reason matters without number, linking the future with the present, and being master of his own acts, guides his ways under the eternal law and the power of God, whose providence governs all things. Wherefore, it is in his power to exercise his choice not only as to matters that regard his present welfare, but also about those which he deems may be for his advantage in time yet to come. Hence, man not only should possess the fruits of the earth, but also the very soil, inasmuch as from the produce of the earth he has to lay by provision for the future.
Pope Leo XIII, Encyclical Rerum Novarum (1891), 6

Rerum Novarum

Equality of All?

There naturally exist among mankind manifold differences of the most important kind; people differ in capacity, skill, health, strength; and unequal fortune is a necessary result of unequal condition. Such inequality is far from being disadvantageous either to individuals or to the community. Social and public life can only be maintained by means of various kinds of capacity for business and the playing of many parts; and each man, as a rule, chooses the part which suits his own peculiar domestic condition.
Pope Leo XIII, Encyclical Rerum Novarum (1891), 14

Rerum Novarum

The Foundation of Human Rights

For they [different classes in society] will understand and feel that all men are children of the same common Father, who is God; that all have alike the same last end, which is God Himself, who alone can make either men or angels absolutely and perfectly happy; that each and all are redeemed and made sons of God, by Jesus Christ, "the first-born among many brethren"; that the blessings of nature and the gifts of grace belong to the whole human race in common, and that from none except the unworthy is withheld the inheritance of the kingdom of heaven. "If sons, heirs also; heirs indeed of God, and co-heirs with Christ." Such is the scheme of duties and of rights which is shown forth to the world by the Gospel. Would it not seem that, were society penetrated with ideas like these, strife must quickly cease?
Pope Leo XIII, Encyclical Rerum Novarum (1891), 21

Freedom for Private Initiative

Pacem in Terris

"However extensive and far-reaching the influence of the State on the economy may be, it must never be exerted to the extent of depriving the individual citizen of his freedom of action. It must rather augment his freedom, while effectively guaranteeing the protection of everyone's essential, personal rights." (Citing John XXIII, Encyclical Mater et Magistra.)

Pope St John XXIII, Encyclical Pacem in terris (1963), 65

The Right to Life and to a Livelihood

Pacem in Terris

But first we must speak of man's rights. Man has the right to live. He has the right to bodily integrity and to the means necessary for the proper development of life, particularly food, clothing, shelter, medical care, rest, and, finally, the necessary social services. In consequence, he has the right to be looked after in the event of ill health; disability stemming from his work; widowhood; old age; enforced unemployment; or whenever through no fault of his own he is deprived of the means of livelihood.

Pope St John XXIII, Encyclical Pacem in Terris (1963), 6

The Right to God

Pacem in Terris

Also among man's rights is that of being able to worship God in accordance with the right dictates of his own conscience, and to profess his religion both in private and in public. According to the clear teaching of Lactantius, "this is the very condition of our birth, that we render to the God who made us that just homage which is His due; that we acknowledge Him alone as God, and follow Him. It is from this ligature of piety, which binds us and joins us to God, that religion derives its name."

Pope St John XXIII, Encyclical Pacem in Terris (1963), 8

Human Rights

Pacem in Terris

A clear proof of the farsightedness of this organization is provided by the Universal Declaration of Human Rights... The preamble of this declaration affirms that the genuine recognition and complete observance of all the rights and freedoms outlined in the declaration is a goal to be sought by all peoples and all nations... It is a solemn recognition of the personal dignity of every human being; an assertion of everyone's right to be free to seek out the truth, to follow moral principles, discharge the duties imposed by justice, and lead a fully human life. It also recognized other rights connected with these.

Pope St John XXIII, Encyclical Pacem in Terris (1963), 75

Man Divided

Gaudium et Spes

The truth is that the imbalances under which the modern world labours are linked with that more basic imbalance which is rooted in the heart of man. For in man himself many elements wrestle with one another. Thus, on the one hand, as a creature he experiences his limitations in a multitude of ways; on the other, he feels himself to be boundless in his desires and summoned to a higher life. Pulled by manifold attractions he is constantly forced to choose among them and renounce some. Indeed, as a weak and sinful being, he often does what he would not and fails to do what he would. Hence he suffers from internal divisions, and from these flow so many and such great discords in society.

Vatican Council II, Pastoral Constitution Gaudium et spes (1965), 10

Development: The New Name for Peace

Populorum Progressio

In God's plan, every man is born to seek self-fulfillment, for every human life is called to some task by God. At birth a human being possesses certain aptitudes and abilities in germinal form, and these qualities are to be cultivated so that they may bear fruit. By developing these traits through formal education of personal effort, the individual works his way toward the goal set for him by the Creator. Endowed with intellect and free will, each man is responsible for his self-fulfillment even as he is for his salvation. He is helped, and sometimes hindered, by his teachers and those around him; yet whatever be the outside influences exerted on him, he is the chief architect of his own success or failure. Utilizing only his talent and willpower, each man can grow in humanity, enhance his personal worth, and perfect himself.

Pope Paul VI, Encyclical Populorum Progressio (1967), 15

On the Nature of Human Sexuality

Familiaris Consortio

Sexuality, by means of which man and woman give themselves to one another through the acts which are proper and exclusive to spouses, is by no means something purely biological, but concerns the innermost being of the human person as such. It is realized in a truly human way only if it is an integral part of the love by which a man and a woman commit themselves totally to one another until death. The total physical self-giving would be a lie if it were not the sign and fruit of a total personal self-giving, in which the whole person, including the temporal dimension, is present: if the person were to withhold something or reserve the possibility of deciding otherwise in the future, by this very fact he or she would not be giving totally.

Pope St John Paul II, Apostolic Exhortation Familiaris Consortio (1981), 11

The Dignity of Woman

Familiaris Consortio

While it must be recognized that women have the same right as men to perform various public functions, society must be structured in such a way that wives and mothers are not in practice compelled to work outside the home and that their families can live and prosper in a dignified way even when they themselves devote their full time to their own family. Furthermore, the mentality which honours women more for their work outside the home than for their work within the family must be overcome. This requires that men should truly esteem and love women with total respect for their personal dignity and that society should create and develop conditions favouring work in the home.

Pope St John Paul II, Apostolic Exhortation Familiaris Consortio (1981), 23

Understanding Man

Centesimus Annus

It is not possible to understand man on the basis of economics alone, nor to define him simply on the basis of class membership. Man is understood in a more complete way when he is situated within the sphere of culture through his language, history, and the position he takes towards the fundamental events of life, such as birth, love, work, and death. At the heart of every culture lies the attitude man takes to the greatest mystery: the mystery of God.

Pope St John Paul II, Encyclical Centesimus Annus (1991), 24

Freedom and Society

Centesimus Annus

Man, who was created for freedom, bears within himself the wound of Original Sin, which constantly draws him towards evil and puts him in need of redemption. Not only *is this doctrine an integral part of Christian revelation;* it also has great hermeneutical value insofar as it helps one to understand human reality. Man tends towards good, but he is also capable of evil. He can transcend his immediate interest and still remain bound to it. The social order will be all the more stable, the more it takes this fact into account and does not place in opposition personal interest and the interests of society as a whole, but rather seeks ways to bring them into fruitful harmony.

Pope St John Paul II, Encyclical Centesimus Annus (1991), 25

Conspiracy against Life

Evangelium Vitae

Looking at the situation from this point of view, it is possible to speak in a certain sense of a war of the powerful against the weak: a life which would require greater acceptance, love, and care is considered useless, or held to be an intolerable burden, and is therefore rejected in one way or another. A person who, because of illness, handicap, or, more simply, just by existing, compromises the well-being or life-style of those who are more favoured tends to be looked upon as an enemy to be resisted or eliminated. In this way a kind of "conspiracy against life" is unleashed.

Pope St John Paul II, Encyclical Evangelium Vitae (1995), 12

A Right to Death on One's Own Terms

Evangelium Vitae

Threats which are no less serious hang over the incurably ill and the dying. In a social and cultural context which makes it more difficult to face and accept suffering, the temptation becomes all the greater to resolve the problem of suffering by eliminating it at the root, by hastening death so that it occurs at the moment considered most suitable.

Pope St John Paul II, Encyclical Evangelium Vitae (1995), 15

Doing Away with Human Beings

`Evangelium Vitae`

We see a tragic expression of all this in the spread of euthanasia—disguised and surreptitious, or practised openly and even legally. As well as for reasons of a misguided pity at the sight of the patient's suffering, euthanasia is sometimes justified by the utilitarian motive of avoiding costs which bring no return and which weigh heavily on society. Thus it is proposed to eliminate malformed babies, the severely handicapped, the disabled, the elderly, especially when they are not self-sufficient, and the terminally ill. Nor can we remain silent in the face of other more furtive, but no less serious and real, forms of euthanasia. These could occur for example when, in order to increase the availability of organs for transplants, organs are removed without respecting objective and adequate criteria which verify the death of the donor.
Pope St John Paul II, Encyclical Evangelium Vitae (1995), 15

The Battle for Life

`Evangelium Vitae`

Aside from intentions, which can be varied and perhaps can seem convincing at times, especially if presented in the name of solidarity, we are in fact faced by an objective "conspiracy against life", involving even international Institutions, engaged in encouraging and carrying out actual campaigns to make contraception, sterilization, and abortion widely available. Nor can it be denied that the mass media are often implicated in this conspiracy, by lending credit to that culture which presents recourse to contraception, sterilization, abortion, and even euthanasia as a mark of progress and a victory of freedom, while depicting as enemies of freedom and progress those positions which are unreservedly pro-life.
Pope St John Paul II, Encyclical Evangelium Vitae (1995), 17

No Right to Kill

`Evangelium Vitae`

To claim the right to abortion, infanticide, and euthanasia, and to recognize that right in law, means to attribute to human freedom a perverse and evil significance: that of an absolute power over others and against others.
Pope St John Paul II, Encyclical Evangelium Vitae (1995), 20

Embryo Research

`Evangelium Vitae`

This evaluation of the morality of abortion is to be applied also to the recent forms of intervention on human embryos which, although carried out for purposes legitimate in themselves, inevitably involve the killing of those embryos. This is the case with experimentation on embryos, which is becoming increasingly widespread in the field of biomedical research and is legally permitted in some countries. Although "one must uphold as licit procedures carried out on the human embryo which respect the life and integrity of the embryo and do not involve disproportionate risks for it, but rather are directed to its healing, the improvement of its condition of health, or its individual survival", it must nonetheless be stated that the use of human embryos or fetuses as an object of experimentation constitutes a crime against their dignity as human beings who have a right to the same respect owed to a child once born, just as to every person.

Pope St John Paul II, Encyclical Evangelium Vitae (1995), 63

Prenatal Diagnosis

Evangelium Vitae

Special attention must be given to evaluating the morality of prenatal diagnostic techniques ... [that] are used with a eugenic intention which accepts selective abortion in order to prevent the birth of children affected by various types of anomalies. Such an attitude is shameful and utterly reprehensible, since it presumes to measure the value of a human life only within the parameters of "normality" and physical well-being, thus opening the way to legitimizing infanticide and euthanasia as well.

Pope St John Paul II, Encyclical Evangelium Vitae (1995), 63

Human Dignity

Laudato Sì

At times we see an obsession with denying any pre-eminence to the human person; more zeal is shown in protecting other species than in defending the dignity which all human beings share in equal measure. Certainly, we should be concerned lest other living beings be treated irresponsibly. But we should be particularly indignant at the enormous inequalities in our midst, whereby we continue to tolerate some considering themselves more worthy than others. ... In practice, we continue to tolerate that some consider themselves more human than others, as if they had been born with greater rights.

Pope Francis, Encylical Laudato Sì (2015), 90

4

QUESTIONS
84–111

The Common Good, Personhood, Solidarity, Subsidiarity

What are the principles of Catholic social teaching?

84

Catholic social teaching has four principles:

the principle of the
dignity of the human person
(personhood)

the principle of the
common good

the principle of
subsidiarity

and the principle of
solidarity.

Dtn 6:5: "You shall love the LORD your God with all your heart, and with all your soul, and with all your might", and Lev 19:18: "You shall love your neighbour as yourself", together make up the so-called **Greatest Commandment of Love.**

,, I exhort you to generous solidarity and to the return of economics and finance to an ethical approach which favours human beings.

POPE FRANCIS, EG 58

With these four principles, we can grasp human society in its entirety and consider this reality truthfully. Why do these principles apply? They apply, in the first place, because they are reasonable. And they apply, secondly, because they result from the Christian faith, which illuminates by reason. Someone who believes wants to obey God's commandments, especially the → GREATEST COMMANDMENT OF LOVE OF GOD AND NEIGHBOUR. Nowadays Christians are confronted with various societal problems. Whether it is a question of relations between individuals, groups, or nations—in every case, with the help of the four principles of Catholic social teaching, we can tell what is truly human, socially beneficial, and just.

→ 160 → 1881, 1883, 1938 ff., 1939 ff.
→ 322, 323, 327, 332

85 *How do the four principles work together?*

All four principles are interrelated. We cannot isolate them from each other or pit one against another. If we apply them together, we can understand a societal reality in depth. An example: the "family" is a social reality that is valuable and worth protecting; in it human beings can develop their *personal dignity*. In itself, a family is already *solidarity* in practice. A family, however, also needs the solidarity of others, because without support from outside it cannot make its irreplaceable contribution to the *common good*. In helping the family, though, higher authorities must not take away what it can do by itself, child-rearing, for example (principle of *subsidiarity*).

→ **161–162** → **2209–2213, 2250** → **370**

86 *Why must we act according to these principles?*

Being human means taking on responsibility. No human being can reasonably situate himself outside of social life. Through the commandment of love of God and love of neighbour, Christians are obliged once again morally to help others, to serve the common good, to help every individual to live a dignified, truly human life, and to protect the intrinsic rights of groups and associations.

→ **163** → **1734 ff.** → **288**

87 *What does "the common good" mean?*

Vatican Council II says that the common good is "the sum of those conditions of social life which allow social groups and their individual members relatively thorough and ready access to their own fulfillment" (GS 26). The goal of the individual is to accomplish good. The goal of society is the common good. "The common good, in fact, can be understood as the so-

> It is impossible for a man to be good unless he is in right relation to the common good.
>
> **ST THOMAS AQUINAS** *Summa theologiae* I-II, q. 92 a.1 ad 3

> But the line dividing good and evil cuts through the heart of every human being. And who is willing to destroy a piece of his own heart?
>
> **ALEKSANDR SOLZHENITSYN** (1918–2008), Russian winner of the Nobel Prize for Literature

> Many people who cannot advise themselves like to give advice to others, like the unfaithful imposters among the preachers: they teach and proclaim the good things that they themselves are unwilling to do.
>
> **CHRÉTIEN DE TROYES** (around 1140–1190), French author

> Give alms ... and do not let your eye begrudge the gift when you make it. Do not turn your face away from any poor man, and the face of God will not be turned away from you.
>
> **TOB 4:7**

> Anything good on earth happens only if someone does more than he must. No one can do for me the good that I do not do.
>
> **HERMANN GMEINER** (1919–1986), founder of the SOS Children's Villages

To love someone is to desire that person's good and to take effective steps to secure it. Besides the good of the individual, there is a good that is linked to living in society: the common good. It is the good of "all of us", made up of individuals, families, and intermediate groups who together constitute society.

POPE BENEDICT XVI, CiV 7

cial and community dimension of the moral good" (*Compendium of Social Doctrine* 164). The common good refers both to the good of *all* human beings and to the good of the *whole* human being. The common good requires, first, the parameters of a functioning governmental order, as it is found in a *constitutional state*. Then there must be concern to maintain the natural means of subsistence. Within this framework are the rights of every human being to food, shelter, health, work, and access to education. There must also be freedom of thought, assembly, and religion. Here the requirements of the common good overlap with universal human rights.

➡ **164** ➡ **1903 ff.** ➡ **326–327**

88   *How does the common good come about?*

And so, my fellow Americans, ask not what your country can do for you, ask what you can do for your country. My fellow citizens of the world, ask not what America will do for you, but what together we can do for the freedom of man.

JOHN F. KENNEDY (1917–1963), Inaugural Address, 20th January 1961

Every human being and every social group has proper interests that are more or less justified. To desire the "common good" means to be capable of thinking beyond one's own needs. We must be interested in the good *of all,* even of people nobody thinks about because they have no voice and no power. The goods of the earth are there for everyone. And if each person thinks only of himself, then coexistence becomes a war of all against all. The common good, however, consists not only of the material or external good of all human beings; it also includes the *comprehensive* good of the human being. Therefore concern about the spiritual good is part of the common good, too. No aspect of human existence can be left out of consideration.

What is not useful to the swarm is not useful to the bee.

CHARLES-LOUIS DE MONTESQUIEU (1689–1755), political philosopher

➡ **168–170** ➡ **1907–1912, 1925, 1927** ➡ **327**

89 How should we deal with the goods of the earth?

God created the world for all. The earth with human aid produces goods and harvests. In principle, they should be at the disposal of all without preferential treatment and be applied for the good of all. Every person has the right to what is vitally necessary, which must not be withheld from him, even though we know that there is a right to property and that there will always be differences in how much people own. If some have more than enough but others lack the bare necessities of life, this calls not only for charity but above all for justice.

→ 171–175 → 2443–2446 → 449

90 *Is private property permissible?*

Yes, it is reasonable for there to be private property. Through his work, a person shapes the earth and makes a piece of it his own. Private property makes people free and independent. It encourages the individual to preserve his property, care for it, and protect it from destruction. In contrast, things owned in common often deteriorate because no one feels responsible for them. Having material goods at our disposal prompts us to take on responsibility and tasks in the community. Thus, the right to private property is an important element of civic freedom. It is the basis of a truly democratic economic order, since a share for everyone in the profits from economic activity becomes possible only through private property.

➡ **176** ➡ **2401** ➡ **426**

 You received without charge,

A person who is deprived of something he can call "his own", and of the possibility of earning a living through his own initiative, comes to depend on the social machine and on those who control it. This makes it much more difficult for him to recognize his dignity as a person and hinders progress towards the building up of an authentic human community.

POPE ST JOHN PAUL II, CA 13

91 *What are the limits of private property?*

The *right to private property* must never be considered absolute. Rather, anyone who owns property must make use of it in a manner consistent with the good of all. This is true of public goods, for example street lights, but it also applies to privately owned things, for instance a mobile phone. Consequently, I must let another person use my phone if he needs help and must make an emergency call. Private property should serve only as an instrument for the better management of the earth's goods. Someone has to feel responsible for particular things. If everyone is responsible for *everything,* in practice no one feels responsible for *anything.* Private property cannot take priority over the common good, since, in principle, all goods must serve all people.

➡ **177, 282** ➡ **2402–2406, 2452** ➡ **427**

A person who can acquire no property can have no other interest but to eat as much and to labour as little as possible.

ADAM SMITH (1723–1790), Scottish economist

Where there is no property, neither is there joy in giving; then no one can have the pleasure of helping his friends, the traveller, or the suffering in their need.

ARISTOTLE (384–322 BC), Greek philosopher and scientist, *Politics,* bk. 2, pt. 5

92   *What are the limits to the joint use of goods?*

Someone who owns private property owns it so that it might be *used jointly.* Here one must think not only of one's fellowmen who are alive right now but also of future generations. This is the reason for the *principle of sustainability.* To conduct sustainable economic activity means that society *must not use up more resources than it can somehow replace or regenerate.* Therefore, in using a resource one must keep in mind not only one's own advantage but also the welfare of all people, in other words, the *common good.* The property owner has the duty to use his goods productively or else to make them available to someone who can make use of them productively, i.e., to make something new that serves all.

→ **178**

give without charge. MT 10:8

> We live in times when an individual in need may also take what he needs to preserve his life and his health, if he cannot obtain it in some other way, through his labour or through begging.

New Year's Eve sermon (1946) by **JOSEF CARDINAL FRINGS** (1887–1978). In the postwar period in Germany, the slang word "fringsen" referred to the pilfering of food or fuel: the Cardinal of Cologne had expressed understanding for the plundering of coal trains, given the inadequate supplies in an icy winter.

93   *What goods do people need in order to be productive?*

Today the duty to make property useful and productive applies not only to land and capital but also increasingly to technical knowledge, in other words, to intellectual property. In fact, the prosperity of the industrial nations is based more and more on this kind of property, whereas the ownership of land and raw materials is becoming increasingly less important for prosperity (John Paul II, CA 32). One example is access to high-yield and special seeds, which is in danger of being controlled by large corporations. Without a universal right of access to these goods, the common good cannot be achieved. The global common good implies that a share in innovations is made possible for people in poorer nations as well.

→ **179** → **2408 ff.** → **429**

> If certain landed estates impede the general prosperity because they are extensive, unused, or poorly used, or because they bring hardship to peoples or are detrimental to the interests of the country, the common good sometimes demands their expropriation.

POPE PAUL VI, *Populorum Progressio* (PP 24)

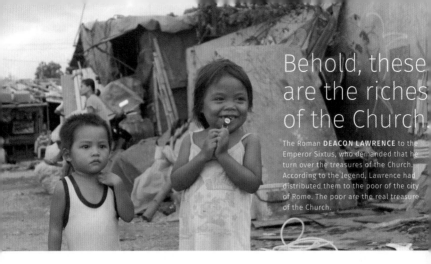

Behold, these
are the riches
of the Church

 The world has
enough for every-
one's need, but not for
everyone's greed.

MAHATMA GANDHI (1869–
1948), Indian politician

If a brother or
sister is poorly
clothed and in lack of
daily food, and one of
you says to them, "Go in
peace, be warmed and
filled," without giving
them the things needed
for the body, what does
it profit? So faith by
itself, if it has no works
is dead.

JAMES 2:15–17

 Oh, how I wish for
a Church that is
poor and for the poor!

POPE FRANCIS,
16th March 2013

94 What does the common good mean for the poor?

The poor must be at the heart of the Church, or else
the Church betrays her mission. In GAUDIUM ET SPES
the Second Vatican Council speaks about a *preferential option for the poor* (GS 1). From this results
the central social obligation of the individual and
of the whole Church to take care of the needs especially of those who are on the peripheries of society.
The Beatitudes in the Sermon on the Mount, Jesus's
own poverty, and his loving care for the poor show
us the way. Standing up for marginalized people is
a direct command of Jesus: "As you did it to one of
the least of these my brethren, you did it to me"
(Mt 25:40). Jesus also warns, however, against the
ideological notion that we can completely do away
with poverty in the world (Mt 26:11). Only at Christ's
Second Coming will this be possible.

➡ **182–183** ➡ **2443–2446** ➡ **448–449**

95 What does the principle of subsidiarity involve?

Every societal task is always assigned in the first
place to the smallest possible group that can
perform it. A group at a higher level may assume

responsibility only if the smaller association is not capable of resolving the problem. If the smaller association needs help, however, the higher level must help. This arrangement is summed up in the →PRINCIPLE OF SUBSIDIARITY and the → OFFER OF ASSISTANCE. For example, if a family has problems, the State can intervene only if the family or the parents are overburdened and cannot resolve them. This principle of subsidiarity is supposed to strengthen the freedom of the individual and of groups and associations and prevent too much centralization. Private initiative should be encouraged, because being able to help oneself is an important component of the dignity of the human person. The principle of subsidiarity was first formulated in 1931, in the Encyclical QUADRAGESIMO ANNO by Pope Pius XI.

→ 185–187 → 1883–1885, 1894 → 286, 323

96   *Does the principle of subsidiarity apply to politics as well?*

Yes. To take the USA example, applying the principle of subsidiarity is indispensable when it is a question, for instance, of determining the relation of local governments to the federal government. Only in cases where a local government cannot resolve a problem by itself may the federal government claim competence. In principle, however, there can be situations in which a higher level must intervene: when, for example, there is a sufficiently large natural disaster or when human rights are violated.

→ 188 → 1883–1885, 1894 → 323, 447

97   *What does the principle of subsidiarity mean for the individual?*

We cannot just leave questions about living together to "the higher-ups". In our situation we must take the initiative in addressing problems and ask for

PRINCIPLE OF SUBSIDIARITY
The superior level (for instance, the State) must not claim competence if the lower level (for example, the family) can solve the problem by itself.

OFFER OF ASSISTANCE
If the lower-level association is overburdened by a problem, the next-higher level must offer help

 [Church authorities] should entrust the layman with tasks that he can perform as well or even better than the priest and allow him to act freely and exercise personal responsibility within the limits set for his work or demanded by the common welfare of the Church.
POPE PIUS XII,
5th October 1957

You don't help people by doing for them what they could and should do for themselves.
ABRAHAM LINCOLN
(1809–1865), United States President

> What you tell me, I forget. What you show me, I remember. What you let me do, I understand.
> **CONFUCIUS** (551–479 BC), Chinese philosopher

help from the next-higher level only if we are over-burdened. Before one does that, of course, person-to-person assistance is appropriate, both for those who offer and for those who receive help. As a matter of principle, a Christian is called to participate actively in society and to exclude no one.

➡ **189** ➡ **1913** ➡ **323, 328**

> ## Self-confidence is the source of confidence in others.
> **FRANÇOIS DE LA ROCHEFOUCAULD** (1613–1680), diplomat and author

98 *How can there be shared responsibility without harmful dependency?*

> Responsibility for oneself is the root of all responsibility.
> **MONG DSI** (372–289 BC), Chinese philosopher

Through *participation*. The participation of citizens is a cornerstone of democracy and therefore important for Christians, also. Christians show solidarity by seeking to participate in civil society and influence its fate. In this way they look after their responsibility to shape the world. The possibility of participating must be guaranteed to all citizens in order to bring about so-called participatory justice (see below).

➡ **190** ➡ **1913–1917**

> The security of the little man is based on the security of the great man; the security of the great man is based on the security of the little man. The little and the great, the noble and the commoners are dependent on one another, so that all can have their joy.
> **LÜ BUWEI** (around 300–236 BC), Chinese political philosopher

99 *What can participation look like in practice?*

Important prerequisites for appropriate participation are a sound education and information. Participation must be in the proper measure and must not be misused to promote merely personal interests. Nor should it consist solely of exercising the right to vote (GS 30–31; CA 51–52). In this regard, the Church's social doctrine especially criticizes authoritarian regimes that see any participation of citizens as a threat. Above and beyond the right to vote, social involvement is demanded of Christians, regardless of

whether this involvement is in the parish, a political party, or a neighbourhood association. Lay people especially should acquire special competence in many societal issues and thus collaborate in shaping the local community (GS 43). Of course, as a Christian one should not just become involved in society personally but should also, in solidarity, make it possible for others to participate. The real *participation of all* is the core of participatory justice, which in turn is a decisive element of social justice in general. The *exclusion* of individuals denies their dignity and thus violates the command to respect the human person.

➡ **151, 189–191, 406** ➡ **1913–1917** ➡ **328**

> Many little people in many little places who do many little things can change the face of the earth.
>
> Xhosa [South African] saying

> The fruit of Silence is Prayer
> The fruit of Prayer is Faith
> The fruit of Faith is Love
> The fruit of Love is Service
> The fruit of Service is Peace
>
> **ST TERESA OF CALCUTTA**
> (1910–1997)

100 *What does the principle of solidarity imply?*

The principle of solidarity gives expression to the social dimension of the human person. No human being can live for himself alone; he is always dependent on others, and not just to receive practical assistance, but also in order to have a conversation partner, to

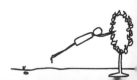

grow by coming to understand the ideas, arguments, needs, and wishes of others, and to be able to develop his personality more completely.

→ **192** → **1939–1942** → **332**

101 *How far does solidarity go?*

In a globalized world, we are glad that boundaries are becoming less important, because the world is coming closer together and communication is possible in real time. Great dangers, however, also lurk in globalization: what happens politically or economically in one part of the world has immediate consequences

for people who live in an altogether different part. Even though the principle of subsidiarity still holds, from an ethical perspective we must learn to think globally. Many questions, such as epidemics or migration, can be dealt with only at the global level if we want to arrive at long-term solutions that are good for all the people on Planet Earth.

→ **192** → **1939–1948** → **332, 376, 395**

102 *How can solidarity be put into practice?*

Solidarity is at the same time a social principle and a moral virtue (*Compendium of Social Doctrine* 193). As a principle of social order, it serves to overcome the "structures of sin" (SRS 36) and

to create a "civilization of love" and consequently of solidarity. As a moral virtue, *solidarity* means deliberate, practical support for the well-being of all people. Vague words of compassion do not help; we must act! "The principle of solidarity requires that men and women of our day cultivate a greater awareness that

99 Justice is "rendering to each one what is due to him", whether to God or to man.

ST THOMAS AQUINAS, *Summa theologiae* II–II, q. 58, art. I

99 I can't stand the pornography of poverty!

BOB GELDOF (b. 1951), Irish rock musician

they are debtors of the society of which they have become part" (*Compendium of Social Doctrine* 195). People can do little by themselves; instead, they are dependent on what others, including their ancestors, have accomplished. As a result, we are obliged to be there for others, too, and to take future generations into consideration in our own actions and decisions.

99 Many people are talking about the poor, but very few people talk to the poor.

ST TERESA OF CALCUTTA (1910–1997)

If one member suffers, all suffer together; if one member is honoured, all rejoice together.

1 COR 12:26

→ 193–195 → 1942 → 323, 328, 332, 447

The deepest essence of love is self-giving.

EDITH STEIN (1891–1942)

 Justice without mercy is unloving; mercy without justice is degrading.

FRIEDRICH VON BODELSCHWINGH (1831–1910), Lutheran theologian and social reformer

A little mercy makes the world less cold and more just.

POPE FRANCIS, 17th March 2013

When I despair, I remember that all through history the ways of truth and love have always won. There have been tyrants and murderers, and for a time, they can seem invincible. But in the end, they always fall. Think of it—always.

MAHATMA GANDHI (1869–1948)

It is no longer enough to speak only of the integrity of ecosystems. We have to dare to speak of the integrity of human life, of the need to promote and unify all the great values.

POPE FRANCIS, LS 224

103 *For a believer, what is the most radical reason to practise solidarity?*

The solidarity of Jesus. No one ever practised greater solidarity than Jesus. Jesus was sent as the living sign of God's solidarity with mankind, which cannot help itself. The Son of God not only declares his solidarity with all mankind; he even lays down his life for us. This definitive self-giving for the sake of others represents the highest possible love and solidarity and should become the standard for Christian action.

 196 ➡ 949–953 ➡ 395

104 *Are the principles of social doctrine the only foundation on which to build a good society?*

No. Christian social doctrine is naturally tied to general values that logically precede it. I must have sound values and commit myself to them personally in order to lead a conscientious life and be able to participate reliably in society. The social principles are then guidelines for shaping society. All values, in turn, are connected with the dignity of the human person, as a primary value that results from man's likeness to God.

➡ 197 ➡ 2419–2425 ➡ 324, 438

105 *What values are important in social doctrine?*

Three values are fundamental: truth, freedom, and justice. Yet truly successful human coexistence requires in addition love and mercy. And so Thomas Aquinas says: "Justice without mercy is cruelty; mercy without justice is the mother of dissolution."

➡ 197 ➡ 1886 ➡ 324

106   *What does freedom mean?*

Being *free* sets man above the animals and in a certain sense even makes him like God. True freedom is not the capacity to choose whatever one wants, good or evil, but rather the capacity to choose the good. Only free human beings can take responsibility. Being personally free makes human beings unique. Within the range of possibilities, someone can freely choose his occupation and his vocation; human beings can come or go, choose this or leave that aside. It is a fundamental human right the exercise of which must not be restricted without good reason. With respect to freedom of expression, human beings must be allowed to articulate freely their own religious, political, and cultural ideas. Everyone must be able to express his own opinion in freedom. For this to happen, there must be a legal order that guarantees a person's freedom and protects it against pressure from the misuse of freedom by others.

→ 199–200 → 1738 → 286, 290

> ❞ The enormous thing granted to a human being is choice, freedom.
>
> **SØREN KIERKEGAARD** (1813–1855), Danish philosopher

> ❞ To serve God is freedom.
>
> **LUCIUS ANNAEUS SENECA** (around 4 BC – AD 65), Roman politician and philosopher

> When you tell the truth you never have to remember later what you lied about.
>
> **WARREN BUFFET** (b. 1930), American businessman

> The truth does not conform to us, but rather we must conform to the truth.
>
> **MATTHIAS CLAUDIUS** (1740–1815), German poet

> As servants of God we commend ourselves in every way: … by genuine love, truthful speech, and the power of God; with the weapons of righteousness for the right hand and for the left.
>
> **2 COR 6:4.7**

> Justice renders to each one what is his, and claims not another's property; it disregards its own profit in order to preserve the common equity.
>
> **ST AMBROSE OF MILAN** (339–397), Doctor of the Church

> Vindicate me, O LORD, my God, according to your righteousness.
>
> **PS 35:24**

> Development, the new name for peace.
>
> **POPE PAUL VI**, PP 76

107 *Why do we need truth in the life of society?*

Truth, translated into my personal life, means truthfulness, honesty. If people do not deal honestly with one another, any society falls apart. When words and actions no longer agree and when we can no longer presume honesty, then mistrust, coldness, and cunning define human coexistence. Another component of truth in the political-economic realm is *transparency*, both of decisions and of actions. This is especially true when it is a question of the use of financial resources.

➡ **198** ➡ **2464–2487** ➡ **452–455**

108 *What is justice?*

Justice is the constant will "to give their due to God and neighbour" (CCC 1807).

➡ **201** ➡ **1807, 2411** ➡ **302**

109 *What sorts of justice are there?*

Distributive justice is a relationship of a community to its members. It allots a fair share to each person or group. *Legal justice* is a relationship of the members to a community. It requires each member of a community to contribute his proper share. *Commutative justice* is a relationship between equals: someone who sells goods should receive a suitable price for them. It guides the distribution of goods through the world market. Together they make up *social justice*. Striving for *social justice* is an important extension of legal justice. While the latter is concerned with obeying the law and a functioning government of laws, *social justice* brings in the overall social question. The goods of the earth must be apportioned justly. And unjust differences between individuals must be balanced out. Moreover, the dignity of the human person must be respected. Especially in economic matters,

persons must not be reduced to their utility and their property. Policies that serve the cause of peace must bring about justice in the comprehensive sense, precisely when it is a question of the just distribution of goods (GS 29). The distribution of goods through the world market must be guided by so-called *commutative justice*: someone who sells goods should receive a suitable price for them.

➡ 201 ➡ 1928, 1943, 2411–2412, 2426–2436
➡ 329, 430, 449

110 *What is the origin of these values?*

All values have their origin in God. Love is not an *attribute* that God has; "God is love" (1 Jn 4:8). Hence

love for others must be the central point of reference for all social activity. If I love, I will be truthful, accept the freedom of other people, and work for justice. Love surpasses justice because I not only give the other person what is due to him but wholeheartedly want to do him good. The fundamental value of "the dignity of the human person" also has its basis in God's love for us. Because God loves each individual person beyond all measure, he created him in his lovable likeness; thus man possesses an inalienable, inherent dignity.

→ 205 → 2212 → 321–324, 332

> If I give away all I have, and if I deliver my body to be burned, but have not love, I gain nothing.
>
> **1 COR 13:3**

> What we do out of love we do most willingly.
>
> **ST THOMAS AQUINAS**
> *Summa theologiae* I–II, q. 114, art. 4, corpus

> ## If love ruled on Earth, there would be no need for laws.
>
> **ARISTOTLE** Nichomachean Ethics III, 7

111 *Why is mere justice not enough?*

Love is more than justice, for it is "patient" and "kind" (1 Cor 13:4). Mercy must be added to justice in order for society to be truly human. *Social justice* is not enough for coexistence, much less mere *legal justice*, since no legislation can generate mutual goodwill among men. *Legal justice* can only punish offenses against human dignity and help educate to virtue, but social *charity* releases creative forces for the common good and, thus, for the comprehensive good of all. This includes just structures that allow room for mercy. Nevertheless, justice is something that mercy cannot be: a basic moral requirement. One can only appeal for mercy; justice can be demanded.

→ 206–207 → 1822–1829, 1844 → 309

> Love is delight in what is good; the proper object of love is the good. To love is to wish good to someone.
>
> **ST THOMAS AQUINAS**
> *Summa theologiae* I–II q. 26, art. 1 corpus, q. 27 art. 1 corpus, q. 26 art 4 corpus

> There is no peace without freedom, no freedom without justice, no justice without love.
>
> **DAN ASSAN** (b. 1946), human rights advocate in Tel Aviv

From important Church documents

THE PRINCIPLES OF THE CHURCH'S SOCIAL TEACHING

Rerum Novarum

The Family as an Example of Subsidiarity

If a family finds itself in exceeding distress, utterly deprived of the counsel of friends, and without any prospect of extricating itself, it is right that extreme necessity be met by public aid, since each family is a part of the commonwealth. In like manner, if within the precincts of the household there occur grave disturbance of mutual rights, public authority should intervene to force each party to yield to the other its proper due; for this is not to deprive citizens of their rights, but justly and properly to safeguard and strengthen them. But the rulers of the commonwealth must go no further; here, nature [i.e., the natural law] bids them stop.

Pope Leo XIII, Encyclical Rerum Novarum (1891), 11

Rerum Novarum

Common Property

And in addition to injustice, it is only too evident what an upset and disturbance there would be in all classes [in a socialist system], and to how intolerable and hateful a slavery citizens would be subjected. The door would be thrown open to envy, to mutual invective, and to discord; the sources of wealth themselves would run dry, for no one would have any interest in exerting his talents or his industry; and that ideal equality about which they entertain pleasant dreams would be in reality the levelling down of all to a like condition of misery and degradation.

Pope Leo XIII, Encyclical Rerum Novarum (1891), 12

Rerum Novarum

The Subsidiary Function of the State and the Common Good

The State must not absorb the individual or the family; both should be allowed free and untrammelled action so far as is consistent with the common good and the interest of others. Rulers should, nevertheless, anxiously safeguard the community and all its members; the community, because the conservation thereof is so emphatically the business of the supreme power that the safety of the commonwealth is not only the first law, but it is a government's whole reason of existence; and the members, because both philosophy and the Gospel concur in laying down [i.e., teaching] that the object of the government of the State should be, not the advantage of the ruler, but the benefit of those over whom he is placed.

Pope Leo XIII, Encyclical Rerum Novarum (1891), 28

The Basis: Solidarity out of Love

Centesimus Annus

In this way what we nowadays call the principle of solidarity ... is clearly seen to be one of the fundamental principles of the Christian view of social and political organization. This principle is frequently stated by Pope Leo XIII, who uses the term "friendship", a concept already found in Greek philosophy. Pope Pius XI refers to it with the equally meaningful term "social charity". Pope Paul VI, expanding the concept to cover the many modern aspects of the social question, speaks of a *civilization of love*. **Pope John Paul II, Pope St John Paul II, Encyclical Centesimus Annus (1991), 10**

The State and Social Principles

Centesimus Annus

The State must contribute to the achievement of these goals [i.e., workers' rights] both directly and indirectly. Indirectly and according to the *principle of subsidiarity*, by creating favourable conditions for the free exercise of economic activity, which will lead to abundant opportunities for employment and sources of wealth. Directly and according to the *principle of solidarity*, by defending the weakest, by placing certain limits on the autonomy of the parties who determine working conditions, and by ensuring in every case the necessary minimum support for the unemployed worker.
Pope St John Paul II, Encyclical Centesimus Annus (1991), 15

Networks of Solidarity

Centesimus Annus

Apart from the family, other intermediate communities exercise primary functions and give life to specific networks of solidarity. These develop as real communities of persons and strengthen the social fabric, preventing society from becoming an anonymous and impersonal mass, as unfortunately often happens today. It is in interrelationships on many levels that a person lives and that society becomes more "personalized".
Pope St John Paul II, Encyclical Centesimus Annus (1991), 49

Social Teaching in Dialogue

Centesimus Annus

In addition, the Church's social teaching has an important interdisciplinary dimension. In order better to incarnate the one truth about man in different and constantly changing social, economic and political contexts, this teaching enters into dialogue with the various disciplines concerned with man. It assimilates what these disciplines have to contribute, and helps them to open themselves to a broader horizon, aimed at serving the individual person who is acknowledged and loved in the fullness of his or her vocation.
Pope St John Paul II, Encyclical Letter Centesimus Annus (1991), 59

Evangelium Vitae

Denial of Solidarity

While the climate of widespread moral uncertainty can in some way be explained by the multiplicity and gravity of today's social problems, and these can sometimes mitigate the subjective responsibility of individuals, it is no less true that we are confronted by an even larger reality, which can be described as a veritable *structure of sin*. This reality is character- ized by the emergence of a culture which denies solidarity and in many cases takes the form of a veritable "culture of death". This culture is actively fostered by powerful cultural, economic, and political currents which encourage an idea of society excessively concerned with efficiency.

Pope St John Paul II, Encyclical Evangelium Vitae (1995), 12

Caritas in Veritate

Charity Goes beyond Justice

Ubi societas, ibi ius [Where there is a society, there is also law]: every society draws up its own system of justice. *Charity goes beyond justice*, because to love is to give, to offer what is "mine" to the other; but it never lacks justice, which prompts us to give the other what is "his", what is due to him by reason of his being or his acting. I cannot "give" what is mine to the other without first giving him what pertains to him in justice. If we love others with charity, then first of all we are just towards them …. On the one hand, charity demands justice: recognition and respect for the legitimate rights of individuals and peoples …. On the other hand, charity transcends justice and completes it in the logic of giving and forgiving. The *earthly city* is pro- moted not merely by relationships of rights and duties, but to an even greater and more fundamental extent by relationships of gratuitousness, mercy, and communion.

Pope Benedict XVI, Encyclical Caritas in Veritate (2009), 6

Caritas in Veritate

Love, Justice, and the Common Good

To desire the *common good* and strive towards it is a *requirement of justice and charity*. To take a stand for the common good is on the one hand to be solicitous for, and on the other hand to avail oneself of, that complex of institutions that give structure to the life of society, juridically, civ- illy, politically and culturally, making it the *pólis,* or "city". The more we strive to secure a common good corresponding to the real needs of our neighbours, the more effectively we love them. Every Christian is called to practise this charity, in a manner corresponding to his vocation and according to the degree of in- fluence he wields in the *pólis*. This is the institutional path—we might also call it the political path—of charity, no less excellent and effective than the kind of charity which encounters the neighbour directly, outside the institutional mediation of the *pólis*. When animated by charity, commitment to the common good has greater worth than a merely secular and political stand would have.

Pope Benedict XVI, Encyclical Caritas in Veritate (2009), 7

Building Bridges to Our Neighbour

Evangelii Gaudium

The individualism of our postmodern and globalized era favours a life-style which weakens the development and stability of personal relationships and distorts family bonds. Pastoral activity needs to bring out more clearly the fact that our relationship with the Father demands and encourages a communion which heals, promotes, and reinforces interpersonal bonds. In our world, especially in some countries, different forms of war and conflict are re-emerging, yet we Christians remain steadfast in our intention to respect others, to heal wounds, to build bridges, to strengthen relationships, and to "bear one another's burdens" (Gal 6:2). Today too, various associations for the defence of rights and the pursuit of noble goals are being founded. This is a sign of the desire of many people to contribute to social and cultural progress.

Pope Francis, Apostolic Exhortation Evangelii Gaudium (2013), 67

Property Should Serve the Common Good

Evangelii Gaudium

Solidarity is a spontaneous reaction by those who recognize that the social function of property and the universal destination of goods are realities which come before private property. The private ownership of goods is justified by the need to protect and increase them, so that they can better serve the common good; for this reason, solidarity must be lived as the decision to restore to the poor what belongs to them. These convictions and habits of solidarity, when they are put into practice, open the way to other structural transformations and make them possible. Changing structures without generating new convictions and attitudes will only ensure that those same structures will become, sooner or later, corrupt, oppressive, and ineffectual.

Pope Francis, Apostolic Exhortation Evangelii Gaudium (2013), 189

5

QUESTIONS
112–133

The Foundation of Society

THE FAMILY

It is not good that the man should be alone.

GEN 2:18

112 *Why does God want us to live together in families?*

God would not want every person to live alone; he created us as social beings. Human persons, therefore, are by nature designed for communion (in the family). This is clear on the very first pages of the Bible in the creation account: God places Eve at Adam's side to be his partner. "The man gave names to all cattle, and to the birds of the air, and to every beast of the field; but for the man there was not found a helper fit for him. So the LORD God … took one of his ribs … and made [it] into a woman and brought her to the man. Then the man said, 'This at last is bone of my bones and flesh of my flesh.'" (Gen 2:20–23)

The meaning of FAMILY:

Father
And
Mother,
I
Love
You.

unknown

➜ 209 ➜ 1877–1880 ➜ 321

113 What significance does the family have in the Bible?

The Bible often deals with family life: in the Old Testament parents are required to hand on to their children experiences of God's love and fidelity and to impart to them the first and most important wisdom in life. The New Testament records that Jesus, too, was born into a specific family. His parents showed him affection and love and raised him. The fact that God looked for a completely "normal" family in which to be born as man and to grow up made the family a special place of God and gave it a unique value as a community.

→ 210 → 531–534 → 68

 Nazareth teach[es] us the meaning of family life, its harmony of love, its simplicity and austere beauty, its sacred and inviolable character; it teach[es] us how sweet and irreplaceable is its training, how fundamental and incomparable its role on the social plane.

POPE PAUL VI, Address in Nazareth 1964

114 How does the Church see the family?

The Church regards the family as the first and most important natural community. The family has special rights and is central to all social life. After all, it is the place where human life comes into being and the place where the first interpersonal relationships develop. The family is the foundation of society; all social arrangements proceed from it. On account of this great significance, the Church sees the family as divinely instituted.

→ 211 → 2207, 2226–2227 → 271, 273

 God blessed them, and God said to them, "Be fruitful and multiply, and fill the earth".

GEN 1:28

The first thing that a human being finds in life, the last thing to which he reaches out his hand, the most precious thing that he has in life, is family.

ADOLPH KOLPING (1813–1865), German Catholic priest and champion of the rights of workers and artisans

115 What is so special about the family?

I am loved unconditionally: that is the irreplaceable experience that people have in a good family. Different generations live together and experience affection, solidarity, appreciation, unselfish commitment, help, and justice. Every member of the family is recognized, accepted, and respected by the others in his dignity, without having to do anything to deserve it. Everyone person is loved, just as he is. The individual

The Church is not a cultural organization ... the Church is the family of Jesus.

POPE FRANCIS, 1st June 2013

> The parents' life is the book that their children read.
>
> **ST AUGUSTINE** (354–430)

> To love means to give and to receive something which can be neither bought nor sold, but only given freely and mutually.
>
> **POPE ST JOHN PAUL II** (1920–2005), Letter to Families, 1994

persons are not means to some end but, rather, ends in themselves. Consequently, in the family a culture of life comes about that nowadays is anything but self-evident. Often today the main question is what someone can do or what he is contributing (for example, money). Often people concentrate first and foremost on material things. This mind-set challenges families and often even destroys them.

➡ 221 ➡ 2207–2208 ➡ 369

> My family was so close-knit that I sometimes had the feeling that we were one person made up of four parts.
>
> **HENRY FORD** (1863–1947), American industrialist, founder of the Ford Motor Company

> Live in such a way that you would not be ashamed to sell the parrot to the town gossip.
>
> **WILL ROGERS** (1879–1935), U.S. humorist and actor

 116 *Does "the family" fit at all into modern society?*

Yes. Frequently in modern societies there are no longer any moral or religious convictions that are shared by all. Moreover, the world has become extremely complex. Every sector of reality functions according to its own rules and regulations. This affects families, too. The Church cares about the welfare and dignity of every individual. This holds all the sectors together. Nowhere are children raised better than in a culture of family life based on high ideals and good relationships. Here individuals can show and learn that mutual respect, justice, dialogue, and love are more important than anything else for successful coexistence. Consequently, the family is not just an institution that fits into modern society but is actually the central place for human integration. It is the source of the necessary social and human prerequisites for the State and for the various sectors of society (e.g., economy, politics, culture).

➡ 222, 223 ➡ 2207, 2208 ➡ 369

To relegate [the family] to a subordinate or secondary role, excluding it from its rightful position in society, would be to inflict grave harm on the authentic growth of society as a whole.

POPE ST JOHN PAUL II (1920–2005), Letter to Families, 1994

117 *What does the family do for the individual?*

To experience family is extremely important for the individual human person. Ideally it is the place where he is born and grows up. In the family he experiences for the first time communion with others who by their very nature wish him well and unreservedly love and respect him. In such a positive atmosphere, every

Healthy people need a happy childhood.

ASTRID LINDGREN (1907–2002), Swedish author of children's books

💬 Children's play should be considered their most important occupation.

MICHEL DE MONTAIGNE (1533–1592), French philosopher and essayist

family member can develop his capabilities and acquire the strength to face whatever life may bring. That is precisely the purpose of an education based on a Christian view of the human person. At the same time, the individual persons in the family experience what it means to take responsibility, since a family member cannot simply live for himself alone. Consequently, every role—whether that of the parents, the grandparents, or the children—always has its duties as well toward the other family members.

➡ 212, 221 ➡ 2224–2230 ➡ 371, 372

Honour your father and your mother, that your days may be long in the land which the LORD your God gives you.

EX 20:12

As well as being a source, the parents' love is also the animating principle and therefore the norm inspiring and guiding all concrete educational activity, enriching it with the values of kindness, constancy, goodness, service, disinterestedness, and self-sacrifice that are the most precious fruit of love.

POPE ST JOHN PAUL II (1920–2005), *Familiaris consortio* 36

A mother is the only human being on earth who already loves you before she knows you.

JOHANN HEINRICH PESTALOZZI (1746–1827), Swiss teacher

Certainly children should have respect for their parents, but certainly parents too should have respect for their children, and they must never misuse their natural superiority. Never violence!

ASTRID LINDGREN (1907–2002)

118 *Does the family also contribute something to society?*

Yes, everything that the family accomplishes internally, for itself and for its own members, is socially relevant, too. After all, a society can thrive only if things go well for the individual members of society, if they feel loved and appreciated. In the family, one can learn that prior to the marketplace logic of exchange there is an entirely different kind of give-and-take, a logic of self-giving and acceptance. The fact

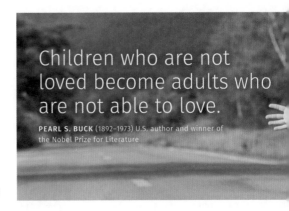

Children who are not loved become adults who are not able to love.

PEARL S. BUCK (1892–1973) U.S. author and winner of the Nobel Prize for Literature

that individuals also learn in the family the meaning of social responsibility and solidarity likewise benefits society as a whole: someone who proves to be responsible and to practise solidarity "in little things" will be more likely do so "in big things", too. Where does one learn devotion to the poor, the sick, or the elderly better than in the family? Where does one better understand people who are desperate, lonely, or abandoned? How does a person become sensitive to structural social ills if his own family does not set an example? The family thereby makes an irreplaceable contribution to the "humanization of society" (C. Kissling).

→ 213, 246 → 2207-2211 → 369, 370

119 *What does the family do for society?*

Family is first of all the place where the continuation of society is ensured. Secondly, the family performs the specific task of socializing and raising children. Cultural, ethical, social, intellectual and religious virtues, values, and traditions are handed down, which are fundamental for every free, conscientious person. Equipped with these tools of a family upbringing, people can assume, with the requisite education, all kinds of responsibilities in society. A third task of the

family is that it cares for all members of the household and offers them a safe, private place in which to grow and relax. Fourth (especially in aging societies), it is becoming increasingly important to provide loving care for household members who are sick or handicapped or no longer able to earn money. Here the view of the nuclear family expands to the previous generation, which can promote profound solidarity and at the same time a sense of identity.

→ 213, 229, 232 → 2207–2209 → 370

120 *Is childrearing the task of the family alone?*

No, certainly not. A family is not a self-contained system that exists only for its own sake. First, however,

The chief thing is to get women to take part in socially productive labour, to liberate them from "domestic slavery", to free them from their stupefying and humiliating subjugation to the eternal drudgery of the kitchen and the nursery.

The abolition of the traditional family structure was strongly advocated by the Communists, and also by **VLADIMIR I. LENIN** (1879-1924), Russian politician and revolutionary. The quotation is from "The Tasks of the Working Women's Movement", a speech he gave in 1919.

The first and fundamental structure for "human ecology" is the family, in which man receives his first formative ideas about truth and goodness and learns what it means to love and to be loved, and thus what it actually means to be a person.
POPE ST JOHN PAUL II (1920–2005), CA 39.

There are two things that children should get from their parents: roots and wings.
JOHANN WOLFGANG VON GOETHE (1749–1832), German poet

> The ancients, when they wished to exemplify illustrious virtue throughout the empire, first ordered well their states. Desiring to order well their states, they first regulated their families. Wishing to regulate their families, they first cultivated themselves. Wishing to cultivate themselves, they first rectified their purposes.
>
> **CONFUCIUS** (551–479 BC)

> The call for State intervention leads to the intrusion of the public authorities into this secluded sphere and leads in the long term to a nationalization of the family community.
>
> **UDO DI FABIO** (b. 1954), judge on the German Constitutional Court

> The family is indisputably and unmistakably the first societal structure that lays the foundation for all the others.
>
> **OSWALD VON NELL-BREUNING** (1890–1991), *Gerechtigkeit und Freiheit* [Justice and Freedom] (1980)

> There is no point in training children. They imitate everything you do anyway.
>
> Witticism

we must remember that parents have the primary right and duty to raise their children themselves and to provide them with a comprehensive education. Only totalitarian states try to take this right away from them. The father and the mother make different contributions, but they are equally important to the formation of children. From this perspective alone, granting adoption rights to homosexual couples is extremely problematic. Next, the social dimension of human beings requires that children have social interaction outside their immediate family; their education should take a more comprehensive form through the collaboration of the family and various institutions, especially the local parish or, for example, sports clubs. Comprehensive education seeks to help make children law-abiding, peaceful citizens who are capable of dialogue, encounter, and solidarity by teaching them to practise the virtues of justice and love. Not only words but above all living examples and models help to achieve this.

➜ **240, 242** ➜ **2223, 2226, 2229**

121 *What role do the elderly play in the family?*

The presence of older people living in the family can prove to be very valuable. They are an example of the ties between the generations, and thanks to their wealth of experience they can make a decisive contribution toward the well-being of the family and of society as a whole. They can transmit values and traditions and support the young. In this way the latter learn not only to care about themselves but to look after others, also. When elderly persons are sick and needy, they need not only medical attention and appropriate care but above all loving treatment and surroundings.

➜ **222** ➜ **2212, 2218** ➜ **371**

122 *Why do children need special protection?*

Children have to be strengthened and defended in every way. "A child is God's greatest gift to the family, to the nation, to the world" (Mother Teresa). Children

> The people who can depend on us support us in life.
> **MARIE VON EBNER-ESCHENBACH** (1830–1916)

 Do not cast me off in the time of old age; forsake me not when my strength is spent.
PS 71:9

are the future of humanity. They are naturally in need of help. Moreover, they often grow up in atrocious conditions. In many parts of the world there is a lack of medical care, appropriate nutrition, elementary education, or even a place to live. Moreover, there are ongoing scandals such as trafficking in children, child labour, the phenomenon of "street children", the deployment of children in wars, the marriage of children, and the (sexual) abuse of children. There must be a decisive campaign on the national and international level against violations of the dignity of boys and girls that occur through sexual exploitation and all forms of violence and in favour of respect for the dignity and rights of every child.

→ 244, 245 → 435

> If you take all the experience and judgement of men over fifty out of the world, there wouldn't be enough left to run it.
> **HENRY FORD** (1863–1947)

> Every child comes with the message that God is not yet discouraged of man.
> **RABINDRANATH TAGORE** (1861–1941), Indian winner of the Nobel Prize for Literature

 123 *What is marriage?*

Marriage is the communion of a man and a woman ordered to the good of the spouses and the procreation and education of offspring (CCC 1601). An essential feature of marriage is the mutual promise of the two spouses to love one another unconditionally and to be faithful to each other. Another essential characteristic of marriage is its indissolubility: the spouses' mutual love and respect should last a lifetime, and they should stand by and support one another in all circumstances of life: "for better or for worse, in sickness and in health", as they promise each other in

> Sons are a heritage from the LORD, the fruit of the womb a reward.
> **PS 127:3**

> There are no great discoveries and advances, as long as there is still an unhappy child on earth.
> **ALBERT EINSTEIN** (1879–1955), winner of the Nobel Prize for Physics

the wedding ceremony. However, even if one or both spouses are unfaithful, their marriage remains. Marriage ends only with the death of one of the spouses.

➡️ **217, 223** ➡️ **2360–2361** ➡️ **416**

124 *What does it mean to marry someone?*

To marry someone means to give oneself completely to that person: husband and wife should live together and be there for each other, with their whole physical and mental constitution. Marriage embraces all areas of life. It is in marriage, where sexual union has its just place, that the love of a man and a woman becomes fruitful. After all, marriage is fundamentally designed to be enlarged into a family with children. Even in marriages in which children are not possible, the union of a man and a woman is the kind of union through which children are conceived. Considering all these aspects, it is not possible to talk about "homosexual marriage". Even the expression "equality in marriage" is ambiguous. Both husband and wife have equal dignity as human persons. But their different and complementary roles are rooted in their very being—even to the level of their chromosomes.

➡️ **217, 218** ➡️ **2362–2363** ➡️ **416**

125 *What significance does marriage have for the family?*

Marriage is the foundation of the family. For Christians, it is a sacrament and, therefore, a great sign from God of salvation. Even before that, however, it

What God has joined together, let no man put asunder.

MT 19:6

❝ Will you honour each other as man and wife for the rest of your lives?"
"Will you accept children lovingly from God, and bring them up according to the law of Christ and his Church?"

Celebrant's questions for the bride and groom

❝ We cannot liberate ourselves from nature.

ROBERT SPAEMANN
(b. 1927)

is the Church's conviction and experience that marriage is the optimal basis for a common life of man, woman, and children. Only in marriage is unconditional reliability guaranteed, a reliability not subject to time or other restrictions. Thus it offers all family members the humanly appropriate protection and room for development they need.

→ 225 → 1655–1657 → 271

126   How is one to evaluate other forms of living together?

The Church quite clearly regards marriage and family as the vocation which corresponds to the deepest longings of man and woman. In this she takes in the current debate a firm stance against the increasing breakdown in the close connection between

sexuality and interpersonal ties, between emotion and responsibility, sexuality and children, partnership and family. Nevertheless, the Church also reaches out with charity to those who live in other ways, and looks for opportunities to make of these forms a path of conversion towards the fullness of the vocation of marriage.

→ 227–228 → 2390–2391 → 425

> It is easier to rule a nation than raise four children.

WINSTON CHURCHILL (1874–1965), British Prime Minister

127 *Is a desire for children part of marriage?*

Yes, absolutely. Just as marriage is part of the family, so too family is part of marriage. The two are interrelated. To simplify, we could say: "No family without marriage and no marriage without family." Marriage is related to the family, which is to say that it is aimed at procreation and childrearing and life with children. Couples who wish to marry should therefore not reject the possibility of having children together at the beginning of their marriage. "Will you accept children lovingly from God and bring them up according to the law of Christ and his Church?" The bride and groom must answer yes to this question posed by the priest. Only then can they contract marriage with one another.

→ 218 → 2373, 2378 → 418, 419

We need to feel the pain of the failure and accompany those persons who have failed in their love, but not condemn them. Behind hair-splitting, behind casuistic thinking there is always a trap hidden. Always! Against people, against us, and against God.

POPE FRANCIS,
28th February 2014

[Today there] is the tendency of many parents to renounce their role in order to be merely friends to their children, refraining from warning and correcting them even when this is necessary for teaching them the truth, albeit with every affection and tenderness. It therefore should be stressed that the education of children is a sacred duty and a shared task of the parents, both father and mother: it requires warmth, closeness, dialogue, and example. In the home parents are called to represent the good Father in heaven, the one perfect model to inspire them.

POPE ST JOHN PAUL II
(1920–2005), 4th June 1999

The couple's legitimate aspirations to parenthood who experience a condition of infertility must there-fore—with the help of science—find an answer that fully respects their dignity as people and as spouses.

POPE BENEDICT XVI, 25th February 2012

The family is experiencing a profound cultural crisis, as are all communities and social bonds. In the case of the family, the weakening of these bonds is particularly se-rious because the family is the fundamental cell of society, where we learn to live with others despite our differences and to belong to one another; it is also the place where parents pass on the faith to their children. Marriage now tends to be viewed as a form of mere emotional satisfaction that can be constructed in any way or modified at will. But the indispensible contribution of marriage to society transcends the feelings and momentary needs of the couple.

POPE FRANCIS, EG 66

128 *What about couples who cannot have children of their own?*

Their marriage is by no means "worth" less, because procreation is not the sole purpose of marriage. Rather, a marriage still has its indissoluble character and its value as a communion, even if married life is not perfected by children—who are often longed for ardently. In this case, the married couple can adopt children or in some other way care for children (for instance, in their extended family or circle of friends). A marriage can be "fruitful" also if a childless couple opens its home to lonely people, conscientiously be-comes involved socially, and shows hospitality.

➡ 218 ➡ 2374, 2379 ➡ 422, 423

129 *If a couple is able to have children, how many should they have?*

Married couples should accept the children that are sent to them by God. That does not mean, however, that every married couple should thoughtlessly have (many) children. Instead—in conformity with the Church's authoritative teaching—the married cou-ple should make their decision for motherhood and fatherhood responsibly, taking into account their health and their economic, spiritual, and social sit-uation. In this they must learn to understand the language of their bodies, making use of methods of natural family planning. Decisions about the interval between births and the number of children are up to the married couple alone, to be made prayerfully and with correctly formed consciences. This is their inalienable right, which they exercise in the sight of God and taking into consideration their duties toward themselves, any children who may already be born, their family, and society.

➡ 218, 234 ➡ 2368–2370 ➡ 419, 420, 421

130 *May governmental family policies try to influence couples' decisions?*

Yes. → FAMILY POLICY certainly may encourage couples to be thoughtful about the number of children they have, in light of the needs of society and the common good. In any case, this must be done with respect for human persons and for the couples' freedom. The policy may—and even should—provide information about the demographic situation, and it can issue regulations that, for example, create economic and other advantages for families with children. Thereby it can create incentives, but ultimately the decision about the number of their children must be left to the couples themselves. No one may deprive them of this freedom of decision.

→ 234, 235

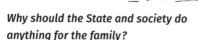

131 *Why should the State and society do anything for the family?*

The family, by its very nature, makes important contributions to society that often go quite unnoticed and unappreciated. The obligation of society and the State to do something for families, too, follows from the fact that the family is the smallest, indispensable unit of society. This is where governmental family policy begins. A nation necessarily depends

! FAMILY POLICY is the set of political measures with which a State improves the circumstances of family life. According to the Catholic understanding, the State has the duty to support families (= long-term communities made up of father, mother, and children) to the best of its ability in a subsidiary way. All governmental attempts to exploit the family, to destabilize it for ideological reasons, or to redefine it (e.g., "wherever there are children there is a family") contradicts Catholic social teaching, for reasons derived from the natural law.

What families need first and foremost, therefore, are not handouts or excessive burdens or life-style advice, but rather a just system of taxation that allows them to raise their children using the income that they themselves have earned.

JUERGEN BORCHERT (b. 1949), German social welfare judge

on potential parents to decide to have children; the State, however, can in no way coerce this decision; it must be made with complete freedom by the citizens. The State thus places its own future in the hands of its citizens, who are entitled to freedom. Again and again surveys show that citizens in principle value the family very highly. Governmental family policy tries to make it possible for them to decide to start a family, in the present societal and political conditions, by shaping economic conditions accordingly.

 238

132 *What can the State and society do for families?*

First, it is important for both society and the State to acknowledge the family as something special and central and therefore to protect and support its unique character. This starts with strengthening the home life of the family, but it also includes respect for human life in every phase, especially for the unborn. When we talk about the State protecting and supporting the family, this can never mean that society or the State, for economic or ideological reasons, takes over or even takes away duties originally belonging to the family and thus narrows its social dimension; instead, the goal of family policy measures, in keeping with the principle of subsidiarity, must be to enable families to perform their own tasks suitably.

➡ **252, 253, 254** ➡ **2211** ▣ **370, 323**

133 ***What is meant specifically by "family policy in keeping with the principle of subsidiarity"?***

An example: in keeping with the principle of subsidiarity, it cannot be the State's task to raise children, because that would take away from parents a task that has belonged to them from the beginning. Rather, in the given circumstances (living conditions, work, and educational opportunities), the State should give families all the necessary assistance. Here it is important to preserve real freedom of choice, for instance, with regard to parental co-operation in dividing up the work of caring for the family and earning a living. The special function of the family in communicating knowledge and the formation of the children can be replaced neither through day care and schools nor through other societal groups, although these institutions can help to support and supplement parental education. The principle of subsidiarity emphasizes at the same time the autonomy of every person and of families. This means that families themselves can and should become involved in political and societal institutions and also join together to stand up for their rights and to strengthen them.

➡ **247** ➡ **2211, 2252** ▣ **323**

❞ Democratizing the family does not mean putting to a vote who the father is.

WILLY BRANDT (1913–1992), German Federal Chancellor

❞ Families have the right to form associations with other families and institutions, in order to fulfill the family's role suitably and effectively, as well as to protect the rights, foster the good, and represent the interests of the family. On the economic, social, juridical, and cultural levels, the rightful role of families and family associations must be recognized in the planning and development of programmes which touch on family life.

Holy See, *Charter of the Rights of the Family*, 1983

❞ The family is the natural and fundamental group unit of society and is entitled to protection by society and the State.

The Universal Declaration of Human Rights, Article 16, Section 3

From important Church documents

THE FAMILY

Rerum Novarum
Fundamental Right to a Family

No human law can abolish the natural and original right of marriage, nor in any way limit the chief and principal purpose of marriage ordained by God's authority from the beginning: "Increase and multiply." Hence we have the family, the "society" of a man's house—a society very small, one must admit, but none the less a true society, and one older than any State. Consequently, it has rights and duties peculiar to itself which are quite independent of the State.

Pope Leo XIII, Encyclical Rerum Novarum (1891), 9

Pacem in Terris
The Right to a Family

The family, founded upon marriage freely contracted, one and indissoluble, must be regarded as the natural, primary cell of human society. The interests of the family, therefore, must be taken very specially into consideration in social and economic affairs, as well as in the spheres of faith and morals. For all of these have to do with strengthening the family and assisting it in the fulfillment of its mission. Of course, the support and education of children is a right which belongs primarily to the parents.

Pope St John XXIII, Encyclical Pacem in Terris (1963), 9

Familiaris Consortio
Families today

On the one hand, in fact, there is a more lively awareness of personal freedom and greater attention to the quality of interpersonal relationships in marriage, to promoting the dignity of women, to responsible procreation, to the education of children. There is also an awareness of the need for the development of interfamily relationships, for reciprocal spiritual and material assistance, the rediscovery of the ecclesial mission proper to the family and its responsibility for the building of a more just society. On the other hand, however, signs are not lacking of a disturbing degradation of some fundamental values: a mistaken theoretical and practical concept of the independence of the spouses in relation to each other; serious misconceptions regarding the relationship of authority between parents and children; the concrete difficulties that the family itself experiences in the transmission of values; the growing number of divorces; the scourge of abortion; the ever more frequent recourse to sterilization; the appearance of a truly contraceptive mentality.

Pope St John Paul II, Apostolic Exhortation Familiaris Consortio (1981), 6

Work and Family

Laborem Exercens

It must be remembered and affirmed that the family constitutes one of the most important terms of reference for shaping the social and ethical order of human work. The teaching of the Church has always devoted special attention to this question, and in the present document we shall have to return to it. In fact, the family is simultaneously a *community made possible by work* and the first *school of work,* within the home, for every person.

Pope St John Paul II, Encyclical Laborem Exercens (1981), 10

Human Ecology and the Family

Centesimus Annus

The first and fundamental structure for "human ecology" is the family, in which man receives his first formative ideas about truth and goodness and learns what it means to love and to be loved, and thus what it actually means to be a person. Here we mean the *family founded on marriage,* in which the mutual gift of self by husband and wife creates an environment in which children can be born and develop their potentialities.

Pope St John Paul II, Encyclical Centesimus Annus (1991), 39

Overcoming Individualism

Centesimus Annus

In order to overcome today's widespread individualistic mentality, what is required is a *concrete commitment to solidarity and charity,* beginning in the family with the mutual support of husband and wife and the care which the different generations give to one another. In this sense the family too can be called a community of work and solidarity. It can happen, however, that when a family does decide to live up fully to its vocation, it finds itself without the necessary support from the State and without sufficient resources. It is urgent therefore to promote not only family policies, but also those social policies which have the family as their principal object, policies which assist the family by providing adequate resources and efficient means of support, both for bringing up children and for looking after the elderly, so as to avoid distancing the latter from the family unit and in order to strengthen relations between generations.

Pope St John Paul II, Encyclical Centesimus Annus (1991), 49

The Family: the place of integral education

Laudato Si

In the family we receive an integral education, which enables us to grow harmoniously in personal maturity. In the family we learn to ask without demanding, to say "thank you" as an expression of genuine gratitude for what we have been given, to control our aggressivity and greed, and to ask forgiveness when we have caused harm. These simple gestures of heartfelt courtesy help to create a culture of shared life and respect for our surroundings.

Pope Francis, Encyclical Laudato Sì (2015), 213

6

Occupation and Vocation

HUMAN WORK

> Choose an occupation
> that you like,
> and you need not
> work another day
> in your life.

Asian proverb

134 *What does it mean for a human being to work?*

> At the beginning of man's work is the mystery of creation.
> **POPE ST JOHN PAUL II**
> (1920–2005), LE 12

To be able to work, to have work, and to be able to accomplish something for oneself and for others is a great source of happiness for many people. To be unemployed, not to be needed, takes the dignity away from a person. Through work man develops his inclinations and abilities and participates in economic, societal, and cultural development. Work plays a major role in God's plan. God commanded man to subdue the earth (Gen 1:28), to protect and cultivate it. Work can be a valuable service to one's fellowmen. Even more: to cultivate the earth in a sustainable way and creatively to develop its further potential makes man like his Creator. Doing simple tasks well also unites a person with Jesus, who was a worker himself.

> Three stonemasons were asked what they were doing. The first said, "I am carving a stone." The second said, "I am working on a Gothic arch window." The third said, "I am building a cathedral."
>
> unknown

→ 275, 287 → 2427-2428 → 444

135 **Is work a punishment from God?**

Every now and then you read that work is God's punishment for the original sin of Adam. But that is not correct. According to the biblical account of creation, work is instead an essential part of man as a creature. In Genesis 2:15 the man receives the instruction to till and keep the Garden of Eden. But after Adam and Eve disobeyed God's commandment not to eat "of the tree of the knowledge of good and evil" (Gen 2:17), in other words, after the Fall, God curses the ground that the man must cultivate. Since then the toil has been burdensome, and man must work hard to feed himself and his family. From the biblical perspective, God's punishment for the Fall is not work itself, but rather the hardship of work.

➡ **255 ff.** ➡ **307** ➡ **50, 66**

136 **Is there an obligation to work?**

God created the earth and left it to man as a precious gift. As the Bible depicts it, human work is man's appropriate, grateful response to this gift. Therefore, when human beings pursue their occupation, and already while they prepare for work as children in school and later as young adults in training, it is not just a matter of being able to earn their own living. Through work, human beings have the privilege of contributing something to the positive development of the world. Thus man in a certain way participates in God's work of creation.

➡ **264–266, 274** ➡ **2427–2428, 2460** ➡ **440**

> Work ennobles man's character as a person.
>
> **JOHN HARDON, SJ**
> (1914–2000), American Jesuit priest and theologian

> If a man is called to be a street sweeper, he should sweep streets even as a Michaelangelo painted or Beethoven composed music or Shakespeare wrote poetry. He should sweep streets so well that all the hosts of heaven and earth will pause to say, "Here lived a great street sweeper who did his job well."
>
> **MARTIN LUTHER KING**
> (1929–1968)

> The soul is nourished by what it is pleased with.
>
> **ST AUGUSTINE** (354–430)

> Work is a good thing for man—a good thing for his humanity—because through work man not only transforms nature, adapting it to his own needs, but he also achieves fulfillment as a human being and indeed, in a sense, becomes "more a human being".
>
> **POPE ST JOHN PAUL II**
> (1920–2005), LE 9

137 How did Jesus regard work?

Jesus was "like us in all things except sin" (Council of Chalcedon, AD 451, quoting Heb 4:15; cf. CCC 467). He lived among fishermen, farmers, and craftsmen, and he himself went through an apprenticeship and then laboured until he was thirty as a carpenter in Joseph's workshop. In his parables, he uses images from commercial life. In his preaching, he praises servants who invest their talents, while he condemns the lazy servant who buries his talent in the ground (see Mt 25:14–30). In school, professional training, and then in one's occupation, work often seems to be a laborious duty. Here we can learn from Jesus and with him take up our cross each day and follow him, who took up his Cross to redeem us.

→ 259, 263 → 2427 → 85, 494

138 How are work and occupational success related to the real goal of human life?

Work is *part* of life, but it is *not* life. This is an important distinction. Nowadays, especially in the highly developed countries of the world, there are many

people who seem to live only for their work. For them work is like an addiction, and therefore these people are called workaholics. Jesus warns people not to let themselves be enslaved by work in this way. The goal of human life is not to pile up money or to earn a reputation, but to attain eternal life with God through prayer, worship, and active love of neighbour. Insofar as man's work is subordinate to this goal, it is part of a Christian life. But when work becomes an end in itself and obscures the real goal of our human existence, its importance has been exaggerated. Yet many people have to take several jobs and work hard in order to feed their family. They are doing a service to their family, therefore, and they do it with God's blessing.

→ 260 → 2426–2428 → 47, 444

139   What does the commandment about Sunday rest have to do with work?

The commandment about rest on the Sabbath or on Sunday is the summit, the high point of biblical teaching about work. By interrupting work and attending

> Your work does not run away if you show your child the rainbow. But the rainbow does not wait until you are finished with your work.
>
> Chinese saying

> What does Sunday cost us? The question itself is already a decisive attack on Sunday. Indeed, Sunday is Sunday precisely because it costs nothing and—in the economic sense—produces nothing. The question about the cost of observing it as a work-free day presupposes that we have already conceptually turned Sunday into a workday.
>
> ROBERT SPAEMANN (b. 1927)

> # They called for manpower and human beings show up.

MAX FRISCH (1911–1991), on the problem of "foreign workers"

> We are firmly convinced that an immense Christian-Social error was made by doing either nothing at all until now or else precisely the wrong thing about the workers.

ADOLPH KOLPING
(1813–1865), German priest who ministered to the urban working class

> The social question concerns the *depositum fidei*.

BISHOP WILHELM EMMANUEL VON KETTELER
(1811–1877), German bishop (*depositum fidei* = deposit of faith, the essential truths of the faith)

Holy Mass on Sunday, man's sights are directed toward the real goal of his life. The commandment to rest on the Sabbath is thus also a bulwark against the (voluntary or compulsory) enslavement of human beings by work. The commandment to keep the Sabbath was established for both purposes: to free man for divine worship, but also to protect mankind, especially the poor, from exploitation by their masters.

➡ **258** ➡ **2185–2188** ➡ **47**

140 *What is "the worker question"?*

Industrialization and the spread of the free-market economy led in the nineteenth century to swift, unprecedented technological and economic development in Europe and the United States. As a result, countless people seeking a better life streamed from the poor villages into the rapidly growing industrial cities in order to work in the modern factories. But all too often their hopes were dashed. In the early phase of industrialization, many factory workers suffered because of inhumane working conditions and inadequate wages. They and their families had too little to live on and too many fatal hazards. Unemployment, disability, and health insurance did not yet exist. In this way, a new social stratum or "class" developed: the proletariat, which was excluded from the benefits

of the growing economic prosperity and so became socially dependent on the rest of society.

→ 267 → 2427–2428, 2460 → 438–439

141 *How did the Church's social teaching come about?*

With the development of her social teaching, the Church tried to respond to the challenge of the worker question. Ever since the early phase of Western industrialization, individual figures like the Bishop of Mainz, Germany, Wilhelm Emmanuel von Ketteler (1811–1877), have dealt with this problem. In the first social encyclical, RERUM NOVARUM (1891), Pope Leo XIII condemned the division of society into social classes and criticized the low wages and poor working conditions prevalent in the early phase of industrialization as an offense against human dignity and social human rights. The pope demanded that workers receive a fair share of the growing economic prosperity and urgently warned against the dangers of class warfare.

→ 267, 268 → 2419–2423 → 438–439

142 *What is the difference between the Church's social teaching and Marxism?*

Karl Marx (1818–1883) also developed his Communist doctrine as a reaction to the worker question. For him, however, the answer was an inevitable class struggle between the proletariat and the bourgeoisie. The bourgeoisie had to be violently dispossessed, and a dictatorship of the proletariat was to be set

The great mistake made in regard to [the social question] is to take up with the notion that class is naturally hostile to class, and that the wealthy and the working men are intended by nature to live in mutual conflict. So irrational and so false is this view that the direct contrary is the truth.
POPE LEO XIII (1810–1903), RN 19

❞ Not religion, but revolution is the opium of the people.
SIMONE WEIL (1909–1943), French philosopher and mystic, who was very involved in political and social activity

❞ The social sense looks so much like the religious sense that it can be mistaken for it.
SIMONE WEIL (1909–1943)

The sources of the dignity of work are to be sought primarily in the subjective dimension, not in the objective one.
POPE ST JOHN PAUL II (1920–2005), LE 6.

❞ The Lord does not regard the importance of works as much as the love with which they are done.
ST TERESA OF AVILA (1515–1582)

In the final analysis it is always man who is the purpose of the work, whatever work it is that is done by man—even if the common scale of values rates it as the merest "service", as the most monotonous, even the most alienating work.

POPE ST JOHN PAUL II
(1920–2005), LE 6

Capital cannot do without labour, nor labour without capital.

POPE LEO XIII (1810–1903), RN 19

I would like to remind everyone, especially governments engaged in boosting the world's economic and social assets, that the primary capital to be safeguarded and valued is man, the human person in his or her integrity.

POPE BENEDICT XVI, CiV 25.2

The social problem knows no bounds.

VICTOR HUGO (1802–1885), French author

You should not strike your subordinates with threatening words as though with a cudgel. Instead, combine words of justice with mercy and apply the ointment of fear of the Lord.

ST HILDEGARD OF BINGEN (1098–1179), German abbess, mystic, and Doctor of the Church

up. In the twentieth century, the Communist ideology brought unimaginable suffering upon mankind. From the very beginning, the Church recognized the dangers of Communism and harshly condemned the teaching of class warfare. The Church's social doctrine and the Christian Social Democratic Movement in Europe have been committed instead to a just balancing of interests among the various participants in the economy and society.

➡ **88–90** ➡ **2424–2425** ➡ **439**

143 *What is the difference between the "objective" and the "subjective" dimension of work?*

Economists speak about the labour productivity of a business or even of an individual. The Church's social teaching distinguishes this "objective" dimension of work from the "subjective" dimension of work. The latter is the dignity that is inherent in all work, because it is accomplished by a human being. Pope John Paul II describes this view of man with his inalienable dignity as the *subject of work* as "the fundamental and perennial heart of Christian teaching on human work" (LE 6). Therefore, we must never treat arrogantly those who do supposedly "menial" jobs, for which one needs no special training or particular qualifications.

➡ **270–271**

144 *What does the principle "labour before capital" mean?*

One consequence of the subjective dimension of work is "the principle of the priority of labour over capital" (LE 12). This is because a human being owns capital as an external object, whereas work is inseparable from the human being who performs it and from his dignity. No reference to the interests of

capital, the demands of competition, or the rigours of globalization can justify demeaning, exploitative wages and working conditions.

→ 277 → 2426 → 442, 445

145 *What does the Church's social teaching mean by demanding the participation of workers?*

At the core of the worker question was the fact that workers shared inadequately in the economic prosperity that society had attained through industrialization and the market economy. In the early phase of industrialization, factory workers were often treated like "human machines". In society they were marginalized. We find the same situation today in many developing and emerging nations. Against this backdrop, one of the central demands of the Church's social teaching has always been genuine participation of workers. This means, on the one hand, their participation in the business: the workers should have a say about their workplace. On the other hand, it means participation in society and government: workers should be able to live as full citizens with all the attendant rights and duties.

→ 281 → 2423

Ownership of the means of production, whether in industry or agriculture, is just and legitimate if it serves useful work. It becomes illegitimate, however, when it is not utilized or when it serves to impede the work of others, in an effort to gain a profit which is not the result of the overall expansion of work and the wealth of society, but rather is the result of curbing them or of illicit exploitation, speculation, or the breaking of solidarity among working people. Ownership of this kind has no justification and represents an abuse in the sight of God and man.

POPE ST JOHN PAUL II
(1920–2005), CA 43

Being out of work or dependent on public or private assistance for a prolonged period undermines the freedom and creativity of the person and his family and social relationships, causing great psychological and spiritual suffering.

POPE BENEDICT XVI, CiV 25

In many cases, poverty results from *a violation of the dignity of human work*, either because work opportunities are limited (through unemployment or underemployment), or "because a low value is put on work and the rights that flow from it, especially the right to a just wage and to the personal security of the worker and his or her family."

POPE BENEDICT XVI, CiV 25

It must be remembered and affirmed that the family constitutes one of the most important terms of reference for shaping the social and ethical order of human work. The family is simultaneously a *community made possible by work* and the first *school of work*, within the home, for every person.

POPE ST JOHN PAUL II
(1920–2005), LE 10

146 *What is to be done about job insecurity?*

Christians are called to treat those in need as they would treat Christ himself. Where workers today are forced to the margins of society because of 'job insecurity' or because they are among the 'working poor' (inadequate wages), they are truly in need. Jobs are insecure when wages are clearly below market levels, when workers can no longer plan their future, or when their rights as workers are infringed. Workers have a right to work and to a fair wage. This holds also for temporary workers and migrants. It is a challenge to everyone when the market forces workers into insecure jobs. The state can and should establish conditions where employers can offer work, for example through a 'secondary job market' in which work necessary for society, but outside the market, can be done. All these measures, however, must respect the principle of subsidiarity; they should be a transitional stage that leads to the primary market and is not in competition with it.

 273, 274 ➡ 1940, 2434 ➡ 444, 447

147 *What should be the relation between work and private property?*

Karl Marx and Friedrich Engels wrote in their 1848 *Communist Manifesto* that the goal of Communism can be summed up as "the abolition of private property". In contrast, the Church in her social teaching has always defended the right to private property. At the same time, though, she has constantly emphasized that God created the earth and its goods to benefit *all* men. Social doctrine calls this the "universal destination of material goods". From this follows the principle *property entails social obligations*. This means that one must not use one's property in a merely selfish way but should apply it for the benefit of all. This is true especially with regard to the relation between property and labour: investments should promote the creation of new jobs and the increase of the common good.

➡️ 282 ➡️ 2402–2406 ➡️ 426–427

 To stop investing in people, in order to gain greater short-term financial gain, is bad business for society.
POPE FRANCIS, LS 218

148 *Is there a right to work?*

For the great majority of people, employment is the most important and often the only source of income. But not just that: work is an essential dimension of human self-realization and participation in society. Conversely, unemployment means more than just the material loss of income. Unemployment often means loneliness, self-doubt, social stigma, and sickness. The social doctrine of the Church therefore speaks about a *moral* right to work. All societal forces—businesses, trade unions, politics—are under an obligation to promote this right to work and to pursue the goal of full employment of the population.

➡️ 155–156, 268 ➡️ 2433–2434 ➡️ 444

 My word of thanks to women thus becomes a *heartfelt appeal* that everyone, and in a special way States and international institutions, should make every effort to ensure that women regain full respect for their dignity and role.
POPE ST JOHN PAUL II
(1920–2005), Letter to Women (1995)

149 *What is the relation between work and family life?*

It often looks as though the working world and family life make conflicting and irreconcilable demands. However, work contributes toward creating a material and moral foundation for family life. Wages ensure the family's livelihood, and parents who hold jobs are an important example to growing children. Nevertheless, for many people, juggling family and occupation is no easy task. This is true precisely when both father and mother wish to or have to pursue an occupation. Employers, unions, and government policies must therefore make a common effort to develop new, flexible models for employment, which make it more practical to combine occupation and family.

❝❝ Never get so busy making a living that you forget to make a life.
unknown

❝❝ One of the most important gifts you can give someone is your time and attention.
unknown

➡️ 294

> Every mom is a working mom!

Traditional wisdom

> A Mother's work is surely in reality the most important work in the world. Your job is the one for which all others exist.

C.S. LEWIS

> A man works from sun to sun, but a woman's work is never done.

A common saying

150 What does Catholic social teaching say on the topic of women in the working world?

In the highly developed countries of the Western world, the emancipation of women has made much progress: the Church welcomes and supports it. Women should be equally entitled to play a role in all areas of society. The prerequisite for this, however, is that the specific situation of women must be taken into account. Pregnant women and mothers in particular need special protection under the law and from society as a whole. This is true especially with regard to the working world. In many parts of the world this is not yet the case. Women in many places are subjected to demeaning discrimination and exploitation. The State, society, and the Church must oppose this injustice resolutely.

→ 295 → 2433

151 What does the Church's social teaching say about the issue of child labour?

> We have not inherited this earth from our parents to do with it what we will. We have borrowed it from our children and we must be careful to use it in their interests as well as our own.

MOSES HENRY CASS (b. 1927), Australian politician

In the early phase of industrialization, the exploitation of children through child labour was one of the great scandals in America and Europe. Even today child labour is widespread in the emerging and developing nations. Often sheer economic deprivation is what forces families to put their children to work for wages. The goal, therefore, must be to create social conditions throughout the world that offer all families a secure means of livelihood without any need for children to contribute to the family income. Under no circumstances should child labour be tolerated

 Whoever causes one of these little ones who believe in me to sin, it would be better for him to have a great millstone fastened round his neck and to be drowned in the depths of the sea. **MT 18:6**

if it harms the children's intellectual and physical development. The exploitation and enslavement of children is an injustice that cries out to heaven.

 296

152 *How do we deal fairly with the phenomenon of migrant workers?*

In today's world there are great imbalances between poor and rich countries and regions. Therefore, many people today leave their homes to find jobs and wages in densely populated areas or in other countries. These people are called migrant workers. If a country decides to welcome migrant workers, then they must not be treated as second-class labourers. In no case may migrant workers be exploited; in their work they must have the same rights and receive the same wages as the local employees. Moreover, they must be respected as human beings who are not just labourers. In particular, the right of migrant workers to bring their families after them must be respected. The State, the business community, and society are

> Deprived of schooling, not only do the children who work in factories lose an economic means of providing for their future, but the very humanity of these neglected young slaves of the mill industry is bent, since they can never lift themselves up to the bright realm of free intellectual development.
>
> **FRANZ JOSEPH VON BUSS** (1803–1878). In 1837, eleven years before the appearance of the book *Das Kapital* by Karl Marx, von Buss gave his so-called factory speech.

> Migrants do not break the law as often as the laws break the migrants.
>
> **HERNANDO DE SOTO** (b. 1941), Peruvian economist

Besides preserving animals and plants, human beings themselves are the ones who must be protected above all.

HANS EHARD (1887–1980), former Bavarian Prime Minister

 Agricultural work involves considerable difficulties, including unremitting and sometimes exhausting physical effort and a lack of appreciation on the part of society, to the point of making agricultural people feel that they are social outcasts and of speeding up the phenomenon of their mass exodus from the countryside to the cities and unfortunately to still more dehumanizing living conditions.

POPE ST JOHN PAUL II (1920–2005), LE 21

 I will listen to both the accuser and the defendant equally.

Oath of an ancient Athenian judge

obliged to make efforts to integrate migrant workers into society comprehensively.

➡ **297 ff.** ➡ **2241**

153 *How does social teaching react to the upheavals in agriculture worldwide?*

More than other branches of the economy, agriculture makes a distinctive mark on the landscape and culture of a society. Therefore, the preservation of a viable farming industry is important even for the highly developed industrial nations. In most countries of the world, however, the agrarian sector is now as always the most important sector of the economy by far. Most of the people work in it, too. This is true particularly of the poor countries and regions of the world. Often the basic problem is that the farmland is in the hands of a few major landowners. Where such land ownership leads to the exploitation of the rural population, is detrimental to the common good, and stands in the way of a positive development of the national economy, the Church's social teaching calls for agrarian reform and a new distribution of the land. Such steps must be taken in an orderly, legal way. Old injustice must not be fought with new injustice.

➡ **299 ff.**

154 *Why must there be special laws concerning labour and employment?*

In a market economy, there is a real balance between the two partners to a contract (and thus room to negotiate the terms of the contract) only if both sides have the same information and the same economic strength. In a contract of employment that is usually not the case. As a rule, the employer is the better informed and economically superior party. This is why the legitimate interests of the employees must be protected by special laws, collectively referred to as

> We should leave behind an earth on which those who come after us can live too. After all, the earth does not consist only of railroads and streets, but also of farmland, etc. There must be a balance between the needs of the farmers and those who build roads. There must be justice among those who use the land.

CARDINAL PETER TURKSON
(b. 1948), President of the Pontifical Council for Justice and Peace, interview on 24th January 2013

employment law. These include, for example, protection from → WAGE EXPLOITATION, the right to have Sundays and annual leave, and entitlement to support in the event of unemployment or illness; protection for mothers was already mentioned earlier.

 301 → **2430, 2433**

! WAGE
● EXPLOITATION
The intentional setting of wages below what is customary and reasonable. This can endanger the livelihood of the worker.

155 *When is a wage just?*

From the beginning, the social teaching of the Church has demanded that a worker's wage be enough to ensure a livelihood for himself and his family. Today this demand is worded a bit differently: the wage must be high enough to make it possible for the employee to participate comprehensively in the life of society. Nevertheless, it is difficult to determine the exact amount of a just wage. One must consider the function and productivity of the individual, but also those of his employer. Moreover, the economic and social setting should be taken into account. Excessively high wages can also endanger overall economic productivity and thus be detrimental to the common good. In any case, there must be fair procedures for setting

> The weak are always anxious for justice and equality. The strong pay no heed to either.

ARISTOTLE (384–322 BC)

You shall not muzzle an ox when it treads out the grain.
DTN 25:4

> I do not pay good wages because I have a lot of money; rather, I have a lot of money because I pay good wages.

ROBERT BOSCH
(1861–1942), German industrialist and inventor, an exemplary employer

> To exercise pressure upon the indigent and the destitute for the sake of gain, and to gather one's profit out of the need of another, is condemned by all laws, human and divine. To defraud anyone of wages that are his due is a great crime which cries to the avenging anger of heaven.

POPE LEO XIII
(1810–1903), RN 20

> The average American CEO still believes that labour has to be the natural, mortal enemy of the manager. That's obsolete thinking. I want labour to understand the inner workings of the company.

LEE IACOCCA (b. 1924), American executive in the auto industry

> What is not possible for the individual can be done by many.

FRIEDRICH WILHELM RAIFFEISEN (1818–1888), German mayor, developer of agrarian policy, founder of the Raiffeisen Co-operatives

wages. Here trade unions play an important role. In a subsidiary way (i.e., playing a secondary role), the State may guarantee a minimum wage. The system of wages as a whole must also be just. With a view to social tranquility in a society, there should be no blatant disproportion between the wage of a simple labourer and the earnings of top executives.

➡ **302 ff.** ➡ **2434** ➡ **332**

156 *What is the importance of trade unions?*

Precisely because there is (usually) an imbalance of power between employer and employees, workers sometimes have to consolidate their forces in trade unions. In this way they can protect their common

> A strike that exerts no economic pressure is not a strike but rather collective begging.

JÜRGEN PETERS, Chairman of IG-Metall, Germany's largest trade union

interests in solidarity with one another. The right to found trade unions is a human right. No one should experience adverse consequences because he is the member of a trade union or is involved in legitimate union activity.

➡ **305–307**

157 *Are employees allowed to strike?*

To some extent, employers and employees pursue conflicting interests, for instance, when discussing

the level of wages and the length of the work week. In order to settle these questions in a mutually satisfactory way, there must be negotiations between the two sides. For this purpose, the employees are represented by their unions. The strike is an important method whereby unions can place the employer under pressure in these negotiations. This method is legitimate, if it is applied peacefully and merely to improve wages and working conditions. The strike must not be contrary to the common good. Necessary community services (e.g., police, fire department, care of the sick) must never be impaired by strikes.

➡ **307** ➡ **2435**

> Civil disobedience becomes a sacred duty when the state has become lawless or corrupt.
> **MAHATMA GANDHI** (1869–1948)

> A strike nevertheless can remain even in present-day circumstances a necessary, though ultimate, aid for the defence of the workers' own rights and the fulfillment of their just desires.
> Second Vatican Council, GS 68

> A demonstration, a protest march, a strike, or civil disobedience might be resorted to, all depending on the actual conditions at the given time.
> **NELSON MANDELA** (1918–2013), first president of South Africa, newspaper article, February 1958

From important Church documents

HUMAN WORK

Wages and Property

Rerum Novarum

It is surely undeniable that, when a man engages in remunerative labour, the impelling reason and motive of his work is to obtain property, and thereafter to hold it as his very own. If one man hires out to another his strength or skill, he does so for the purpose of receiving in return what is necessary for the satisfaction of his needs; he therefore expressly intends to acquire a right full and real, not only to the remuneration, but also to the disposal of such remuneration, just as he pleases. Thus, if he lives sparingly, saves money, and, for greater security, invests his savings in land, the land, in such case, is only his wages under another form; and, consequently, a working man's little estate thus purchased should be as completely at his full disposal as are the wages he receives for his labour. But it is precisely in such power of disposal that ownership obtains, whether the property consist of land or chattels. Socialists, therefore, by endeavouring to transfer the possessions of individuals to the community at large, strike at the interests of every wage-earner, since they would deprive him of the liberty of disposing of his wages, and thereby of all hope and possibility of increasing his resources and of bettering his condition in life. What is of far greater moment, however, is the fact that the remedy they propose is manifestly against justice. For, every man has by nature the right to possess property as his own.

Pope Leo XIII, Encyclical Rerum Novarum (1891), 4

No Common Interest between Wealthy and Workers?

Rerum Novarum

The great mistake made in regard to the matter now under consideration is to take up with the notion that class is naturally hostile to class, and that the wealthy and the working men are intended by nature to live in mutual conflict. So irrational and so false is this view that the direct contrary is the truth. Just as the symmetry of the human frame is the result of the suitable arrangement of the different parts of the body, so in a State is it ordained by nature that these two classes should dwell in harmony and agreement, so as to maintain the balance of the body politic. Each needs the other.

Pope Leo XIII, Encyclical Rerum Novarum (1891), 15

Workers Are Not Slaves

Rerum Novarum

The following duties bind the wealthy owner and the employer: not to look upon their work people as their bondsmen, but to respect in every man his dignity as a person ennobled by Christian character.

They are reminded that, according to natural reason and Christian philosophy, working for gain is creditable, not shameful, to a man, since it enables him to earn an honourable livelihood; but to misuse men as though they were things in the pursuit of gain, or to value them solely for their physical powers—that is truly shameful and inhuman. Again justice demands that, in dealing with the working man, religion and the good of his soul must be kept in mind. Hence, the employer is bound to see that the worker has time for his religious duties; that he be not exposed to corrupting influences and dangerous occasions; and that he be not led away to neglect his home and family, or to squander his earnings. Furthermore, the employer must never tax his work people beyond their strength, or employ them in work unsuited to their sex and age.

Pope Leo XIII, Encyclical Rerum Novarum (1891), 16

Injustice Crying Out to Heaven

Rerum Novarum

Wealthy owners and all masters of labour should be mindful of this—that to exercise pressure upon the indigent and the destitute for the sake of gain, and to gather one's profit out of the need of another, is condemned by all laws, human and divine. To defraud any one of wages that are his due is a great crime which cries to the avenging anger of heaven.

Pope Leo XIII, Encyclical Rerum Novarum (1891), 17

Jesus the Worker

Rerum Novarum

As for those who possess not the gifts of fortune, they are taught by the Church that in God's sight poverty is no disgrace, and that there is nothing to be ashamed of in earning their bread by labour. This is enforced by what we see in Christ Himself, who, "whereas He was rich, for our sakes became poor"; and who, being the Son of God, and God Himself, chose to seem and to be considered the son of a carpenter—nay, did not disdain to spend a great part of His life as a carpenter Himself.

Pope Leo XIII, Encyclical Rerum Novarum (1891), 20

Work and the Human Person

Mater et Magistra

Work ... must be regarded not merely as a commodity, but as a specifically human activity. In the majority of cases a man's work is his sole means of livelihood. Its remuneration, therefore, cannot be made to depend on the state of the market. It must be determined by the laws of justice and equity.

Pope St John XXIII, Encyclical Mater et Magistra (1961), 18

Work and Human Development

Gaudium et Spes

Remuneration for labour is to be such that man may be furnished the means to cultivate worthily his own material, social, cultural, and spiritual life and that of his dependents, in view of the function and productiveness of each one, the conditions of the factory or workshop, and the common good.

Vatican Council II, Pastoral Constitution Gaudium et Spes (1965), 67

Laborem Exercens

Work—a Fundamental Human Act

The Church is convinced that work is a fundamental dimension of man's existence on earth. She is confirmed in this conviction by considering the whole heritage of the many sciences devoted to man: anthropology, paleontology, history, sociology, psychology and so on; they all seem to bear witness to this reality in an irrefutable way. But the source of the Church's conviction is above all the revealed word of God, and therefore what is a *conviction of the intellect* is also a *conviction of faith.* The reason is that the Church—and it is worthwhile stating it at this point—believes in man: she *thinks of man* and addresses herself to him *not only* in the light of historical experience, not only with the aid of the many methods of scientific knowledge, but in the first place in the light of the revealed word of the living God.

Pope St John Paul II, Encyclical Laborem Exercens (1981), 4

Laborem Exercens

Man as the subject of work

Man has to subdue the earth and dominate it, because as the "image of God" he is a person, that is to say, a subjective being capable of acting in a planned and rational way, capable of deciding about himself and with a tendency to self-realization.

Pope St John Paul II, Encyclical Laborem Exercens (1981), 6

Laborem Exercens

Work is for Man

However true it may be that man is destined for work and called to it, in the first place work is "for man" and not man "for work" …. Each sort [of work] is judged above all by the *measure of the dignity* of the subject of work, that is to say, the person, *the individual who carries it out* …. In the final analysis it is always man who is *the purpose of the work,* whatever work it is that is done by man—even if the common scale of values rates it as the merest "service", as the most monotonous, even the most alienating work.

Pope St John Paul II: Encyclical Laborem exercens (1981), 6

Laborem Exercens

Work and Occupation

Work constitutes a foundation for the formation of *family life,* which is a natural right and something that man is called to. These two spheres of values—one linked to work and the other consequent on the family nature of human life—must be properly united and must properly permeate each other. In a way, work is a condition for making it possible to found a family, since the family requires the means of subsistence which man normally gains through work. Work and industriousness also influence the whole *process of education* in the family, for the very reason that everyone "becomes a human being" through, among other things, work, and becoming a human being is precisely the main purpose of the whole process of education.

Pope St John Paul II, Encyclical Laborem Exercens (1981), 10

Laborem Exercens

Fair Wage as a Criterion of Justice

In every system, regardless of the fundamental rela-tionships within it between capital and labour, wages, that is to say, *remuneration for work*, are still a *practical means* whereby the vast majority of people can have access to those goods which are intended for common use: both the goods of nature and manufactured goods. Both kinds of goods become acces-sible to the worker through the wage which he receives as remuneration for his work. Hence, in every case, a just wage is the concrete means of *verifying the justice* of the whole socioeconomic system and, in any case, of checking that it is functioning justly. It is not the only means of checking, but it is a particularly important one and, in a sense, the key means.

Pope St John Paul II, Encyclical Laborem Exercens (1981), 19

Centesimus Annus

Praise for Unions

Finally, "humane" working hours and adequate free-time need to be guaranteed, as well as the right to express one's own per-sonality at the workplace without suffering any affront to one's conscience or personal dignity. This is the place to mention once more the role of trade unions, not only in negotiating contracts, but also as "places" where workers can express themselves. They serve the development of an authentic culture of work and help workers to share in a fully human way in the life of their place of employment.

Pope St John Paul II, Encyclical Centesimus Annus (1991), 15

Evangelii Gaudium

Unemployment and Exclusion from Society

Today everything comes under the laws of competi-tion and the survival of the fittest, where the powerful feed upon the power-less. As a consequence, masses of people find themselves excluded and mar-ginalized: without work, without possibilities, without any means of escape. Human beings are themselves considered consumer goods to be used and then discarded. We have created a "throw-away" culture which is now spreading. It is no longer simply about exploitation and oppression, but something new. Exclusion ultimately has to do with what it means to be a part of the society in which we live; those excluded are no longer society's underside or its fringes or its disenfranchised—they are no longer even a part of it. The excluded are not the "exploited" but the outcast, the "leftovers".

Pope Francis, Apostolic Exhortation Evangelii Gaudium, 53

7

QUESTIONS
158–194

Welfare
and Justice
for All

ECONOMIC LIFE

> **In the economic and social realms, too, the dignity and complete vocation of the human person and the welfare of society as a whole are to be respected and promoted. For man is the source, the centre, and the purpose of all economic and social life.**
>
> Vatican Council II, GS 63

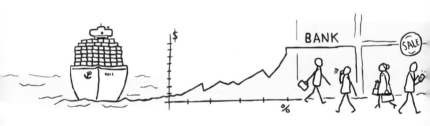

 158 *What do we mean by "economic activity"?*

ECONOMIC ACTIVITY is "the totality of arrangements and procedures for the systematic, ongoing, and secure satisfaction of human needs for those goods and services that enable individuals and social entities to develop as God wills." (Cardinal Josef Höffner)

By → ECONOMIC ACTIVITY we mean the area of our social interactions in which people provide for their material needs and for those of their fellow human beings. Economic life therefore involves the production, the distribution, and the consumption of goods and services.

→ 332 → 2426, 2427

159 *What is the goal of economic activity?*

The goal of economic activity is to supply us with all the material things that we need in order to live. The resources for this purpose—raw materials, machines, land and soil, human labour, for example—are limited. Therefore we must create economic arrangements, in other words, organize economic activity in such a way that these limited resources are used as efficiently and reasonably as possible. The source, focus, and end of all economic activity is the free human being. As always, when we engage in social action, the dignity of the human person and the development of the common good are central (cf. GS 63).

➡ 334, 346, 375 ➡ 2426 ➡ 442

160 *How are economic activity and ethics interrelated?*

The economy functions according to its own laws. One type of economy, the market economy, is increasingly accepted worldwide. It is just like in a real "marketplace": suppliers and consumers meet and negotiate freely with each other about prices, quantities, and the quality of the products. The market economy has proved to be very efficient, but it is ethically acceptable only if it is a social market economy accompanied by a constitutional State. Hence, first of all, there must be clear rules guaranteed by the government, and, secondly, provisions must be made also for those who cannot offer anything in that marketplace, for example, because they have no job or no money. Furthermore there are human experiences that cannot be dealt with justly by the logic of the marketplace: suffering, sickness, and disability, for example. The fact that the economy functions according to its own laws does not mean that the laws of the marketplace are not subject to God's laws and commandments. Ethics is an essential component of good economic activity. Unethical business is in the long run economically wrong, also. It is equally true that uneconomical business, for instance wasting resources, is unethical.

➡ 330–333 ➡ 2426, 2431 ➡ 442–443

> If you can trust a person, you don't need a contract. If you cannot trust him, a contract is useless.
>
> **JOHN PAUL GETTY** (1892–1976), American oil magnate and art patron, the richest man in the world in his day

> Why do Roman bridges historically last for a long, long time? The key reason was that the people who designed the bridge had to stand underneath it before the traffic went on.
>
> **PREM WATSA** (b. 1950), Canadian investor

> There are many human needs which find no place on the market. It is a strict duty of justice and truth not to allow fundamental human needs to remain unsatisfied and not to allow those burdened by such needs to perish.
>
> **POPE ST JOHN PAUL II** (1920–2005), CA 34

> A moral code that supposes that it can skip over the subject of economic laws is not morality but moralism, that is, the opposite of morality.
>
> **JOSEPH CARDINAL RATZINGER/POPE BENEDICT XVI**, *The Market Economy and Ethics* (1986)

161 *Is affluence "unethical"?*

No. To increase prosperity can be a noble ethical purpose. But this purpose is morally good only when it is pursued in a way consistent with the *global development of all human beings in solidarity;* not when only a few individuals profit from the increased prosperity. Development means the holistic, comprehensive development of human beings. This includes faith and family, education and health, and many other values. It cannot always be merely a matter of greater consumption. In a certain way "consumerism" makes people even poorer.

➡ **334** ➡ **2426**

> We must give as long as we have, for we too have a generous Giver.
>
> **BRIDGET OF SWEDEN**
> (1303–1373), mystic and co-patroness of Europe

> Without internal forms of solidarity and mutual trust, the market cannot completely fulfill its proper economic function.
>
> **POPE BENEDICT XVI**, CiV 35

162 *Is the Church critical of economic activity?*

The Church has a fundamentally positive view of economic activity. She critiques economic activity only when commerce sets itself up as an absolute. This happens, for example, when labourers are exploited and co-opted or when people neglect to use the earth's resources in a sustainable way. The Church supports economic activity when human beings can thereby enjoy at least a modest prosperity and have no need to fear poverty. Catholic social doctrine wants everyone to participate actively in bringing about economic progress, improving economic production, and distributing material goods (cf. GS 63, 65).

➡ **373–374** ➡ **2423–2425** ➡ **442**

163 *Can work in business be a vocation?*

Yes. Work in commerce and business can be an authentic vocation from God: people who in their specialized area of responsibility place themselves at the service of their fellow human beings and of society

Just as the commandment "Thou shalt not kill" sets a clear limit in order to safeguard the value of human life, today we also have to say "thou shalt not" to an economy of exclusion and inequality. Such an economy kills.

POPE FRANCIS, EG 53

are a blessing for all. God entrusted the earth to us, "to till it and keep it". In our work we can obey God's will and in some small area contribute to the perfecting of creation (Gen 2:15 ff.). If we act justly and lovingly, we will use the good gifts of the earth and our own talents for the good of our fellow human beings who are entrusted to us (Mt 25:14–30; Lk 19:12–27).

Charity is at the heart of the Church's social doctrine. Every responsibility and every commitment spelled out by that doctrine is derived from charity.

POPE BENEDICT XVI, CiV 2

➡ **326** ➡ **2427–2428** ➡ **442**

164 *What does the Bible say about poverty and riches?*

Anyone who follows Jesus must never forget that first and foremost we are supposed to be "rich toward God" (Lk 12:21). To become rich in material things is not a particularly Christian goal in life. And to be materially rich is not a sure sign of God's special grace. Jesus teaches us to pray: "Give us this day our daily bread" (Mt 6:11). With these words we ask the Father for all that we need for our earthly life. We do not strive for luxurious possessions but for the goods required for a happy life in moderate prosperity, the support of a family, works of charity, and participation in culture and education, as well as further development.

→ 323, 326 → 2443–2446 → 449

165 *Is poverty always bad?*

If "poverty" means involuntary need and doing without vitally necessary means, then poverty is an evil. The fact that one part of humanity goes hungry and another throws excess food away is a scandal and a sin crying out to heaven. It is difficult to say, in wealthy countries, where the boundary line of material poverty runs, in other words, what should be regarded as a minimum subsistence level. Relative poverty—not living in excess—is not necessarily a negative thing. It can lead people to recognize their true needs in God's sight and to approach God in an attitude of petition and trust. When Christians take the Gospel seriously, again and again there is a deliberate, voluntary renunciation of material wealth: many wish to be able to serve God with a free heart. In general it is true: anyone who wants to follow Jesus must "be poor in God's sight", i.e., be interiorly detached from possessions (Mt 5:3). Nothing should have priority over love for God.

→ 324 → 2437–2440 → 448

166 Is prosperity always good?

To be able to live without material cares is a great privilege, for which one should thank God every day. Someone who lives this way can assist those who, for whatever reason, are not so fortunate in life. Wealth, however, can also lead to spiritual self-satisfaction, presumption, and arrogance. Unlike the poor person, the rich person is often tempted to attribute his fortunate circumstances to his own accomplishments. When having leads to greed, it is often accompanied by hardheartedness. Jesus addresses woeful words to the rich man who is fixated on material things: "Fool! This night your soul is required of you" (Lk 12:20).

→ **325** → **2402–2404**

> Some people spend money that they don't have, for things that they don't need, to impress people that they don't like.
>
> **DANNY KAYE** (1913–1987), American entertainer

> The love of money is the root of all evils; it is through this craving that some have wandered away from the faith and pierced their hearts with many pangs.
>
> **1 TIM 6:10**

> ## From greed spring all crimes and wrongdoings.
>
> **CICERO** (106–43 BC)

167 Why does Jesus say that we should not be anxious about tomorrow (Mt 6:34)?

Jesus does not mean thereby to discredit diligent planning. In another passage, after all, he praises wise stewardship and dependable work. Moreover, Jesus himself lived as a manual labourer and worked for others. Anxious worrying about the future, in contrast, is incompatible with a Christian's basic trust.

→ **523**

> You can't have everything. Where would you put it?
>
> **STEVEN WRIGHT** (b. 1955), American comedian

The Works of Mercy

Counsel the doubtful.

Console the sorrowful.

Admonish the sinner.

Instruct the ignorant.

SPIRITUAL WORKS

Forgive all injuries.

Pray for the living and the dead.

Bear wrongs patiently.

Feed the hungry.

Welcome the stranger.

Clothe the naked.

Visit the sick.

CORPORAL WORKS

Visit the imprisoned.

Bury the dead.

Give drink to the thirsty.

168 How does a Christian react to his own poverty?

He will do all that he can to free himself and his own family from poverty through conscientious, persistent work. Often "evil" structures and unjust forces that limit opportunities for property ownership, self-support, and material progress for the poor have to be overcome by working together with others.

→ 325 → 2443–2446 → 449–450

169 What should I do about other people's poverty?

Because God loves every individual human being "unto death on the cross", Christians look at their fellowmen in a new light. Even in the poorest of the poor they recognize Christ, their Lord. Christians are therefore deeply motivated to do everything possible to alleviate the suffering of others. In doing so they take as their guide the →WORKS OF MERCY. One can help person-to-person. But it is also possible, through donations, indirectly to help poor people to survive and to live in dignity. Much more important, however, is assistance that enables the poor person to free himself from his poverty, for example, by finding him a job or by giving him a better education. In doing so, no one should feel overburdened, but no one should feel too easily exempt. Businessmen make an important contribution toward the fight against poverty by creating jobs and humane working conditions.

→ 329 → 2447 → 449–450

170 Can we bring about "the Kingdom of God" through material progress?

If we work passionately and perseveringly for comprehensive human development and to preserve the environment, we can accomplish much but not

 The great challenge before us … is to demonstrate that … the principle of gratuitousness and the logic of gift as an expression of fraternity can and must find their place within normal economic activity.
BENEDICT XVI, CiV 36

 We can no longer trust in the unseen forces and the invisible hand of the market. Growth in justice requires more than economic growth, while presupposing such growth: it requires decisions, programmes, mechanisms, and processes specifically geared to a better distribution of income, the creation of sources of employment, and an integral promotion of the poor which goes beyond a simple welfare mentality.
POPE FRANCIS, EG 204

 Today, it is the case that some economic sectors exercise more power than states themselves. But economics without politics cannot be justified, since this would make it impossible to favour other ways of handling the various aspects of the present crisis.
POPE FRANCIS, LS 196

[If private property were abolished,] the sources of wealth themselves would run dry, for no one would have any interest in exerting his talents or his industry; and that ideal equality about which they entertain pleasant dreams would be in reality the leveling down of all to a like condition of misery and degradation.

POPE LEO XIII
(1810–1903) RN 15

remake paradise. Jesus says: "My kingship is not of this world" (Jn 18:36). The Kingdom of God therefore must not be confused with material or earthly progress. Nevertheless, to the extent that economic progress "can contribute to the better ordering of human society, it is of vital concern to the Kingdom of God" (GS 39).

➡ 55, 323–326 ➡ 2419–2420, 2426

171 *Is capitalism compatible with human dignity?*

In view of the spectacular failure of the central planning economy in the Soviet system, John Paul II wrote: "If by 'capitalism' is meant an economic system which recognizes the fundamental and positive role of business, the market, private property, and the resulting responsibility for the means of production, as well as free human creativity in the economic sector, then the answer is certainly in the affirmative, even though it would perhaps be more appropriate to speak of a 'business economy', 'market economy', or simply 'free economy'. But if by 'capitalism' is meant a system in which freedom in the economic sector is not circumscribed within a strong juridical framework which places it at the service of human freedom in its totality, and which sees it as a particular aspect of that freedom, the core of which is ethical and religious, then the reply is certainly negative" (CA 42).

➡ 335 ➡ 2425 ➡ 442

 It is through work that man, using his intelligence and exercising his freedom, succeeds in dominating the earth and making it a fitting home. In this way, he makes part of the earth his own, precisely the part which he has acquired through work; this is the *origin of individual property*.

POPE ST JOHN PAUL II
(1920–2005), CA 31

172 *Is there such a thing as a "Christian economic model"?*

No. The Church is supposed to proclaim the Gospel and not enter a competition for the best economic model and technological solutions. The Church's demand that the economy should serve man and the

Capitalism does not mean too many capitalists, but too few capitalists.

G.K. CHESTERTON (1874–1936) English writer

common good is a reasonable demand in keeping with human dignity.

→ 335 → 2420–2422 → 23

173 *How do we achieve an economic order that serves man and the common good?*

It depends primarily on integrating the factors of *justice* and *love of neighbour* into everyday business. Christians have not only the opportunity but also the duty to improve institutions and living conditions until they are humane. Before a Christian improves others, though, he works on himself. Only then will his commitment to optimizing economic circumstances and societal institutions be credible.

→ 42 → 1888 → 327–329

174 *Is entrepreneurial private property an injustice?*

No. An entrepreneur, like any other person, has the natural right to the fruits of his labour and to the means for obtaining these fruits (means of production). This right is what stimulates the creative, entrepreneurial freedom from which everyone involved

The Church does not have technical solutions to offer and does not claim "to interfere in any way in the politics of States".
POPE BENEDICT XVI, CiV 9

The worship of the ancient golden calf (cf. Ex 32:1–35) has returned in a new and ruthless guise in the idolatry of money and the dictatorship of an impersonal economy lacking a truly human purpose.
POPE FRANCIS, EG 55

How could we do good to our neighbour if everyone owned nothing?
CLEMENT OF ALEXANDRIA (ca. 150–210), early Greek theologian

God gave the earth to the whole human race for the sustenance of all its members, without excluding or favouring anyone. This is *the foundation of the universal destination of the earth's goods.*

POPE ST JOHN PAUL II, CA 31

MORTGAGE
The pledge of real estate by a debtor to a creditor as security for a debt (especially one incurred in purchasing the property). Just as the owner of a mortgaged house must make regular payments to the lender bank, so too the owner of private property must make sure that it is used in a socially beneficial way.

It's never too early to teach your children about the tool of money. Teach them how to work for it and they learn pride and self-respect. Teach them how to save it and they learn security and self-worth. Teach them how to be generous with it and they learn love.

JUDITH JAMISON (b. 1943), American dancer and choreographer

in the economic process benefits. Creating property motivates one to make great efforts; since private property "adds incentives for carrying on one's … charge, it constitutes one of the conditions for civil liberties" (GS 71). On the other hand, drastic economic inequalities are social explosives. And often they are really unjust, too, for instance when employees do not receive a sufficient share of the profits. Exploitation is still the order of the day in many countries. The vast economic superiority of some can lead to the inferiority and disadvantage of others. Private property, therefore, is subject to a "social → MORTGAGE": property should be used for the common good of all, because God created material goods for everyone. It is the state's task justly to regulate and enforce this social requirement of property.

→ **176–184, 328–329** → **2403, 2427–2430** → **443**

175 *Is money bad in itself?*

No. Money is a good human invention, but it can be abused. Money is a means of exchange, a measure of value, a reserve for the future, and a means with which to support what is good. Money must never become an end in itself. Jesus says explicitly: "You cannot serve both God and → MAMMON" (Mt 6:24). Money can become an idol and addictive. Someone who avariciously pursues money becomes the slave of his greed.

→ **328** → **2424, 2449** → **355**

176 *Is it permissible to make a profit?*

Yes. Profit is an initial indication of the success of an enterprise, but not yet a sufficient proof that the enterprise serves society. In order to run a business in a sustainable way, the justifiable pursuit of profit must be harmonized with the indispensable protection of the dignity of the human person. Profit gained on the basis of exploitation or the violation of social justice and workers' rights is injustice.

→ 340 → 2443–2446 → 449

177 *Is a "free market" a good thing?*

In a free market, people can offer and obtain goods and services freely within a legal, ethical framework. Consumers ultimately determine what is produced, at what price, and in what quantity, unless monopolies

> **Markets are like parachutes; they function only when they are open.**
> **HELMUT SCHMIDT** (b. 1918), former German Federal Chancellor

and cartels disrupt the law of supply and demand. The "free market" has generally proved that it can set economic development in motion and sustain it in the long term. Moreover, in a free market, resources are used more efficiently than in a planned economy. There are also, however, "markets" that are unethical, for example, the drug trade, human trafficking in all its forms, illegal weapons sales, etc. Efficiency, though, is not everything. Not infrequently the free market can lead to situations where those with fewer financial resources can be put at a disadvantage or exploited by those with greater resources, e.g., through forcing workers to accept unfairly low wages. When this happens, the weaker party has to be helped; on the hand by the state through its laws, and on the other hand through societal organizations such as trade unions.

MAMMON
Aramaic = *mamona*. Wealth used immorally or dishonest gain. Disparaging term for money.

> Some people regard private enterprise as a predatory tiger to be shot. Others look on it as a cow they can milk. Not enough people see it as a healthy horse, pulling a sturdy wagon.
> **WINSTON CHURCHILL** (1874–1965), in a speech given on 29th October 1959

It would appear that, on the level of individual nations and of international relations, the *free market* is the most efficient instrument for utilizing resources and effectively responding to needs.
POPE ST JOHN PAUL II CA 34

Just as social in-equalities down to the level of poverty exist in rich countries, so, in parallel fashion, in the less developed countries one often sees manifestations of selfishness and a flaunting of wealth which is as disconcerting as it is scandalous.

POPE ST JOHN PAUL II, SRS 14

A free market is only acceptable when it is also a market that serves the whole community. But there are also 'markets' which are unethical, e.g, drug trafficking, human trafficking in all its forms, and illegal trafficking in weapons, etc.

➡ **347** ➡ **2425–2426** ➡ **442**

178 *Is competition in the free market an offense against love of neighbour?*

It depends on the nature of the competition. If "competition" is understood as the systematic destruction of one's competitor, then it is an offense against love of neighbour. In contrast, if competition is the sporting attempt to do better than one's opponent, then it is an effective means of attaining important goals of justice: prices fall, entrepreneurs comply better with the needs of consumers, resources are used more sparingly, entrepreneurial incentive and innovative skill are rewarded, etc. Moreover, Christians throughout the world have established forms of collaboration that are not based on competition, for instance in → CO-OPERATIVES, which combine fraternal assistance and efficiency.

➡ **347** ➡ **2423–2425, 2430** ➡ **442**

CO-OPERATIVE
An association of persons who do business together and thereby achieve a social benefit. The first long-standing co-operatives in Britain were founded in the mid-nineteenth century.

179 *What are the limits of the free market?*

Many people have no access at all to the market and cannot satisfy their fundamental needs. They are poor, have nothing to offer, and cannot buy anything. Again and again we must make it clear that a human being not only *has something* but above all is *someone*—one of our brothers or sisters who has an inalienable dignity. "It is a strict duty of justice and truth not to allow fundamental human needs to remain unsatisfied, and not to allow those burdened by such needs to perish" (John Paul II, CA 34). Moreover, the free market is limited by the fact that there are

 As needs proliferate and life becomes more expensive and everyone wants to and has to have a lot of things in order to live in his own way, to the same extent public credit and general trust diminish, speculators perform somersaults, and dishonesty and deceit gain ground.

ADOLPH KOLPING (1813-1865), German Catholic priest who organized support for young workers

numerous goods that have no price and therefore cannot be sold: a human being himself (prostitution, exploitation, human trafficking), his health (the industrialization and commercialization of medicine), his body parts (the organ trade), or else friendship, forgiveness, family relationships, etc.

 349 ➡ 2431 ➡ 442

180 What does globalization mean for the economy?

Economically, the world is growing more and more interconnected. The fall of barriers after the end of the Cold War, the improvement of transportation, and especially the digital revolution have led to a situation in which businesses can communicate worldwide in real time and produce globally. Funds flow at lightning speed all over the earth. Manufacturing facilities are relocated to the most profitable site. New markets are constantly opening up, etc.

➡ 361 ➡ 2438–2440 ➡ 446–447

 Globalization must not be a new version of colonialism. It must respect the diversity of cultures which, within the universal harmony of peoples, are life's interpretive keys.

POPE ST JOHN PAUL II (1920–2005), Address on 27th April 2001

Politics must not be subject to the economy, nor should the economy be subject to the dictates of an efficiency-driven paradigm of technocracy. Today, in view of the common good, there is urgent need for politics and economics to enter into a frank dialogue in the service of life, especially human life.

POPE FRANCIS, LS 189

No one discovers new continents without having the courage to lose sight of old shores.

ANDRÉ GIDE (1869–1951), French writer

181 Is the globalization of the economy beneficial?

Globalization has benefits but it also has costs. We are still not coping adequately with this new reality ethically or technologically. On the one hand, globalization is connected with the hope of a worldwide development and improvement of material and cultural

> Future project for the Church: give globalization a soul.

RENÉ RÉMOND (b. 1918), French historian

The challenge, in short, is to ensure a globalization in solidarity, a globalization without marginalization.

POPE ST JOHN PAUL II (1920–2005), Message for the World Day of Peace 1998

Economic activity, especially the activity of a market economy, cannot be conducted in an institutional, juridical, or political vacuum. On the contrary, it presupposes sure guarantees of individual freedom and private property, as well as a stable currency and efficient public services.

POPE ST JOHN PAUL II (1920–2005), CA 48

Never tell a man how to do something. Tell him what to do and let him surprise you with his ingenuity.

GEORGE SMITH PATTON (1885–1945), American general

living conditions. On the other hand, we are confronting tremendous movements of migration and flight from the countryside, along with the loss of cultural identities. Cities with a million or more inhabitants can become uncontrollable and scarcely inhabitable population centres, inequality is aggravated, and the exploitation of the poor increases instead of diminishing. In an age of globalization, solidarity between peoples and generations must be practised with new intensity.

→ 362–366 → 2438–2440 → 446–447

182 What is the government's role in the economy?

The government and international communities of States (e.g., the United States of America or the European Union) create the framework for the economy. In doing so, the State must be guided first of all by the principle of subsidiarity (see nos. 94–96 above) and help participants in the economy to *help themselves*. What business organizations can accomplish must not be organized by the government (privatization). When such assisted self-help is not possible, the State must act according to the *principle of solidarity* (see nos. 99–102 above): the unemployed must not fall through the cracks, and provisions must be made for retirees and those in need of special care. The most important thing is to protect the weakest. The State's intervention must be carefully weighed: neither too strong (*command economy* or *statism*) nor too restrained (*laissez-faire*). The State's main task in the economic realm is to establish a legal framework and a tax structure; moreover, a welfare system must aid those who are not capable of earning their own livelihood.

➡ **351–355** ➡ **2430–2431** ➡ **447–448**

183 *What is the role of groups, unions, foundations, and associations?*

There are non-profit institutions, founded and run by private individuals, that pursue goals that are of general interest: sports clubs, regional associations, environmental protection groups, religious associations etc. These are forms of co-operative activity that have their roots in civil society. They create solidarity and are very important for society. They should be fostered and protected by the State in its laws and taxation policies.

➡ **357** ➡ **2429–2433** ➡ **447–448**

> United there is little we cannot do. Divided there is little we can do.
>
> **JOHN F. KENNEDY** (1917–1963), U.S. President

> The rise and growth of associations and movements mostly made up of young people can be seen as the work of the Holy Spirit, who blazes new trails to meet their expectations and their search for a deep spirituality and a more real sense of belonging. There remains a need, however, to ensure that these associations actively participate in the Church's overall pastoral efforts.
>
> **POPE FRANCIS,** EG 105

> Chose an avocation, an inconspicuous, perhaps a secret avocation. Open your eyes and seek another human being in need of a little time, a little friendliness, a little company, a little work. It may be a lonely, an embittered, a sick, or an awkward person for whom you can do something, to whom you can mean something. Or else a good cause needs volunteer workers, people who can give up a free evening or run errands. Be prepared for disappointments also! But do not abandon your quest for the avocation, for that sideline in which you can act as a human being for other human beings. There is one waiting for you, if only you really want it.
>
> **ALBERT SCHWEITZER** (1875–1965)

> Where would we be today if somebody had said to Columbus, "Christopher, stay here. Wait with your discovery trip, until our most important problems are solved—war and famine, poverty and crime, environmental pollution and illnesses, illiteracy and racism"?
>
> **BILL GATES** (b. 1955)

184 *What is a business?*

A business is a unit of production that requires equipment, premises, money, etc., and a society of persons (John Paul II, CA 43). A business should supply people with goods that are truly good and with services that really serve. Founding a business often demands unusual daring, innovative creativity, and a heightened sense of responsibility.

➡ 338 ➡ 2426 ➡ 443

> After careful consideration of your invention, we have come to the conclusion that it has no commercial possibilities.
>
> From the letter by financier **J. P. MORGAN** to Alexander Graham Bell after the latter had demonstrated the telephone to him.

185 *What human qualities does a good business foster?*

"When managed well, businesses actively enhance the dignity of employees and the development of virtues, such as solidarity, practical wisdom, justice, discipline, and many others. While the family is the first school of society, businesses, like many other social institutions, continue to educate people in virtue" (Pontifical Council for Justice and Peace, "The Vocation of the Business Leader", 3).

➡ 331–335 ➡ 2426–2428 ➡ 443

> I have to sell something to other people, my customers. I must line up coworkers. I must convince suppliers that I am the right partner for them. And so I must be able to sell my product. Someone who thinks that selling is beneath him should not start a business.
>
> **NORMAN RENTROP** (b. 1957), German entrepreneur and main sponsor of Bibel-TV, an interdenominational Christian TV network.

186 *Why is the economy a place and a school of humanity?*

Many employees and employers work much more than duty demands. They do this out of a sense of responsibility and out of love for their job and for the people who rely on the service they provide. Even employers do not always act in profit-oriented ways: investments are often an act of generosity, for investing means giving up immediate consumption and using funds to create jobs. Then, too, more and more people work in so-called non-profit organizations, which pursue social goals in an entrepreneurial spirit. Volunteering, too, is a form of work inspired by charity.

➡ 365–367 ➡ 2426–2428 ➡ 443

187 *When does a business work successfully?*

Success consists first but not exclusively in the efficient earning of profit. A business is good when it persistently creates something that is good for other people and for society. The State sets up the legal framework. It is not enough for a business to make donations from its profits; the important thing is to act justly, humanely, in a socially and environmentally conscious way already within the economic activity, at the heart of the business itself and of its processes and goals.

⇒ 332, 340 ⇒ 2426–2427 ⇒ 443

188 *How does one act justly in business?*

In economic activity, one acts justly by giving the other his due. This consists chiefly in the faithful fulfillment of contracts, the honouring of agreements, the punctual and proper delivery of goods, and payment within the agreed time. In order to be just, contracts must be entered into freely, which means without deceit, fear, or coercion. Someone who as the more powerful negotiating partner forces his terms on the other acts unjustly.

⇒ 340 ⇒ 2411 ⇒ 430

189 *What is a fair price?*

Fundamentally, a fair price is what is agreed upon in free negotiations through the interaction of supply and demand. Many factors, however, can distort this free agreement: deception, a lack of information, a monopoly position of the seller or the buyer, an emergency situation affecting one of the partners, etc. Usury (the charging of excessive interest on a loan) and exploitation are sins against justice and charity.

⇒ 340 ⇒ 2414, 2434, 2436

The Church's social doctrine holds that authentically human social relationships of friendship, solidarity, and reciprocity can also be conducted within economic activity, and not only outside it or "after" it.
POPE BENEDICT XVI, CiV 36

When you are thirsty, it is already too late to dig a well.
Proverb

Businesses should "create goods which are truly good and services which truly serve."
Pontifical Council for Justice and Peace, "The Vocation of the Business Leader", 40

Both the market and politics need individuals who are open to reciprocal gift.
POPE BENEDICT XVI, CiV 39

The one who has the profit must also bear the loss. The more those responsible for investments are liable for them, the more carefully they are made.
WALTER EUCKEN (1891–1950), German economist

190 *What are the "sins" of business?*

Unfortunately there is a lot of lying, trickery, swindling, and fraud in the business world. Those who act in this way destroy a firm's real capital: trust. Without trust, the business cannot function: when someone gives his word or signs a contract, you must be able to rely on it. One gains trust through reliability and earns it through virtuous conduct. In the business world, one must guard especially against: greed, corruption, and any form of injustice, such as theft, fraud, usury, exploitation, etc.

 343 ➡ 2408–2414 ➡ 428, 430

191 *The speculative financial market per se is a sinful structure, is it not?*

No, not in principle. If they are oriented toward the common good, the financial market and the banks perform an important service: they make available

the capital required for enterprises and businesses. The debtor must pay interest as the price for the liquidity that is offered. Moreover, the mechanism of speculation is good in itself, for it serves to equalize quantities and prices from one region to the next and to balance out times of shortage or surplus. Of course in recent years these instruments have been abused disastrously. The financial market is inflated. "Investors" have been speculating without anything of real value backing up their money. In a few seconds unimaginable sums are gained or lost, without any genuine work behind it.

→ 368 → 2426

192 How can the financial market regain trust?

Besides a voluntary commitment to ethical principles, the greatest possible transparency of transactions is the most effective way of leading the banking and financial sector out of the worst crisis in its

> It is impossible to make everything good unless all men are good, and that I don't expect to see for quite a few years yet.
>
> **ST THOMAS MORE**
> (1478–1535), English Lord-Chancellor, philosopher, martyr

Financial crises are triggered when ... those working in the economic sector lose trust in its modes of operating and in its financial systems. Nevertheless, finance, commerce, and production systems are contingent human creations which, →

→ if they become objects of blind faith, bear within themselves the roots of their own downfall. Their true and solid foundation is faith in the human person. For this reason all the measures proposed to rein in this crisis must seek, ultimately, to offer security to families and stability to workers and, through appropriate regulations and controls, to restore ethics to the financial world.

POPE BENEDICT XVI, 30th March 2009

Development is the new name for peace.

POPE PAUL VI (1897–1978), quoted in SRS 10

history. Furthermore, the international financial market must be regulated within a binding legal framework.

➡ 369–372 ➡ 2430–2432 ➡ 430

193 *Why is "development" more than "economic growth"?*

Development is a broader term than "economic growth". Besides the prospect of welfare and security, people need a comprehensive vision of development: in the family, in the faith, through education, through good medical care. In wealthy nations many people still dream about universal prosperity. Nowadays, however, no State can address the problems by itself and solve them alone. One of the tasks of the international economy is the realization of a *comprehensive, co-operative development for humanity*, in other words, for every human being and for the *whole* human being. This is to the benefit of the wealthy countries, too. It is not true that the rich must always become richer and the poor, poorer. In a humane economic system, economic growth for some leads to the improvement of the situation of others as well.

→ 373–374 → 2426–2433 → 443–444, 446–448

 194 *What is corruption and what can one do about it?*

Corruption—the misuse of the power and the resources one has been entrusted with for personal advantage—is a cancer that destroys society from within. Those who have no power are deprived of access to benefits they are entitled to, e.g., security, education, health care, work, advancement. Often victims become perpetrators when they succeed in acquiring some small measure of power themselves. Forms of corruption include bribery, embezzlement, cronyism, misuse of resources, and much more. Corruption is widespread and has devastating consequences. Even Church institutions are not free from "the sweet poison of corruption" (Pope Francis). Corruption contradicts the fundamental principles of social justice; it cheats people out of their natural rights; it harms the common good and tramples on the dignity of the human person. It is everyone's responsibility to fight against corruption, but especially those in politics. A first protection against corruption is maximum transparency in the distribution of resources and opportunities. Christian persons and communities living free of corruption in the midst of corrupt societies can be a leaven for the renewal of the whole society.

→ 411 → 2407–2414 → 428

Of all the mistakes made in bringing up children, the belief in inherited limits to development is the worst.

ALFRED ADLER (1870–1937), Austrian psychologist

An increased sense of God and increased self-awareness are fundamental to any *full development of human society.*

CCC **2441**

If we find a dead animal and it is corrupted, ... it 'stinks', corruption 'stinks'! A corrupt society stinks! A Christian who allows corruption to enter is not Christian, they stink!

POPE FRANCIS, 21st March 2015

Corruption has become natural, to the point of becoming a personal and social statement tied to customs, common practice in commercial and financial transactions, in public contracting, in every negotiation that involves agents of the State. It is the victory of appearances over reality and of brazenness over honourable discretion. The Lord, however, does not tire of knocking at the doors of the corrupt..

POPE FRANCIS, 23rd October 2014

From important Church documents

ECONOMIC LIFE

Warning to the Rich
Rerum Novarum

Therefore, those whom fortune favours are warned that riches do not bring freedom from sorrow and are of no avail for eternal happiness, but rather are obstacles; that the rich should tremble at the threatenings of Jesus Christ - threatenings so unwonted in the mouth of our Lord - and that a most strict account must be given to the Supreme Judge for all we possess.
Pope Leo XIII, Encyclical Rerum Novarum (1891), 22

Wealth Exists for All
Rerum Novarum

"Man should not consider his material possessions as his own, but as common to all, so as to share them without hesitation when others are in need. Whence the Apostle [says], 'Command the rich of this world ... to offer with no stint, to apportion largely.' " True, no one is commanded to distribute to others that which is required for his own needs and those of his household .... It is a duty, not of justice (save in extreme cases), but of Christian charity—a duty not enforced by human law.
Pope Leo XIII, Encyclical Rerum Novarum (1891), 19

The Limits of the Welfare State
Centesimus Annus

By intervening directly and depriving society of its responsibility, the Social Assistance State leads to a loss of human energies and an inordinate increase of public agencies, which are dominated more by bureaucratic ways of thinking than by concern for serving their clients, and which are accompanied by an enormous increase in spending.
Pope St John Paul II, Encyclical Centesimus Annus (1991), 48

The Dangers of Globalization
Caritas in Veritate

The global market has stimulated first and foremost, on the part of rich countries, a search for areas in which to outsource production at low cost with a view to reducing the prices of many goods, increasing purchasing power, and thus accelerating the rate of development in terms of greater availability of consumer goods for the domestic market. Consequently, the market has prompted new forms of competition between States as they seek to attract foreign businesses to set up production centres, by means of a variety of instruments, including favourable fiscal regimes and deregulation of the labour market. These processes have led to a *downsizing of social security systems* as the price to be paid for seeking greater competitive advantage in the global market, with consequent grave danger for the rights of workers, for fundamental human rights, and for the solidarity associated with the traditional forms of the social State. Systems of social security can lose the capacity to carry out their task, both in emerging countries and in those that were among the earliest to develop, as well as in poor countries. Here budgetary policies, with cuts in social spending often made under pressure from international financial institutions, can leave citizens powerless in the face of old and new risks; such powerlessness is increased by the lack of effective protection on the part of workers' associations. Through the combination of social and economic change, *trade union organizations* experience greater difficulty in carrying out their task of representing the interests of workers, partly because governments, for reasons of economic utility, often limit the freedom or the negotiating capacity of trade unions. Hence traditional networks of solidarity have more and more obstacles to overcome.

Pope Benedict XVI, Encyclical Caritas in Veritate (2009), 25

Caritas in Veritate The Principle of Gratuity and the Logic of Gift

The great challenge before us, accentuated by the problems of development in this global era and made even more urgent by the economic and financial crisis, is to demonstrate, in thinking and behaviour, not only that traditional principles of social ethics like transparency, honesty, and responsibility cannot be ignored or attenuated, but also that in *commercial relationships* the *principle of gratuitousness* and the logic of gift as an expression of fraternity can and must *find their place within normal economic activity*. This is a human demand at the present time, but it is also demanded by economic logic. It is a demand both of charity and of truth.

Pope Benedict XVI, Encyclical Caritas in Veritate (2009), 36

Caritas in Veritate The Poor and the Life of Excess

Many people today would claim that they owe nothing to anyone, except to themselves. They are concerned only with their rights, and they often have great difficulty in taking responsibility for their own and other people's integral development .... On the one hand, appeals are made to alleged rights, arbitrary and non-essential in nature, accompanied by the demand that they be recognized and promoted by public structures, while, on the other hand, elementary and basic rights remain unacknowledged and are violated in much of the world. A link has often been noted between claims to a "right to excess", and even to transgression and vice, within affluent societies, and the lack of food, drinkable water, basic instruction, and elementary health care in areas of the underdeveloped world and on the outskirts of large metropolitan centres.

Pope Benedict XVI, Encyclical Caritas in Veritate (2009), 43

Evangelii Gaudium

The Dictatorship of an Impersonal Economy

The current financial crisis can make us overlook the fact that it originated in a profound human crisis: the denial of the primacy of the human person! We have created new idols. The worship of the ancient golden calf (cf. Ex 32:1–35) has returned in a new and ruthless guise in the idolatry of money and the dictatorship of an impersonal economy lacking a truly human purpose. The worldwide crisis affecting finance and the economy lays bare their imbalances and, above all, their lack of real concern for human beings; man is reduced to one of his needs alone: consumption.

Pope Francis, Apostolic Exhortation Evangelii Gaudium (2013), 55

Evangelii Gaudium

Prosperity for All

While the earnings of a minority are growing exponentially, so too is the gap separating the majority from the prosperity enjoyed by those happy few. This imbalance is the result of ideologies which defend the absolute autonomy of the marketplace and financial speculation. Consequently, they reject the right of states, charged with vigilance for the common good, to exercise any form of control. A new tyranny is thus born, invisible and often virtual, which unilaterally and relentlessly imposes its own laws and rules. Debt and the accumulation of interest also make it difficult for countries to realize the potential of their own economies and keep citizens from enjoying their real purchasing power. To all this we can add widespread corruption and self-serving tax evasion, which have taken on worldwide dimensions. The thirst for power and possessions knows no limits. In this system, which tends to devour everything which stands in the way of increased profits, whatever is fragile, like the environment, is defenceless before the interests of a deified market, which become the only rule.

Pope Francis, Apostolic Exhortation Evangelii Gaudium (2013), 56

🙶 Man at the centre of economic activity

The long-term measures that are designed to ensure an adequate legal framework for all economic actions, as well as the associated urgent measures to resolve the global economic crisis, must be guided by the ethics of truth. This includes, first and foremost, respect for the truth of man, who is not simply an additional economic factor or a disposable good, but is equipped with a nature and a dignity that cannot be reduced to simple economic calculus. Therefore concern for the fundamental material and spiritual welfare of every human person is the starting point for every political and economic solution and the ultimate measure of its effectiveness and its ethical validity.

Moreover, the goal of economics and politics is to serve humanity, beginning with the poorest and most vulnerable wherever they may be, even in their mothers' wombs. Every economic and political theory or action must set about providing each inhabitant of the planet with the minimum wherewithal to live in dignity and freedom, with the possibility of supporting a family, educating children, praising God, and developing one's own human potential. This is the main thing; in the absence of such a vision, all economic activity is meaningless.

In this sense, the various grave economic and political challenges facing to-day's world require a courageous change of attitude that will restore to the end (the human person) and to the means (economics and politics) their proper place. Money and other political and economic means must serve, not rule, bearing in mind that, in a seemingly paradoxical way, free and disinterested solidarity is the key to the smooth functioning of the global economy.

I wished to share these thoughts with you, Prime Minister, with a view to high-lighting what is implicit in all political choices, but can sometimes be forgot-ten: the primary importance of putting humanity, every single man and woman, at the centre of all political and economic activity, both nationally and inter-nationally, because man is the truest and deepest resource for politics and economics, as well as their ultimate end.

From a letter by Pope Francis to the British Prime Minister, David Cameron, dated 15th June 2013

8

QUESTIONS
195–228

Power and Morality

THE POLITICAL
COMMUNITY

> It is evident that
> a city is a natural
> production
> and that man is naturally
> a political animal.

ARISTOTLE, Politics, bk.1, chap.2

> The administration of the government must be conducted for the benefit of those entrusted to one's care, not of those to whom it is entrusted.

MARCUS TULLIUS CICERO
(106–43 BC) Roman politician

> The budget should be balanced. Public debt should be reduced. The arrogance of the generals should be tempered and controlled. Assistance to foreign lands should be curtailed lest Rome become bankrupt.

TAYLOR CALDWELL (1900–1985), Anglo-American novelist, imaginatively summarizing the philosophy of Cicero

195 *What is a political community?*

A political community regulates the public affairs of a society, the *res publica,* as the Romans described it, in contrast to private interests. In antiquity it was considered honourable to care about public affairs as though they were one's own. In Aristotle's view, man is a "political animal": one is truly a human being when one helps shape public life and consequently lives as a *citizen.*

→ 47, 68, 106 → 1880–1882, 1910 → 139

196 *How "political" is a human being in Christianity?*

In contrast to the ancient authors, Christianity emphasizes above all the unconditional worth of the human person, independent of his accomplishments in public and political life. Even a handicapped or elderly person has the dignity of being created in God's image and likeness. Hence all political thought in Christianity is measured against the God-given dignity of the human person. A human being is both an *individual* and a *social being*. He lives in a threefold circle of relationships: 1) to himself, 2) to his fellow human beings, and 3) to God. Man is the measure and object of politics.

→ 384, 388 → 1879, 1881 → 440

197 How important is politics?

For Christians the "State" always comes after the person, or else after the community of persons that today we call *civil society*. First a person finds himself and his dignity in his relationship to God, then he achieves fulfillment in relation to his fellowmen. These two dimensions are closely interconnected. In any case, man should come into his own first, then society, and finally the political organization of the State.

→ 417–420 → 1883–1885 → 440

198 How much of a State does man need?

Despite the priority of the person, we cannot do without the State. It has subsidiary—and therefore auxiliary—significance, yet is indispensable in bringing about and securing any sort of order in society. It would be wonderful if the wishes and demands of individuals and of societal groups automatically coalesced in a vision of the common good. But society is pulled back and forth by multiple special interests. This causes bitter conflicts, battles, rivalry, and competition. The strong try to trump the weak. In such a situation, who is supposed to create order, if not the *State?* Its most important tool is the *law*. Without curtailing people's freedom arbitrarily or more than

> By blood, I am Albanian. By citizenship, I am Indian. By faith, I am a Catholic nun. As to my calling, I belong to the world. As to my heart, I belong entirely to the Heart of Jesus.
>
> **ST TERESA OF CALCUTTA** (1910–1997)

> The most important criterion of the State must always be the development of the powers of the individual citizens in their individuality.
>
> **WILHELM VON HUMBOLDT** (1767–1835), German scholar and politician

TRANSCENDENCE
That which surpasses what went before, ultimately God, who surpasses everything conceivable.

> There are not two sorts of decency, and what a decent man is not allowed to do, a decent State must not do either.
>
> **THEODOR FONTANE** (1819–1898), German author

> Politics is a strong and slow boring of hard boards. It takes both passion and perspective.
>
> **MAX WEBER** (1864–1920), German sociologist and national economist

necessary, the constitutional State creates a framework that is at the service of the common good. In the
best case, the State is the secure sphere in which the
human person can freely develop.

➡ 418 ➡ 1880, 1882 ➡ 326, 376–377

199 How is civil society structured?

Civil society often appears to be no more than a
"market" in which supply, demand, and competition
rule. However, there are also non-profit social ini-
tiatives (unions, associations, foundations, interest
groups). They thrive on solidarity and volunteering
and cultivate values in society that are indispensable
for its cohesiveness: warmth, closeness, fellowship,
concern for the plight of the weak, fraternity. In order
to distinguish volunteer commitments from the public and private sector, these groups are also called the
third sector. A State can govern only when it can build

Crown Court

> **"**
> # The high destiny of the individual is to serve rather than to rule.
>
> **ALBERT EINSTEIN** (1879–1955)

on committed individuals and loyal associations that actively share responsibility with it.

→ **419, 420** → **1880** → **447**

> **"** If not us, who?
> If not here, where?
> If not now, when?
>
> **JOHN F. KENNEDY**

200

What are the origins of the Christian understanding of State and government?

The Christian notion of State, government, and authority is rooted in the Old Testament. In ancient Israel, political thought revolved around *God and "his people"*. It was about Yahweh and about keeping the covenant. The fact that there was a "king", too, happened as a divine concession. The king, of course, was not supposed to wield power for his own sake but, rather, was supposed to look out for social justice, make just judgements, perform service for the poor, and so on. Things were supposed to be regulated in a "God-pleasing" way. The question of how to regulate public concerns reasonably appeared in Greek

> I will save them from all the backslidings in which they have sinned, and will cleanse them; and they shall be my people, and I will be their God.
>
> **EZEK 37:23b**

philosophy from the time of Herodotus and Plato. "Render to ... Caesar the things that are Caesar's, and to God the things that are God's" (Mt 22:21). The conversion of Emperor Constantine to Christianity was a turning point in the relationship of Church and State, which is analyzed in greater detail in the works of Augustine.

➡ 377, 378 ➡ 1897, 1900, 1904 ➡ 140, 376

201 *What are the theological origins of the common good?*

From ancient Israel down to the Christian Middle Ages, the *bonum commune* (= common good) was more a theological than a political concept. For Thomas Aquinas, the common good consisted first in the communion of the saints with God. Divine ordinances and human order are co-ordinated with one another. In this regard, Thomas starts from the political reality, for example, from the definition of what a law is. The pragmatic concern about the common good slowly emerged from the shadow of theocentrism and sought social arrangements in which an individual could live his life in communion with God. The important thing, now as always, is that the "good" for which the political community strives must not be opposed to the "good" of persons but, rather, must provide the appropriate general framework for their development. In this sense, the "political common good" has the function of serving the person or civil society.

➡ 389 ➡ 1905–1912 ➡ 296, 327–328

202 *Does the political community rely on fundamental values?*

Contemporary democracies are no longer founded on the attempt to be faithful to God and his covenant. Religiously neutral modern democracies are

What does the LORD your God require of you, but to fear the LORD your God, to walk in all his ways, to love him, to serve the LORD your God with all your heart and with all your soul.

DTN 10:2

Politics, though often denigrated, remains a lofty vocation and one of the highest forms of charity, inasmuch as it seeks the common good. I beg the Lord to grant us more politicians who are genuinely disturbed by the state of society, the people, the lives of the poor! It is vital that government leaders and financial leaders take heed and broaden their horizons, working to ensure that all citizens have dignified work, education and healthcare.

POPE FRANCIS, EG 205

animated by respect for the dignity of the human person and for individual rights and freedoms, which rest upon freedom of religion and freedom of opinion. Even modern states cannot dispense with the fundamental moral assumptions that are supported and fostered not least importantly by religious convictions. It was possible for today's appreciation of the human person and his freedoms to develop only because Christianity existed, which liberated people from absolute subjugation to the political commonwealth. Indeed, in Christianity the State is expected to acknowledge and protect the unique value of the individual person. The State is also expected to combat → RELATIVISM and secure moral and religious values by law.

⇨ **386, 407** ⇨ **333**

203 *On what is political power based?*

If the *human person is the fundamental value* of the political community, then he is also the sole reason for the legitimacy of political power. Political power thus is not the individual, arbitrary will of the one who happens to rule, who supposes that he is responsible only to himself. Power to govern, rather, is *legitimized by the people.* Those who hold authority, like the human persons who legitimize them, are *capable of the truth* thanks to their faculty of reason; they can recognize with certainty the validity of values and also the One who guarantees that the good is absolutely good: God. Catholic social doctrine rejects a general → SCEPTICISM that claims that truth and universal moral values are ultimately unknowable. Augustine characterized a political community that tried to get by without "justice" as a "band of robbers".

⇨ **395–397** ⇨ **2236–2237**

RELATIVISM
the view that there are no absolute values and that values are a matter of cultural or social consensus

Without justice, what else is the state but a great band of robbers?
ST AUGUSTINE

Freedom is not the power of doing what we like, but the right of being able to do what we ought.
LORD ACTON (1834–1902), English historian

SCEPTICISM
the intellectual attitude that declares it ultimately impossible to know truths and values

204 *What does democracy owe to the ancient Greeks?*

Much; the ancient Greeks invented the word itself (*demos* = people, *-kratos* = rule). Often, however, the origin of democracy is connected exclusively with Greek antiquity. Aside from the fact that only one-quarter of the population ("free" Greek men) had the right to vote, it was less highly esteemed than monarchy or aristocracy by almost all Greek philosophers and statesmen. The ideal was considered the "philosopher king", who could discern the political common good better than the "blind masses". The fundamental value of the human person did not yet define political thought.

205 *Is democracy a result of Christianity?*

To a great extent, yes. Only Christianity radically democratized something that in Greece had been reserved to a few and made it a fundamental element of human existence: *the dignity* that every person has, independently of his origins and his birth. Every individual stands in a direct relationship to God. This removes him from the reach of any political community that tries to make totalitarian claims on him. The dignity of every individual person is the real ethical foundation for the democratization of participation in political decision making. Moreover, modern democracy is based on human rights, which guarantee, for example, that human life will not be destroyed or minorities oppressed through arbitrary majority decisions.

→ 395–399 → 140

206 *Which is the ultimate authority: the State or the individual citizen?*

Christianity has always emphasized that the ultimate binding authority is the conscience of the individual person. Immoral laws must not be obeyed, even if a State commands it. Democracy is not better than a monarchy or the aristocracy because it is more efficient but, rather, because it has a different → ETHOS based on human rights and is a better organizational framework for the fulfillment of the human person.

→ 398, 399, 1881, 1892 → 2242, 2288 → 322

207 *Is Christianity a "political religion"?*

At no time did Jesus allow himself to be politically co-opted. Thus he did not join the Zealots, who wanted to liberate Israel by force from political subjugation to the Romans. Jesus wanted the salvation and the freedom of all mankind. He was concerned about the fundamental restoration of man in his relation to his Creator. Consequently, his Good News was more than politics, although it has eminently political implications for the individual as well as for society. First of all, though, we must separate the political and the religious dimensions, as Jesus also did with his pronouncement: "Render ... to Caesar the things that are Caesar's, and to God the things that are God's" (Mt 22:21). The distinction between religion and politics was difficult for the ancient world to understand and put into practice—and it still is today for broad sectors of the Muslim world.

→ 49–51 → 2244–2246 → 376

> It is easier to build a city in the air than to found a State without a God.
>
> **PLUTARCH** (AD 45–120)
> Greek historian

ETHOS
a set of values, an attitude shaped by the awareness of moral values

> My devotion to truth has drawn me into the field of politics; and I can say without hesitation, and yet in all humility, that those who say that religion has nothing to do with politics do not know what religion means.
>
> **MAHATMA GANDHI**
> (1869–1948)

> Let no one hide behind God while planning and carrying out acts of violence and oppression! May no one use religion as a pretext for actions against human dignity and against the fundamental rights of every man and woman, above all, the right to life and the right of everyone to religious freedom!
>
> **POPE FRANCIS**
> 21st September 2014,
> Tirana, Albania

> Either this man was, and is, the Son of God, or else a madman or something worse. You can ... spit at him and kill him as a demon or you can fall at his feet and call him Lord and God, but let us not come with any patronising nonsense about his being a great human teacher. He has not left that open to us. He did not intend to.

C. S. LEWIS (1868–1963)

208 *How did Jesus "reign"?*

The Old Testament expected the Messiah to be a political saviour. When the Messiah came in the person of Jesus Christ, the people of Israel saw, not a conquering ruler, but a "king" who by his word and sacrifice unmasked injustice and through his surrender showed in his own body what torture and governmental and religious injustice do and how people can be destroyed by them. Power, wealth, and influence? Jesus turns these features of a political career upside down: he did not come to rule, but to serve. With that Jesus introduced a new standard for everyone who takes on responsibility: "Whoever would be great among you must be your servant" (Mt 20:26).

➡ **13, 379, 382–383** ➡ **450, 668, 840, 1884**

All authority in heaven and on earth has been given to me.
MT 28:18

> God is dead.

FRIEDRICH NIETZSCHE (1844–1900)

> Religion is the opium of the people.

KARL MARX (1818–1883), German philosopher and revolutionary socialist

> Marx is dead! Jesus lives!

NORBERT BLÜM (b. 1935)

PARADOX
a statement that is seemingly contradictory

209 *Was Jesus on the Cross a complete failure?*

Jesus was nailed to the Cross because he was misunderstood both politically and religiously. The Jewish authorities saw him as a blasphemer, whereas the Romans interpreted his claims to kingship politically. The crucifixion, however, was not the failure of his mission but, rather, its completion. Jesus redefined the standards for exercising political power. In the → PARADOX of the Cross—God's power manifested in the powerlessness of his tortured Son—all worldly claims to dominion are called into question. A political order that ensures freedom is needed, but it is legitimate only if it actually does this and protects its citizens. Moreover, the exercise of Christian authority will take the form of love and service.

➡ **379, 410** ➡ **439, 664, 711–714, 840** ➡ **101**

210 ### What difference does it make when politics "serves"?

Catholic social teaching emphasizes that *all public office is service.* Someone who serves the common good is not looking out primarily for his own welfare but for that of the political community entrusted to him, and he performs his political function according to ethical criteria. This is decisive in the fight against corruption. Moreover, someone who serves has in view the concrete human person in his misery and need. Nor does the excessive bureaucratization of states or communities of states serve the free, subsidiary development of persons and smaller societal units. Simple people are often at a disadvantage, because the complexity of bureaucratic procedures is beyond them. Good management is a great good; good management serves the common good. Excessive bureaucracy (= rule by office), in contrast, can dehumanize those who practise it, too, it turns men into "functionaries and mere cogs in the administrative machine" (Hannah Arendt).

→ **411, 412** → **1888–1889** → **448**

> The essence of totalitarian government, and perhaps the nature of every bureaucracy, is to make functionaries and mere cogs in the administrative machinery out of men, and thus to dehumanize them. And one can debate long and profitably on the rule of Nobody, which is what the political form known as bureaucracy truly is.
>
> **HANNAH ARENDT** (1906–1975), Jewish German-American philosopher

> Politics cannot be holy, but it is by no means condemned to being dirty.
>
> **JOACHIM GAUCK** (b. 1940), German Federal President

> Every political party exists for the people, not for itself.
>
> **KONRAD ADENAUER** (1876–1967), first Chancellor of the German Federal Republic

211 ### How do political parties "serve", and to what end?

The purpose of political parties is to organize the formation of political opinion and to be instruments of the political participation of all citizens. This works, though, only if the parties themselves are democratically structured, first of all, and secondly if they adopt a *role of service*, i.e., if they keep the common good in view. The Church appreciates it when the faithful

> People always want me to take sides in politics; well, then, I am on my side.
>
> **JOHANN WOLFGANG VON GOETHE** (1749–1832), German poet and dramatist

Today, when the networks and means of human communication have made unprecedented advances, we sense the challenge of finding and sharing a "mystique" of living together, of mingling and encounter, of embracing and supporting one another, of stepping into this flood tide which, while chaotic, can become a genuine experience of fraternity, a caravan of solidarity, a sacred pilgrimage. Greater possibilities for communication thus turn into greater possibilities for encounter and solidarity for everyone. If we were able to take this route, it would be so good, so soothing, so liberating and hope-filled!

POPE FRANCIS, EG 87

Perfectionism, the system that considers perfection in human things possible and sacrifices present goods for the imagined future perfection, is a result of ignorance.

ANTONIO ROSMINI (1797–1855), Italian philosopher

become involved in political parties and stand up for the realization of Christian values in a democracy. Christian charitable activity itself, however, "must be independent of parties and ideologies. It is not a means of changing the world ideologically, and it is not at the service of worldly stratagems, but it is a way of making present here and now the love which man always needs" (Pope Benedict XVI, DCE 31b).

→ 413 → 898–900 → 447–448

212 *Why must political reporting follow ethical rules?*

The genuine formation of opinion is achieved in a democracy only when there is *objectivity and freedom of information.* If the political authority orchestrates the news and misuses it for ideological or propagandistic purposes, this violates a fundamental right of the human person, namely, his inalienable claim to participation in society. Independent sources of political news are an essential component of the common good, not only because politics itself does not work otherwise, but also because the human being as a person is designed for the truth. Furthermore, it is important for all groups in society, even minorities, to be considered in public communications.

→ 414–416 → 2494 → 459

213 *Are Christians not harming themselves when they defend the democratic system?*

The democratic system is the system in which fundamental Christian principles are best preserved. In its political ethics, however, Christianity advocates no particular religious opinions but, rather, general governmental principles founded on right reason. "Whatever is true, honourable, just, pure, lovely, gracious, if there is any excellence [or] anything worthy of praise, think about these things" (cf. Phil 4:8). This is true also when Christians thereby get themselves into an apparently contradictory situation: on the one hand, they desire the most widespread acceptance of fundamental values, including freedom of religion and freedom of conscience. On the other hand, they put up with the fact that a majority may not think, act or make decisions according to those values. Christians can only patiently work to convince their fellow citizens to adopt other views.

➡ 421–423 ➡ 2105 ff. ➡ 440

214 *What does the principle of laicity [radical secularism] mean?*

The Church is critical of →LAICISM/SECULARISM because it seeks to exclude religion from public life. In contrast, the Church appreciates a co-operative form of secularism that carefully distinguishes between the proper responsibilities of Church and State, but strives for a positive co-operation for the good of men. Christians are obliged to support in a special way constitutional freedom, political participation, basic principles of the welfare state, freedom of conscience, and religious tolerance. Secularists repeatedly point out that in Europe democratic principles not infrequently had to gain acceptance against ecclesiastical and Christian resistance. But the principle

> I have three things I'd like to say today. First, while you were sleeping last night, 30,000 kids died of starvation or diseases related to malnutrition. Second, most of you don't give a shit. What's worse is that you're more upset with the fact that I said shit than the fact that 30,000 kids died last night.

TONY CAMPOLO (b. 1935), American sociologist and Baptist minister, during a sermon

SECULARISM
(from Latin *saeculum* = a generation, the spirit of the age) = a political tendency that pursues such a strict separation of Church and State that religion is seen merely as a "private matter" and must be excluded from public debate.

> Peaceful coexistence between different religions is favoured by the laicity of the state, which, without appropriating any one confessional stance, respects and esteems the presence of the religious dimension in society, while fostering its more concrete expressions.

POPE FRANCIS, 27th July 2013

> ❞ Ideology is a vaccine that immunizes a person against clear thinking.
>
> unknown

⛪ If in a given region the state does not carry out its responsibilities, some business groups can come forward in the guise of benefactors, wield real power, and consider themselves exempt from certain rules, to the point of tolerating different forms of organized crime, human trafficking, the drug trade, and violence, all of which become very difficult to eradicate. If politics shows itself incapable of breaking →

of the dignity due each person, upon which modern democracy is rooted in the Christian view of man.

➡ 396, 421, 422 ➡ 2105, 2442 ➡ 440

215 *What is the chief concern of political ethics?*

"The human person is the foundation and purpose of political life" (*Compendium of the Social Doctrine of the Church* 384). This is the central theme of Christian political ethics. There are no political or ideological values for which human beings can be demoted to "means" by which to attain more valuable ends. In all totalitarian systems of the twentieth century, persons were sacrificed for ideologies. Even the principle of religion itself can be misused. Indeed, there are also religiously motivated ideologies and forms of terrorism, as we all know. The priority of the human person still must be defended again and again.

➡ 384 ➡ 1881 ➡ 322

→ such a perverse logic and remains caught up in inconsequential discussions, we will continue to avoid facing the major problems of humanity.
POPE FRANCIS, LS 197

❗ **NATURAL LAW**
● a rule and measure of acts directing them to their proper end and promulgated by being in man's very nature. It is man's participation in God's eternal law and be be known by reason alone.

216 *How does genuine authority function?*

Without authority, any human community falls apart. Of course authority must not be arbitrary; it serves to direct people toward the common good in freedom. Nor should the common good consist of an arbitrary determination; rather, it must be something toward which all (should) be inclined out of reasonable self-interest because it is good for all. If this is the case, then Christians are obliged in conscience to obey the authority. All political authority exists on the basis of the dignity of the human conscience. Therefore, all politics that is guided by ethical principles makes the concept of conscience the central category of the exercise of political authority.

→ **393, 394** → **1897–1899** ⬚ **325**

217 *By what is authority bound?*

All authority is bound by the → NATURAL LAW, which expresses the fundamental ethical values that are immediately evident to human reason. If any authority enacts laws and regulations that contradict these values, it creates an unjust "law"—in other words, a law that obliges no one. On account of the validity of the natural law, Nazi war criminals, for example, could not argue that they had merely acted according to the law and had obeyed the commands of a legitimate authority. Today these insights have been enshrined in international law.

→ **394–398, 407** → **1902** ⬚ **325–326**

218 *Why are conscientious objection and resistance legitimate?*

No legal or political system can ever claim that it is ultimately binding. The responsibility of the individual conscience surpasses the scope of political power. With due regard to the objective moral order and the common good, no one should be compelled to do something that is diametrically opposed to his fundamental convictions. This starts with conscientious objection to military service and extends as far as the question: Can it ever be legitimate to kill a ruler who is formally legitimate? All Christian authors, from Augustine and Thomas Aquinas on, affirmed this, although only with the utmost reservations and under very narrowly defined conditions.

→ **399–401** → **2242** ⬚ **377**

In all cultures there are examples of ethical convergence, some isolated, some interrelated, as an expression of the one human nature, willed by the Creator; the tradition of ethical wisdom knows this as the natural law. This universal moral law provides a sound basis for all cultural, religious, and political dialogue, and it ensures that the multi-faceted pluralism of cultural diversity does not detach itself from the common quest for truth, goodness, and God.
POPE BENEDICT XVI, CiV 59

His conscience was clean. He never used it.
STANISLAW JERZY LEC (1909–1966), Polish wit

The distrust of wit is the beginning of tyranny.
EDWARD ABBEY (1927-1989), American author

Our democracy has only one great fault: it is not democratic.
GILBERT KEITH CHESTERTON (1874–1936)

When men become godless, then governments are perplexed, lies—limitless, debts—innumerable, consultations—inconclusive; then enlightenment is mindless, politicians—unprincipled, Christians—devoid of prayer, morals—unrestrained, fashions—shameless, conferences—endless, and prospects—hopeless.

ANTOINE DE SAINT-EXUPÉRY (1900–1944), French author

Why do we follow the majority? Is it because they have more reason? No, because they have more power.

BLAISE PASCAL (1623–1662), French mathematician and philosopher

Democracy is a device that insures we shall be governed no better than we deserve.

GEORGE BERNARD SHAW (1856–1950)

We have no secret recipe for the third millennium, we do not have to invent anything new, but merely must not stop proclaiming the old message, less with words than through the loving witness of our lives.

CARDINAL FRANZ KÖNIG (1905–2004), Archbishop of Vienna

---

219 *Can one be a politician and at the same time a Christian?*

It is an honour for any Christian to serve society by becoming involved in politics. Politics are always about what is "feasible": the means of doing what is necessary are not always available, and sometimes the majorities do not exist to transform even fundamental Christian options into policy. Christian politicians should not be blamed if they have to engage in compromises. Nevertheless, there are decisions for which a Christian politician, for reasons of conscience, definitely cannot share responsibility. The fundamental values of the human person—life, freedom, dignity—are non-negotiable for a Christian politician. No politician, for example, can describe himself as a Christian and at the same time justify abortion.

➡ **394–399, 407** ➡ **899, 2242**

220 *Must the Church agree with all democratic decisions?*

The Church's option in favour of democracy does not mean that she also must agree with all decisions that a democratic society makes. In her ethical judgement she often takes a stand opposed to the decisions of elected officials. For example, can the Church approve of legalized abortion or research on human embryos? The Church has the duty to criticize such developments. Here Christians are required to become actively involved in politics, to stand up for the values of human rights and the sanctity of human life, and to convert them into political decisions.

➡ **407** ➡ **1922** ➡ **441**

221 *Does the Church therefore have reservations about democracy after all?*

The Church reserves the right to distance herself critically from all forms of political organization. She

> ❝ Whenever you find yourself on the side of the majority, it is time to pause and reflect.
>
> **MARK TWAIN** (1835–1910), American humorist

prefers and supports democratic forms of government, but she does not idealize them. Democracy, too, is a system that is not impervious to mistakes and errors. Catholic social doctrine is concerned about the fundamental ethical principles of social life and not about "technical questions" of political organization.

→ 407 → 1920–1923

> ❝ The true spirit of 1789 consists not in the idea that a thing is just because the people declare it so, but rather in this: that in certain circumstances, the will of the people corresponds to justice better than anyone else's will
>
> **SIMONE WEIL**

222 *How far do the rights of the majority extend in a democracy?*

If the fundamental value of every political community is the human person, then even democratic or legislative majorities cannot justly make any political decision whatsoever. Politics is inseparably connected

with law and rights, especially with fundamental personal and civil rights. These must never be denied to minorities. Of course this creates duties, too, for the minorities, even if they feel that they are not represented in the political decisions.

→ 387, 407

 223 *What does the Church say about the separation of powers and the constitutional State?*

The Church has explicitly pronounced in favour of the principle of the separation of powers. Only when the → Judicial, Legislative and →Executive branches exist independently of one another is a constitutional State possible. This in turn is the prerequisite for the dignified development of human beings, for instance, inasmuch as they enjoy freedom of conscience and of religion. In particular, the existence of an independent judiciary is considered in Catholic social ethics the test of an ethically justified political system. The principle of the constitutional State is regarded as something so fundamental that the Church makes herself subject to this principle: Catholic social teaching agrees that religious freedom, for instance, cannot be exclusively advantageous to the Catholic Church. Religious freedom must be guaranteed for all religious communities.

→ 408, 422

 224 *What connects and what separates Church and State?*

Like the State, the Church on earth is a community with a visible organizational structure, yet they are mutually independent and self-governing. The Church is no longer politically bound up with the State, as was the case in the centuries of the "alliance of throne and altar". In this sense, the autonomy and independence

of Church and State are especially emphasized. The political and the spiritual common good can be separated to a great extent, even though there will always be points of mutual contact. For this reason, Church and State must work together well. Despite the obligation to obey laws, the Church reserves the right to act as a moral corrective and to criticize the State when she sees ethical principles being violated.

→ 424, 425, 427 → 2244–2245 → 140

225 *On what ethical principles should the Church's productive coexistence with the State be based?*

The Church demands what is implied by the universal principles of religious freedom: freedom of expression and teaching, freedom of public worship and organizational freedom, freedom to appoint her own officials, freedom to construct houses of worship, the right to own private property and also to associate for various educational, cultural, medical, and charitable purposes.

→ 426 → 2246

" The loftier the pretensions of power, the more meddlesome, inhuman, and oppressive it will be. Theocracy is the worst of all possible governments.
C.S. LEWIS

" Even as a non-believer I fear a godless society.
GREGOR GYSI (b. 1948), German leftist politician

[The Church] must always open up afresh to the cares of the world. In the concrete history of the Church, however, a contrary tendency is also manifested, namely that the Church becomes self-satisfied, settles down in this world, becomes self-sufficient and adapts herself to the standards of the world. Not infrequently, she gives greater weight to organization and institutionalization than to her vocation to openness towards God, her vocation to opening up the world towards the other.

POPE BENEDICT XVI, address in Freiburg, 25th September 2011

How is it possible that thousands and thousands of people are bored with the church and pass it by? Why did it come about that the cinema really is often more interesting, more exciting, more human and gripping than the church? Is it really just other people's fault and not ours, too?

DIETRICH BONHOEFFER (1906–1945), German Evangelical Lutheran pastor, killed in a Nazi concentration camp

No problem is solved when we idly wait for God to undertake full responsibility.

MARTIN LUTHER KING (1929–1968)

226 *Is the law a sufficient framework for people and for institutions to coexist?*

No. In order for people to get along and for institutions to work together well, it is never enough to define "social justice" merely in terms of principles, rights, and duties. Also needed is something like fellowship among citizens, "civic spirit" or "social charity". A Christian social ethic worthy of the name does not stop at principles, rights, and duties. It also calls us to take to heart our real-life neighbour with his problems and needs and thus to obey Christ's command to love our neighbour as ourselves for love of God.

→ 390 → 2212–2213 → 332

Love can't be coerced.

BORIS PASTERNAK (1890–1960), Russian winner of the Nobel prize in literature

227 *How does one show "civic spirit"?*

Civic spirit is above all solidarity in practice. A society that cares only for "justice" in the abstract is cold and inhumane. Back in the Middle Ages, Thomas Aquinas knew that justice without love is ultimately horrible. For justice looks only at the universal; it does not regard the human being in his particularity. But that is precisely the distinctive Christian characteristic: the fact that Christians do not judge everyone alike. They know that the other person has a name, a face, and a whole individual history.

→ 390–392 → 2212–2213 → 327–329

228 *How should we treat those who have broken the law?*

Because a human being is always a person, solidarity with incarcerated citizens should not be withdrawn. Punishment should not humiliate and debase. Its purpose is to restore and protect public order, to change the guilty for the better, and it is a form of reparation. The Church opposes all governmental re-actions that disregard the criminal's human dignity, such as torture and disproportionate punishment. Moreover, she advocates less time-consuming trials.

→ 402–405 → 2266–2267 → 331–332

I was in prison and you visited me. Then the righteous will answer him, "Lord, when did we see you in prison and visit you?" And the King will answer them, "Truly, I say to you: as you did it to one of the least of these my brethren, you did to me."

Based on **MT 25:35–40**

From important Church documents

THE POLITICAL COMMUNITY

Man and the State

Rerum Novarum

Nature accordingly must have given to man a source that is stable and remaining always with him, from which he might look to draw continual supplies. And this stable condition of things he finds solely in the earth and its fruits. There is no need to bring in the State. Man precedes the State and possesses, prior to the formation of any State, the right of providing for the substance of his body.

Pope Leo XIII, Encyclical Rerum Novarum (1891), 6

Church and State: Both for Mankind

Rerum Novarum

The Church improves and betters the condition of the working man by means of numerous organizations; does her best to enlist the services of all classes in discussing and endeavouring to further in the most practical way the interests of the working classes; and considers that for this purpose recourse should be had, in due measure and degree, to the intervention of the law and of State authority.

Pope Leo XIII, Encyclical Rerum Novarum (1891), 13

The State Exists for All

Rerum Novarum

There is another and deeper consideration which must not be lost sight of. As regards the State, the interests of all, whether high or low, are equal. The members of the working classes are citizens by nature and by the same right as the rich; they are real parts, living the life which makes up, through the family, the body of the commonwealth; and it need hardly be said that they are in every city very largely in the majority. It would be irrational to neglect one portion of the citizens and favour another, and therefore the public administration must duly and solicitously provide for the welfare and the comfort of the working classes; otherwise, that law of justice will be violated which ordains that each man shall have his due. To cite the wise words of St Thomas Aquinas: "As the part and the whole are in a certain sense identical, so that which belongs to the whole in a sense belongs to the part." Among the many and grave duties of rulers who would do their best for the people, the first and chief is to act with strict justice—with that justice which is called *distributive*—toward each and every class alike.

Pope Leo XIII, Encyclical Rerum Novarum (1891), 27

How Binding Are Governmental Laws?

Pacem in Terris

Governmental authority, therefore, is a postulate of the moral order and derives from God. Consequently, laws and decrees passed in contravention of the moral order, and hence of the divine will, can have no binding force in conscience, since "it is right to obey God rather than men" (Acts 5:29). Indeed, the passing of such laws undermines the very nature of authority and results in shameful abuse. As St Thomas teaches, "In regard to the second proposition, we maintain that human law has the rationale of law in so far as it is in accordance with right reason, and as such it obviously derives from eternal law. A law which is at variance with reason is to that extent unjust and has no longer the rationale of law. It is rather an act of violence" (*Summa theologiae* I/II, q. 93, a. 3, ad 2).

Pope St John XXIII, Encyclical Pacem in Terris (1963), 30

What the State Must Provide
Pacem in Terris

The public administration must therefore give consider-able care and thought to the question of social as well as economic progress and to the development of essential services in keeping with the expansion of the productive system. Such services include road-building, transportation, communications, drinking-water, housing, medical care, ample facilities for the practice of religion, and aids to recreation. The government must also see to the provision of insurance facilities, to obviate any likelihood of a citizen's being unable to maintain a decent standard of living in the event of some misfortune or greatly increased family responsibilities. The government is also required to show no less energy and efficiency in the matter of providing opportunities for suitable employment, graded to the capacity of the workers. It must make sure that working men are paid a just and equitable wage and are allowed a sense of responsibility in the industrial concerns for which they work. It must facili-tate the formation of intermediate groups, so that the social life of the people may become more fruitful and less constrained. And finally, it must ensure that everyone has the means and opportunity of sharing as far as possible in cultural benefits.

Pope St John XXIII, Encyclical Pacem in Terris (1963), 39

Politics as Religion
Centesimus Annus

In fact, where self-interest is violently suppressed, it is replaced by a burdensome system of bureaucratic control which dries up the wellsprings of initiative and creativity. When people think they possess the secret of a perfect social organization which makes evil impossible, they also think that they can use any means, including violence and deceit, in order to bring that organization into being. Politics then becomes a "secular religion" which operates under the illusion of creating paradise in this world. But no political society—which possesses its own autonomy and laws—can ever be confused with the Kingdom of God.

Pope St John Paul II, Encyclical Centesimus Annus (1991), 25

9

One World
–
One
Humanity

THE INTERNATIONAL
COMMUNITY

> The world has a
> lively feeling of unity
> and of compelling
> solidarity of mutual
> independence.
>
> Vatican Council II, GS 4

In view of the increasingly close ties of mutual dependence today between all the inhabitants and peoples of the earth, the apt pursuit and efficacious attainment of the universal common good now require of the community of nations that it organize itself in a manner suited to its present responsibilities.

Vatican Council II, GS 84

If globalization is to succeed, it must succeed for poor and rich alike. It must deliver rights no less than riches. It must provide social justice and equity no less than economic prosperity and enhanced communication.

KOFI ANNAN (b. 1938), U.N. General Secretary from 1997–2006

229 *What does "globalization" actually mean?*

Much has changed drastically in the last hundred years. Today's world offers many of us improved living conditions and, thanks to technological progress, has grown together into "One World"; so, for example, we can travel everywhere by aeroplane within a few hours and communicate with everyone on earth simply and without cost by Internet. Because of these accelerated exchanges, it is possible for industry to supply many more products less expensively. Transportation has become so inexpensive and fast that it is worth it, for example, in the manufacture of jeans, to grow the cotton for them in the U.S. and have the fabric woven from it in India; the jeans are then sewn in Cambodia and sold in Europe. Thus, a simple object often travels around the whole globe before it gets to the consumer.

Meanwhile, everything is more and more closely connected and interdependent.

 1911 → **446**

230 *What social problems does globalization bring with it?*

Accelerated globalization does not mean, however, that all countries are equally developed and all people can benefit from its networking. Quite the contrary: problems like poverty, hunger, lack of education, poor health care, and human rights violations are still breaking news. Poorer countries are often extremely dependent on how much the better developed countries produce in them or buy from them. At the same time, the wages paid to workers in poor countries are often extremely low. For example, a seamstress in Bangladesh receives only two or three cents for a T-shirt that in the U.S. costs about five dollars. This gives rise to injustices that are often responsible for the fact "that many are deprived of fundamental *human rights*" (cf. Synod of Bishops, 1971, "Justice in the World", 9). Globalization, therefore, not only has advantages but also aggravates many problems or even causes them in the first place.

→ **442** → **446**

231 *Is globalization fate?*

No, we should not think about globalization fatalistically. It is man-made and therefore can also be shaped by man according to moral standards.

 448

232 *Are we part of the way in which the world is changing?*

Because in a globalized world everyone and everything is connected, even our everyday actions

> Whereas the standard of living is high [for some], [others] are subject to extreme poverty.
>
> **POPE ST JOHN XXIII** (1881–1963), MM 157

> Globalization, for all its risks, also offers exceptional and promising opportunities, precisely with a view to enabling humanity to become a single family, built on the values of justice, equity and solidarity. For this to happen, a complete change of perspective will be needed: it is no longer the well-being of any one political, racial or cultural community that must prevail, but rather the good of humanity as a whole. The pursuit of the common good of a single political community cannot be in conflict with the *common good of humanity*.
>
> **POPE ST JOHN PAUL II** Message for the Celebration of the World Day of Peace (1st January 2000), 5-6.

> Today more than in the past, the Church's social doctrine must be open to an international outlook.
>
> **POPE ST JOHN PAUL II** (1920–2005), SRS 42

For he delivers the needy when he calls, the poor and him who has no helper. He has pity on the weak and the needy, and saves the lives of the needy. From oppression and violence he redeems their souls; and precious is their blood in his sight.

PS 72:12–14

" No effect in nature is without a rational basis. Discover the rational basis, and you do not need to experiment.

LEONARDO DA VINCI (1452–1519), Italian painter, architect, and natural scientist

If globalization is viewed from a deterministic standpoint, the criteria with which to evaluate and direct it are lost. As a human reality, it is the product of diverse cultural tendencies, which need to be subjected to a process of discernment.

POPE BENEDICT XVI, CiV 42

" Globalization is not a natural phenomenon. It was intended and made by human beings. Therefore human beings can also change and shape it and guide it onto the right paths.

JOHANNES RAU (1931–2006), President of the Federal Republic of Germany

can have far-reaching consequences. With every purchase, for example, we indirectly come into contact with those who manufactured our product somewhere in the world or packed it for transport. In paying for a product, we also help pay for the work of all those persons. Thus the group of people for whom we share responsibility extends beyond the circle of our acquaintances, friends, and family. Thanks to better communications, we simply know more about each other. We can take the initiative and become informed about worldwide topics and opinions. Environmental problems caused in one particular place in the world often have repercussions on the entire world. Again and again this makes clear to us the fact that our world does not function only within the boundaries of our own country, but that we live together in the world with many different cultures and religions.

→ 446, 447

233 *Is the Church concerned about these problems?*

Yes. The Church has "the duty of scrutinizing the signs of the times and of interpreting them in the light of the Gospel. Thus, in language intelligible to each generation, she can respond to the perennial questions which men ask about this present life and the life to come and about the relationship of the one to the other. We must therefore recognize and understand the world in which we live, its explanations, its longings, and its often dramatic characteristics" (GS 4). So the Church tries again and again to see the current situation of the world and to make practical recommendations according to Jesus's message of the brotherly love of all men. In doing so, she is particularly concerned about the poor, the weak, and the exploited. The Church always reminds the politicians of individual countries that they bear responsibility not only for their own nations but for all mankind. She advocates policies that have peace and development

The bread which you do not use is the bread of the hungry; the garment hanging in your wardrobe is the garment of him who is naked; the shoes that you do not wear are the shoes of the one who is barefoot. The acts of charity that you do not perform are so many injustices that you commit.

ST BASIL THE GREAT (330–379)

And the LORD said, "Behold, they are one people, and they have all one language; and this is only the beginning of what they will do; and nothing that they propose to do will now be impossible for them. Come, let us go down, and there confuse their language, that they may not understand one another's speech." So the LORD scattered them abroad from there over the face of all the earth, and they left off building the city. Therefore its name was called Babel, because there the LORD confused the language of all the earth; and from there the LORD scattered them abroad over the face of all the earth.

GEN 11:6–9

as their goal. Implementing such policies requires the collaboration of the various states. This is why the Church supports international organizations such as the United Nations, where trusting international co-operation can grow.

➡ 433–455 ➡ 1927

234 *Where should global assistance begin?*

There are many problems that we can do something about only if we work together. For this purpose there must be an increase of *solidarity* and mutual *responsibility* on earth. Catholic social teaching cites as the reason for this mutual responsibility the idea of the "unity of the human family". God is the Creator of every single human being; therefore, he is the Father of all mankind. We human beings can regard each other as brothers and sisters who are connected with one another in one *family*. In a family, the members trust one another, are there for each other, and help each other. In the same way, the entire population of the world should feel connected with one another.

➡ 1947–1948

235 *What arguments does the Bible give for the unity of mankind?*

The Book of Genesis shows God as the Creator, who brought the whole world and all mankind out of nothingness into being. Man does not appear only as an individual; rather, he stands in relation to his fellowman and to other living creatures, and he can act responsibly. God gives human beings what they need to live a dignified life. In God's covenant

with Noah (cf. Gen 9:1–17), it becomes clear that, despite sin, violence, and injustice, God is there for human beings. The idea of the human family is seen in the covenant with Abraham, too. Abraham is considered the father of many nations (Gen 17). And, since Christ, a "son of Abraham", is also the "new Adam", all human beings are Abraham's offspring; therefore God made this covenant with us, too. The multitudes and varieties of peoples are regarded in the Book of Genesis as the result of God's creative action. However, the story of the Tower of → BABEL (see Gen 11:1–9) shows how inadequately human beings can deal with this variety.

→ 428–430

236 *How should human beings treat one another?*

People in the world should regard themselves as a community and accept certain differences between individuals and peoples, since this variety is to be seen as wealth. This becomes increasingly important in times of globalization. We are bound together as "members of a common family", Pope St John XXIII writes (MM 157). Values such as truth, solidarity, and freedom, which are indispensable in our everyday relationships, become more and more important globally, too, with the increasing interconnectedness of relations and dependencies. Only in the

> If someone brings a bit more love and goodness into the world, a little more light and truth, then his life has a meaning.

ALFRED DELP SJ (1907–1945), Executed by the Nazis as a resistance fighter

The name

BABEL

itself etymologically means "confusion"— perhaps a reference to the confused relations among the peoples of the world.

> Relations between States must furthermore be regulated by justice.

POPE ST JOHN XXIII (1881–1963), PT 91

Seek first the kingdom of God and his righteousness, and all these things shall be yours as well.

MT 6:33

At one extreme, we find those who doggedly uphold the myth of progress and tell us that ecological problems will solve themselves simply with the application of new technology and without any need for ethical considerations or deep change. At the other extreme are those who view men and women and all their interventions as no more than a threat, jeopardizing the global ecosystem, and consequently the presence of human beings on the planet should be reduced and all forms of intervention prohibited. Viable future scenarios will have to be generated between these extremes, since there is no one path to a solution.

POPE FRANCIS, LS 60

absence of violence, war, discrimination, intimidation, or deception is it possible to get along well. Therefore, the Church demands that economic and social globalization proceed together with a globalization of justice. Jesus Christ brought fundamental justice to the earth, and we, as his followers, have a special obligation to further this cause by our actions.

▶ **431, 433** ▶ **1912**

237 *What does this mean in terms of our use of the world's resources?*

Again and again Catholic social teaching points to the "unity of the human family" and the related "universal destination of goods". This means that God, as the Creator of the world, destined the earth's resources to provide for the livelihood and needs of all human beings. Excessive inequality in the distribution of the world's goods, in contrast, is a scandal.

COMMANDMENTS FOR A FUTURE WITHOUT HUNGER

1. You shall co-operate so that everyone on earth has enough to eat.

2. You shall not gamble away your neighbour's bread by speculation.

3. You shall not hoard what the hungry need to eat.

4. You shall honour the earth, so that you, your children, and everyone on earth might prosper.

5. You shall live in such a way that your life-style is not at the expense of others.

6. You shall not covet your neighbour's land and property.

7. You shall reduce hunger with your agrarian policies and not increase it.

8. You shall challenge corrupt regimes and their underlings.

9. You shall help prevent armed conflicts and wars.

10. You shall combat hunger effectively with developmental aid.

Caritas Austria

DIGRESSION

WHAT IS POVERTY?

Former World Bank President Robert McNamara once defined "absolute poverty" broadly as "conditions of deprivation that fall below any rational definition of human decency". According to the most commonly used metric, anyone with a daily income of below a certain amount in U.S. dollars (currently $1.25 per day, according to the World Bank) is living in absolute poverty. By this standard, 14.5 percent of the world population (or 1.29 billion) lived in such inhumane conditions in 2011. Other measurements (such as those of the International Development Association) take into account not only per-capita income but also calorie intake, average life expectancy, child mortality rates, as well as the birthrate of a country.

In contrast there is also the notion of *relative* poverty. This considers the living situation of a human being, or the fact that he is supplied with fewer material and immaterial resources, in comparison to the welfare of the society in which he lives. According to the World Health Organization, people experience relative poverty if they have at their disposal each month less than 60 percent of the median income in their native land.

For Christian men and women it is unacceptable for poverty and hunger to be the fate of millions of people, while others lead a live of excess and waste. The foodstuffs of this world, for example, are not self-evidently the property of those who can pay the most for them. Rather, they are the basis for the life of all human beings.

→ 447, 448 → 2407, 2415 → 436

238 *Why do the poor deserve special attention?*

Christ turned especially to those who were at the margins of society. That is why the Church, too, professes a "preferential option for the poor". The poor are often the ones who have the fewest opportunities to influence the shaping of society and of their own living conditions. The Church stands by them and is concerned about putting an end to injustice, discrimination, and oppression. Justice, in the sense in which Catholic social teaching understands it, demands the participation of all people in the central social, political, cultural, and economic activities in life. Programmes for the poor must not be designed from the top down, because those who are affected usually know best what they need. Given complex relationships of dependency and the increasing interconnectedness of the world economy, it is not easy to find concrete solutions that permanently do away with the causes of poverty.

→ 449 → 2443–2446 → 449

239 *How does global solidarity become generally binding?*

For Christians, who believe in God as the Creator of the world, it should be self-evident that solidarity and justice cannot apply only to "our family", "our country", "our culture", or "our religion". If we want to justify this Christian attitude toward other cultures and religions without using faith-based arguments, we can best explain this universal demand for solidarity and justice by reminding people of their claim to freedom: I am free when I myself can determine what I do and how I live. Now if I myself want to be free, then I should grant this also to my fellow human beings, from the perspective of justice and of the fundamental equality of all human beings. Just as I do not want anyone in the world to determine my fate, so too I must acknowledge that no one else wants me to determine his fate. One speaks in this context of a general right to a reasonable explanation. Everyone has a right to have laws, to which he will be subject, be explained in a reasonable and intelligible way.

→ 437 → 1939–1942 → 332

240 *What specifically follows from this claim to freedom?*

If I admit that other people have rights, I thereby also assume duties. On the one hand, there are negative duties, in other words, duties not to perform certain actions, for example, not to enslave or otherwise exploit someone. On the other hand, though, there are also positive duties: in particular cases I should not only avoid something, but do something, for example, help someone nearby who is in dire need. In other situations, perhaps I do not know right away how I can help, for example, a starving child in Africa. Of course, with regard to more distant needs like that, I also have a moral duty to help. But how should I do it? And do I have this duty toward everyone who needs help? That would obviously demand too much of me. Often I cannot help directly. But I do have, for example, the possibility of supporting organizations and institutions that can take on this task. By supporting relief organizations through volunteer work or financial contributions, one can do much to help improve human living conditions in general. If more

> Justice renders to each one what is his and claims not another's property; it disregards its own profit in order to preserve the common equity.
>
> **ST AMBROSE OF MILAN** (339–397), Doctor of the Church

> I simply decided that I had enough money.
>
> **CHARLES FENNEY** (b. 1931), co-founder of the Duty Free Shop chain, when asked why he donated $600,000,000 to assorted charitable organizations

> Despotism is a sort of arbitrary political or social rule without sufficient justification. By unjust social and political circumstances we mean those circumstances in which individuals or groups rule over others, or have advantages over them for which there is no good reason that could be given to those who are ruled over or disadvantaged.
>
> **RAINER FORST** (b. 1964), German philosopher

> There can be no such thing as responsibility to oneself, strictly speaking, because in that case one can always dispense oneself.
>
> **ROBERT SPAEMANN** (b. 1927)

Act in such a way that the effects of your actions are compatible with the persistence of genuine human life on earth.

HANS JONAS (1903–1993), German philosopher

 Remember: the opposite of love is not hate but indifference. The opposite of faith is not arrogance but indifference. The opposite of hope is not despair but indifference. Indifference is not the beginning of a process, it is the end of a process.

ELIE WIESEL (b. 1928), American Nobel Peace Prize winner

and more people think this way, then much can be accomplished in the fight against poverty in the world.

➡ **1934–1935** ➡ **330**

 241 *How can people's self-interest be mobilized?*

In situations where there is no consciousness of global solidarity, it may help to appeal to the self-interest of people or of nations, in other words, the advantage to be gained from something. We speak then about self-interest "correctly understood". It is often the case that international collaboration ultimately is worthwhile for everyone. Let us take the example of natural resources. One country alone cannot stop worldwide soil or water depletion. Concentrating on conservation in one's own country and saying, "We do not care what the others do", is no solution. The environment is a global, public good ("global common property"); protecting it takes global co-operation. Such international collaboration to protect the environment is in the self-interest, correctly understood, of all countries. For only if all countries participate

You shall not see your brother's donkey or his ox fallen down by the way, and withhold your help from them; you shall help him to lift them up again. DTN 22:4

in conservation, for instance through sustainable agriculture, can the cause be advanced, which leads to better conditions in each individual country. Similarly the fight against poverty is in the interest of all, since in that way migration is reduced, violent conflicts are repressed, and the economy can grow.

➡ **481–484** ➡ **1911, 1913–1914**

DIGRESSION

GOODS BELONGING TO THE WORLD COMMUNITY

These are goods, the use of which benefits everyone worldwide; no one has a specific right or ownership claim to them, because no one can or should be excluded from using them (non-exclusivity). These characteristics make it difficult to allocate these goods.

What specifically is understood as global common property varies: some take it to mean only goods in the environmental area. Others have a broader understanding of the term and see human rights or the world cultural heritage as part of these global goods. The United Nations has developed a common understanding of global public goods, in other words, of what all human beings are jointly responsible for: peace and international security, the defence of human rights, international justice, health, knowledge, and information as well as the protection of the environment, of biological diversity, and of forests and oceans as a minimal consensus. To these may be added economic stability, the availability of food and welfare for all, disarmament and the non-proliferation of atomic weapons, as well as the fight against terrorism.

In the Middle Ages people complained when they had to tithe, which means to give one tenth of their income or their produce to the landowner. Today more than one-third of the price of goods and services goes to servicing capital for the owners of financial and real capital. The fact that most of us—at any rate here in Germany—are nevertheless economically better off than in the Middle Ages is due to the industrial revolution, the increasing automation of the economy, an enormous plundering of the raw materials available, and the exploitation of the Third World.

MARGRIT KENNEDY (1939-2013), German ecologist and architect

 To manage the global economy; to revive economies hit by the crisis; to avoid any deterioration of the present crisis and the greater imbalances that would result; to bring about integral and timely disarmament, food security, and peace; to guarantee the protection of the environment and to regulate migration: for all this, there is urgent need of a true world political authority, as my predecessor Blessed John XXIII indicated some years ago. [GT 225] Such an authority would need to be →

242   *How can worldwide co-operation become a reality?*

For global problems that cannot be solved by individual countries at the national level, what is needed are organizations and co-operative institutions that assist with the management of the common property, propose rules for all countries, monitor observance of them, and report non-compliance or violations. Again and again the Church advocates the building up of an international community, since only in this way can the idea of the *unity of the human family* be translated into political action, also. In any case, this community must be voluntary on the part of all the participating countries and must not under any circumstances be compulsory. It should be a community with authority, which, on the one hand, respects the fact that every State has its own jurisdiction, according to the principle of subsidiarity, but, on the other, can address major problems in the world, inasmuch as it is "endowed with the power to safeguard on behalf of all security, regard for justice, and respect for rights" (GS 82). A first step in this direction was made in 1945, when the United Nations Organization (UN) was founded. Since then the Catholic Church has advocated the idea of the United Nations, supported its initial human rights policies, and called for its further development.

→ 434, 435, 441 → 1919 → 325, 326

243 *What are the minimal ethical standards for international co-operation?*

If individual countries want to live in a globally responsible, binding community, the most important thing is mutual trust and then a minimum of common values and norms. Included among these are human rights, but also values such as justice, solidarity, and freedom. The international community must see to it that through their joint decisions all people have the opportunity to share equally in worldwide development. All these fundamental values are obligatory not only for Christians. They apply to all.

→ 433, 439, 448 → 1924, 1925

244 *How are these values to become generally accepted in the international community?*

Generally acknowledged fundamental values and human rights must be the foundation for both the decisions and the communications of the international community. Building on them, members must formulate rules on which they can rely in their business and negotiations. Rules are needed when people want to negotiate something and reach a decision together.

→ regulated by law, to observe consistently the principles of subsidiarity and solidarity, [and] to seek to establish the common good.
POPE BENEDICT XVI, CiV 67

99 There is an urgent need to explore, with the full and intense co-operation of all, and especially of the wealthier nations, ways whereby the human necessities of food and a suitable education can be furnished and shared with the entire human community.
Vatican Council II, GS 87

99 Might makes right is the mightiest injustice.
MARIE VON EBNER-ESCHENBACH (1830–1916)

99 Prayers do not change the world. But prayers change human beings. And human beings change the world.
ALBERT SCHWEITZER (1875–1965)

> The force of a law depends on the extent of its justice. Now in human affairs a thing is said to be just, from being right, according to the rule of reason. But the first rule of reason is the law of nature. Consequently every human law has just so much of the nature of law as it is derived from the law of nature. But if in any point it deflects from the law of nature, it is no longer a law but a perversion of law.

ST THOMAS AQUINAS
Summa Theologiae
I–II, q. 95, a. 2

More than ever before, the rule that "might makes right" must be replaced at the international level by respect for the law.

 436, 438  1954, 1929–1930  333

245 *Who needs this international community?*

Everyone. Yet countries are dependent on an international community to varying degrees. Highly developed countries need it more in order to be able to make economic agreements more securely or to gain access to raw materials and less in order to make a decent life possible for their populations. But that is precisely why developing countries need the international community. Ultimately all people have the same right to development and access to vitally essential goods (food, clothing, education, etc.). All people also have a right to live in peace and freedom. Mutual support is therefore necessary. The necessity of an international community must not become a pretext for the creation of new dependencies and more complicated exploitative mechanisms between rich and poor countries.

→ 446, 447

246 *With which organizations does the Church get along well?*

Since the 1940s the world has been determined to build an international community. In 1945 the United Nations was founded, and a few years later it issued the Universal Declaration of Human Rights. Then in the early 1990s the World Trade Organization was formed. Many other organizations, which are more or less closely connected with the system of the United Nations, try to solve global problems (→ GLOBAL GOVERNANCE).

247 *What is the Vatican's role in international politics?*

As a worldwide Church, the Catholic Church has a global structure and centuries of global experience. As a State, the Holy See can participate in international politics. The Holy See can therefore send ambassadors (nuncios), conclude treaties with other States, take part in supra-governmental organizations (for example, the United Nations and its subsidiary organizations), and mediate in international conflicts. The objective of all this activity is to promote the co-operation of the international community, to support it on its path toward the greater common good within the human family, to demand human rights and human dignity for all, and to assist and accompany all mankind on the way to justice and peace.

→ 444, 445

" It is incomprehensible how the rich nations try to justify their attempts to grasp still more of the earth's goods, when as a result either the other nations never emerge from their miserable plight or else the physical foundations of life on earth run the risk of being destroyed.

Document *Iustitia in mundo* (IM) 64, of the Synod of Bishops, "Justice in the World" (1971)

GLOBAL GOVERNANCE refers to political processes at the international level for solving problems that affect the whole world, some of which were recently caused by globalization. For this purpose co-operative efforts should be made to form structures and organizations that are to take charge of solving the problems. The concept of global governance, however, does not imply a world government. The individual states still remain autonomous states.

The Issue of Migration

> These are the first efforts at laying the foundations on an international level for a community of all men to work for the solution to the serious problems of our times, to encourage progress everywhere, and to obviate wars of whatever kind.

Vatican Council II, GS 84, on international institutions

248 *Why is migration a controversial issue?*

> Every day human interdependence grows more tightly drawn and spreads by degrees over the whole world. As a result the common good … today takes on an increasingly universal complexion and consequently involves rights and duties with respect to the whole human race. Every social group must take account of the needs and legitimate aspirations of other groups, and even of the general welfare of the entire human family.

Vatican Council II, GS 26

There can be many reasons for leaving one's native land: the poverty and misery of the population, lack of freedom and democracy, political persecution as well as conflicts and wars in the native land, or simply the desire to live in another culture or place. Besides the migrants who live legally in the countries to which they immigrated, there are also many "illegal aliens", who often stay in hiding in society because they have no residence permit. The lives of these people are often marked by a constant fear of discovery, arrest, and deportation. As a result, they are sometimes deprived of fundamental rights. People without a residence permit often do not risk seeking medical care, resisting exploitative working arrangements, or sending their children to school—their fear of being discovered and deported is too great. But the Church says quite clearly: even people without residence permits have human rights, which must not be denied them.

> The most important hour is always the present; the most important human being is the one facing you now; the most important deed is love.

MEISTER ECKHART (1260–1328), German theologian and mystic

249 *How should migrants be treated, in keeping with the unity of the human family?*

Often migrants are turned away from countries even when that means tolerating human rights violations.

Thus many people drown while travelling from Africa to Europe or, after arrival, are sent to camps with degrading conditions or else are often sent back without sufficient examination of their legal claims. As Christians see them, however, these people are not just citizens of a country but are always members of the human family as well. That is why it is a moral duty to provide refuge for those who in their homeland are subject to persecution or suffer from dire need. People do not leave their homeland without a reason. As long as there is no real international collaboration

 "Where is ... your brother ...?" Today no one in our world feels responsible; we have lost a sense of responsibility for our brothers and sisters. We have fallen into the hypocrisy of the priest and the levite whom Jesus described in the parable of the Good Samaritan: we see our brother half dead on the side of the road, and perhaps we say to ourselves: "poor soul ...!", and then go on our way. It's not our responsibility, and with that we feel reassured, assuaged.

POPE FRANCIS in Lampedusa, 8th July 2013

> We are all foreigners—almost everywhere.
European bumper sticker

for the truly just development of all nations, people will seek to migrate to other countries looking for a better life.

➡ **297, 298** ➡ **1911**

 250 *How is the Catholic Church involved in this area?*

For many years, throughout the world, the Catholic Church has been an advocate for migrants, including the group of "undocumented" or "illegal" aliens. In doing so, she cites the preferential option for the poor and Jesus's identification with the marginalized and the forgotten. Catholic teaching can be summarized in a number of key points. First, people have the right to migrate in order to

> Let all guests who arrive be received like Christ, for He is going to say, "I came as a guest, and you received Me" (Mt 25:35). And to all let due honour be shown, especially to the domestics of the faith and to pilgrims.

ST BENEDICT OF NURSIA (480–547), Rule

Migrants and refugees are not pawns on the chessboard of humanity. They are children, women and men who leave or who are forced to leave their homes for various reasons, who share a legitimate desire for knowing and having, but above all for being more. The sheer number of people migrating from one continent to another, or shifting places within their own countries and geographical areas, is striking. The reality of migration ... needs to be approached and managed in a new, equitable, and effective manner; more than anything, this calls for international co-operation and a spirit of profound solidarity and compassion.

POPE ST JOHN PAUL II, Message for the World Day of Migrants and Refugees, 5th August 2013

His irregular legal status cannot allow the migrant to lose his dignity, since he is endowed with inalienable rights, which can neither be violated nor ignored.

POPE ST JOHN PAUL II (1920–2005), Message for the World Migration Day, 1996, par. 2

When a stranger sojourns with you in your land, you shall not do him wrong. The stranger who sojourns with you shall be to you as the native among you, and you shall love him as yourself; for you were strangers in the land of Egypt: I am the LORD your God.

LEV 19:33

support themselves and their families. Second, nations have the right to regulate their borders. Third, refugees and asylum seekers should be given protection. Fourth, human dignity and human rights of undocumented migrants should be respected. Regarding this last point, as the U.S. and Mexican bishops have stated, "Regardless of their legal status, migrants, like all persons, possess inherent human dignity that should be respected. Often they are subject to punitive laws and harsh treatment from enforcement officers from both receiving and transit countries. Government policies that respect the basic human rights of the undocumented are necessary" (*Strangers No Longer: Together on the Journey of Hope*, A Pastoral Letter Concerning Migration from

> **O LORD my God, in you I take refuge: Save me from all my pursuers, and deliver me.**
>
> **PS 7:2**

the Catholic Bishops of Mexico and the United States [2003], no. 38; cf. nos 35–37). It is not enough to help only in individual cases; it is also the Church's task to prompt legislators to pass more humane laws.

The Issue of Fair Trade

251 *What problems arise in regard to worldwide trade?*

In the wake of globalization, trade relations between countries throughout the world have also become closer. This has helped some countries; in many others, nevertheless, it has aggravated social and ecological

> If I have a dream about the church, it is the dream of open doors for the foreigners who speak, eat, and smell different. I want to live, not in a fortress that others cannot set foot in, but rather in a house with many doors. A home that we possess only for ourselves makes us narrow and stuffy. Every guest brings with him into the house something that we ourselves do not have.

DOROTHEE SÖLLE (1929–2003), German Lutheran-Evangelical theologian

A theory of fairness in international trade should answer at least three questions. What, at the basic level, are we to assess as fair or unfair in the trade context? What sort of fairness issue does this basic subject of assessment raise? And, what moral principles must be fulfilled if trade is to be fair in the relevant sense?

AARON ADAMS American professor of political philosophy

problems. Of course, in selecting my purchases as an individual consumer, I have very few opportunities to influence the way trade is structured. Therefore, it is important for national governments to deal with this problem or else for organizations to be founded that advocate trade structures that are more just.

➡ 362–364

252 *What is fair trade?*

Fair trade refers to commerce that is conducted according to definite principles of *justice* (fairness). Various fair trade organizations determine these

The balance of business expenditures shifts from product research to market research, which means orienting business away from making products of value and toward making consumers feel valuable. The business of business becomes pseudo-therapy; the consumer, a patient reassured by psychodramas.

NEIL POSTMAN (1931–2003), American media theorist

principles and co-ordinate the trade relations. They promote greater justice in international trade inasmuch as they strengthen the rights of the producers (such as small farmers and plantation owners) and contribute to a *sustained* development in the countries in question. In order to achieve this, they commit themselves to a *dialogue* between the trade partners, to greater *transparency* about production and trade relations, and also *respect* for all the actors involved.

 You be the change that you wish for this world.
Attributed to **MAHATMA GANDHI**

253 What measures are taken to promote fair trade?

First, opportunities are created for economically disadvantaged producers to take an active part in the trade system in the first place and to become more independent. Socially just production methods, good work conditions (pay, hours, prohibition of child labour, etc.), and also equal rights for women are fostered. At the same time, environmental standards are developed. Long-term "partnership" relations between countries should also be established.

> A man's wisdom can be measured by the care with which he reflects on the future or the end.
>
> **GEORG CHRISTOPH LICHTENBERG** (1742–1799), German scientist

> Inventions have long since reached their limit, and I see no hope for further developments.
>
> **JULIUS SEXTUS FRONTINUS,** Roman engineer in the year 10 BC

254 How does fair trade work?

Fair trade helps to fight poverty on several continents, especially in rural areas. The living conditions of producers and labourers in various developing countries are thereby improved and made more dignified. Furthermore, fair trade can contribute to changes in heavily one-sided relationships of power and thus help reduce the number of dependencies.

> When the tree begins life, it is not tall immediately. Once it is tall, it does not immediately blossom. Once it blossoms, it does not immediately bear fruit. Once it bears fruits, they are not immediately ripe. Once they are ripe, they are not immediately eaten.
>
> **BL. EGIDIO OF ASSISI** (d. 1262), companion of St Francis

255 Is fair trade enough to solve problems of poverty?

No, not by far. Fair trade must be further developed in order for its positive effects to unfold. It is not enough if individual organizations and firms commit themselves to the appropriate principles. In the long term, all trade relations worldwide must

> He has a right to criticize, who has a heart to help.
>
> **ABRAHAM LINCOLN** (1809–1865)

be guided by the criteria of fair trade. For that to happen, it is essential that members of the international community also work for this cause politically and support fair trade more intensively or commit themselves to the promotion of responsible, humane trade relations in solidarity with all peoples. They have made a good start. The important thing in the next few years will be for more and more people to exert pressure on the political and economic forces by demanding, buying, and using fair trade products.

> Wherever we look upon this earth, the opportunities take shape within problems.

NELSON A. ROCKEFELLER (1908–1979), U.S. Vice-President

> Someone sits in the shade today because someone planted a tree a long time ago.

WARREN BUFFETT (b. 1930)

> To see clearly, it is often enough to change the direction of your gaze.

ANTOINE DE SAINT-EXUPÉRY (1900–1944)

> "Adam, where are you?" "Where is your brother?" These are the two questions which God asks at the dawn of human history, and which he also asks each man and woman in our own day, which he also asks us. But I would like us to ask a third question: "Has any one of us wept because of this situation and others like it?" Has any one of us grieved for the death of these brothers and sisters? Has any one of us wept for these persons who were on the boat? For the young mothers carrying their babies? For these men who were looking for a means of supporting their families? We are a society which has forgotten how to weep, how to experience compassion—"suffering with" others: the globalization of indifference!

POPE FRANCIS in Lampedusa, 8th July 2013

From important Church documents

THE INTERNATIONAL COMMUNITY

Pacem in Terris
The Right to Emigrate and Immigrate
Every human being has the right to freedom of movement and of residence within the confines of his own State. When there are just reasons in favour of it, he must be permitted to emigrate to other countries and take up residence there (cf. Pius XII, Christmas Eve Message 1952). The fact that he is a citizen of a particular State does not deprive him of membership in the human family, nor of citizenship in that universal society, the common, world-wide fellowship of men.
Pope St John XXIII, Encyclical Pacem in Terris (1963), 12

Pacem in Terris
The Refugee's Rights
For this reason, it is not irrelevant to draw the attention of the world to the fact that these [political] refugees are persons and all their rights as persons must be recognized. Refugees cannot lose these rights simply because they are deprived of citizenship of their own States. And among man's personal rights we must include his right to enter a country in which he hopes to be able to provide more fittingly for himself and his dependents. It is therefore the duty of State officials to accept such immigrants and—so far as the good of their own community, rightly understood, permits—to further the aims of those who may wish to become members of a new society.
Pope St John XXIII, Encyclical Pacem in Terris (1963), 57

Centesimus Annus
Development for All in Solidarity
Finally, development must not be understood solely in economic terms, but in a way that is fully human. It is not only a question of raising all peoples to the level currently enjoyed by the richest countries, but rather of building up a more decent life through united labour, of concretely enhancing every individual's dignity and creativity, as well as his capacity to respond to his personal vocation, and thus to God's call. The apex of development is the exercise of the right and duty to seek God, to know him and to live in accordance with that knowledge.
Pope St John Paul II, Encyclical Centesimus Annus (1991), 29

Centesimus Annus
Fair Access to the Marketplace
Even in recent years it was thought that the poorest countries would develop by isolating themselves from the world market and by depending only on their own resources. Recent experience has shown that countries which did this have suffered stagnation and recession, while the countries which experienced development were those which succeeded in

taking part in the general interrelated economic activities at the international level. It seems therefore that the chief problem is that of gaining fair access to the international market, based not on the unilateral principle of the exploitation of the natural resources of these countries but on the proper use of human resources.

Pope St John Paul II, Encyclical Centesimus Annus (1991), 33

Economic Opportunity

Centesimus Annus

Love for others, and in the first place love for the poor, in whom the Church sees Christ himself, is made concrete in the *promotion of justice*. Justice will never be fully attained unless people see in the poor person, who is asking for help in order to survive, not an annoyance or a burden, but an opportunity for showing kindness and a chance for greater enrichment. Only such an awareness can give the courage needed to face the risk and the change involved in every authentic attempt to come to the aid of another. It is not merely a matter of "giving from one's surplus", but of helping entire peoples which are presently excluded or marginalized to enter into the sphere of economic and human development. For this to happen, it is not enough to draw on the surplus goods which in fact our world abundantly produces; it requires above all a change of life-styles, of models of production and consumption, and of the established structures of power which today govern societies.

Pope St John Paul II, Encyclical Centesimus Annus (1991), 58

Truth and Development

Caritas in Veritate

Development, social well-being, the search for a satisfactory solution to the grave socio-economic problems besetting humanity, all need this truth. What they need even more is that this truth should be loved and demonstrated. Without truth, without trust and love for what is true, there is no social conscience and responsibility, and social action ends up serving private interests and the logic of power, resulting in social fragmentation, especially in a globalized society at difficult times like the present.

Pope Benedict XVI, Encyclical Caritas in Veritate (2009), 5

An Increasingly Globalized Society

Caritas in Veritate

In an increasingly globalized society, the common good and the effort to obtain it cannot fail to assume the dimensions of the whole human family, that is to say, the community of peoples and nations, in such a way as to shape the earthly city in unity and peace, rendering it to some degree an anticipation and a prefiguration of the undivided *city of God*.

Pope Benedict XVI, Encyclical Caritas in Veritate (2009), 7

10

QUESTIONS
256–269

Safeguarding
Creation

THE ENVIRONMENT

> ❞ God himself is the Creator of the world, and creation is not yet finished. God works.

POPE BENEDICT XVI, 12th September 2008

256 *What contribution can Christians make toward a humane environment?*

 We are not God. The earth was here before us and it has been given to us.... Each community can take from the bounty of the earth whatever it needs for subsistence, but it also has the duty to protect the earth and to ensure its fruitfulness for coming generations.

POPE FRANCIS, LS 67

Christians are not environmentalists if their commitment is limited to moral appeals made to others. It is just as unhelpful to talk constantly about global problems instead of paying close attention to one's own environment and the possibilities present in it. Christian environmental ethics, therefore, is not built on smug appeals. Instead, it tries to provide orientation concerning individual and societal conflicts that need to be resolved. For this purpose, there must be first of all a precise analysis of cause-and-effect connections, risks, and prospects. Only then can guiding principles be effective. Christians make a valuable contribution to the preservation of the ecosystem when they care for creation instead of venting frustration about the environment. The courage to hope must be combined with the search for knowledge and the readiness to act.

→ 180 → 373, 2415–2418 → 50

257 *What does it mean to "be good stewards of creation"?*

We have not yet managed to adopt a circular model of production capable of preserving resources for present and future generations, while limiting as much as possible the use of non-renewable resources, moderating their consumption, maximizing their efficient use, reusing and recycling them.

POPE FRANCIS, LS 22

"Being good stewards of creation" cannot mean that we as Christians are supposed to preserve all of nature as an object of our care. Nature is an open, continuously evolving system and not an array of static conditions to be maintained. Only when there

is a more exact theological, ecological, economic, aesthetic, or cultural description of what aspects of nature are worth preserving can there be meaningful reflections about what should be protected and tended, and when, why, and how that can be done.

➡ **166, 180, 461, 465–468** ➡ **344, 354, 2415–2418**
➡ **57, 288**

258 *Isn't ecology a technical challenge for specialists?*

No. As Pope St John Paul II emphasized at a world conference for sustainable development in Johannesburg in 2002, every Christian has an "ecological vocation", which "in our time is more urgent than ever". The main concept of his address was "ecological humanity". Central to this is the dignity of the human being. This involves understanding the themes "respect for life", "work", and "responsibility" in reference to God, the good Creator of a world that is good in itself. "Peace with God the Creator" means "peace with all of creation" (John Paul II, Message for the World Day of Peace 2010). Every Christian must know that the "lack of due respect for nature" and the "plundering of natural resources" that results from it are a threat to world peace.

➡ **472** ➡ **2415–2418** ➡ **436–437**

> A valley, a cliff, a grove. Listen, don't touch anything, no stone, no blade of grass, no tree. Leave the grains of sand in their place, and the mountains. What do you want to change? What can you do better? The west wind arises all by itself and carries the blossoms. Before man changes the world, it is perhaps more important that he doesn't destroy it.
>
> **PAUL CLAUDEL** (1868–1955), French writer

 A person who could afford to spend and consume more but regularly uses less heating and wears warmer clothes, shows the kind of convictions and attitudes which help to protect the environment.
POPE FRANCIS, LS 211

" Don't blow it—good planets are hard to find.

Quoted in *Time*

With due respect for the autonomy and culture of every nation, we must never forget that the planet belongs to all mankind and is meant for all mankind; the mere fact that some people are born in places with fewer resources or less development does not justify the fact that they are living with less dignity.
POPE FRANCIS, EG 190

The sparkling of the Mediterranean Sea, the grandeur of the North African desert, the luxuriant green of the forests of Asia, the breadth of the Pacific Ocean, the horizon over which the sun rose and set, and the majestic splendour of Australia's natural beauty that I was able to enjoy in recent days—all this aroused a profound reverence.
POPE BENEDICT XVI, after the flight to Sydney, 17th June 2008

The human environment and the natural environment deteriorate together; →

259 ***What does the Church have to contribute to the topic of ecology?***

The Church has no special ecological competence. In his encyclical LAUDATO SÌ, Pope Francis speaks of the earth as the "common home" of all men. He praises all who strive to take responsibility for the upkeep of this home and challenges Christians to a radical ecological conversion. "The urgent challenge to protect our common home includes a concern to bring the whole human family together to seek a sustainable and integral development, for we know that things can change. The Creator does not abandon us; he never forsakes his loving plan or repents of having created us. Humanity still has the ability to work together in building our common home. Here I want to recognize, encourage and thank all those striving in countless ways to guarantee the protection of the home which we share (LS, 13)".

 166, 473 ➡ **283, 2456** ➡ **57**

260 ***What is integral ecological development?***

Pope Francis says; "We are faced not with two separate crises, one environmental and the other social, but rather with one complex crisis which is both social and environmental. Strategies for a solution demand an integrated approach to combating poverty, restoring dignity to the excluded, and at the same time protecting nature" (LS 139). And in another place

he says: "That is why it is no longer enough to speak only of the integrity of ecosystems. We have to dare to speak of the integrity of human life, of the need to promote and unify all the great values" (LS 224).

→ 166, 481 → 282, 354, 2456 → 426–437

261 *Where can we find what the Church has to say about environmental ethics?*

The Church's central text on ecology is Pope Francis's encyclical Laudato Si' (2015). It offers a comprehensive analysis of the ecological threat, with reference to many scientific studies, and it describes the causes of the crisis. These consist not only in the striking political impotence ("subject[ion] of politics to technology and finance") and the mindless economic exploitation of the earth which results. The core reason for the problem is to be sought in man himself, in a general disturbance of his relationship with creation (" ...my relationship with my own self, with others, with God, and with the earth"). Conversion restores man, who has to learn "that everything is interconnected, and that genuine care for our own lives and our relationships with nature is inseparable from fraternity, justice and faithfulness to others" (LS 70). So genuine ecology is at the same time protection of the environment, human ecology, social ecology, and cultural ecology. Human freedom, says Pope Francis, can "limit and direct technology; we can put it at the

→ we cannot adequately combat environmental degradation unless we attend to causes related to human and social degradation. In fact, the deterioration of the environment and of society affects the most vulnerable people on the planet: "Both everyday experience and scientific research show that the gravest effects of all attacks on the environment are suffered by the poorest"

POPE FRANCIS, LS 48^

Cultivating and caring for creation is an instruction of God which he gave not only at the beginning of history, but has also given to each one of us; it is part of his plan; it means making the world increase with responsibility, transforming it so that it may be a garden, an inhabitable place for us all.

POPE FRANCIS,
5th June 2013

We are God's creatures, made in his image and likeness, endowed with an inviolable dignity, and called to eternal life. Wherever man is diminished, the world around us is also diminished; it loses its ultimate meaning and strays from its goal. What emerges is a culture, not of life, but of death. How could this be considered "progress"?

POPE BENEDICT XVI,
19th July 2008

The brutal consumption of Creation begins where God is not, where matter is henceforth only material for us, where we ourselves are the ultimate demand, where the whole is merely our property and we consume it for ourselves alone … where we must possess all that is possible to possess.

POPE BENEDICT XVI,
6th August 2008

When the food was shared fairly, with solidarity, no one was deprived of what he needed, every community could meet the needs of its poorest members. Human and environmental ecology go hand in hand.

POPE FRANCIS,
5th June 2013

service of another type of progress, one which is healthier, more human, more social, more integral" (LS 112). In addition to LAUDATO SÌ, the encyclicals POPULORUM PROGRESSIO (1967) and CARITAS IN VERITATE (2009) are also important documents for the relationship between social responsibility and ecological protection of the environment.

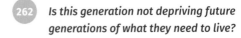 466–471 ➡ 282, 454 ➡ 436–437

262 *Is this generation not depriving future generations of what they need to live?*

To some extent that is true. And only a movement towards solidarity can change that. And so Pope Francis says: "Once we start to think about the kind of world we are leaving to future generations, we look at things differently; we realize that the world is a gift which we have freely received and must share with others. Since the world has been given to us, we can no longer view reality in a purely utilitarian way, in which efficiency and productivity are entirely geared to our individual benefit" (LS 159).

➡ 319, 470, 478 ➡ 299 ➡ 56–57

Usually paradise shows that it is paradise only after we are driven out of it.

HERMANN HESSE (1877–1962), German-Swiss poet, novelist, and painter

> We must not look at nature as an enemy to dominate and overcome, but rather learn again to co-operate with nature. She has four and a half billion years of experience. Ours is considerably shorter.

HANS-PETER DÜRR
(1929–2014), German physicist

263 · Sustainability – a new social principle?

With the help of the fundamental social principles → PERSONHOOD →SOLIDARITY and → SUBSIDIARITY (see nos. 83–102), one can understand the structures of society and align them with ethical criteria. Given the particular challenges of the present time, it seems appropriate to add another principle to these: the principle of sustainability. This principle of sustainability relates to and puts into action the traditional principles of social ethics with regard to human living conditions and the survival of the earth itself. When people discuss sustainability, they are talking about safeguarding in the long term the stability of the earth's ecosystem and its natural ability to regenerate its resources.

> The resources of creation [are] an immense gift of God to humanity. Humanity is duty-bound to protect this treasure and to counter the indiscriminate use of the earth's goods.

POPE BENEDICT XVI,
27th September 2008

→ 160–163 → 2415–2418 → 436

264 · Why does sustainability require "personhood"?

> I would therefore like us all to make the serious commitment to respect and care for creation, to pay attention to every person, to combat the culture of waste and of throwing out so as to foster a culture of solidarity and encounter.

POPE FRANCIS,
5th June 2013

Concern about the earth's ecosystem is not an end in itself; ultimately we must be working for the unconditional dignity of the human person. Man is the

centre of the world, not nature and not animals, even though we know that it benefits man when care is taken to keep nature intact and when animals have species-appropriate habitats. Protecting nature and protecting mankind are two sides of the same coin for Christian ethics.

➡ 456–457; 473 ➡ 354 ➡ 57

265 Why does sustainability require "solidarity"?

Sustainability is a challenge that can only be met by common effort. Without practical solidarity in the immediate vicinity, sustainability would remain a frustrating topic for a few idealists, while others shamelessly used up resources ("After me, the deluge!"). And without all the many institutions that have been created to fight poverty in solidarity or to safeguard natural resources, sustainability would be an empty, politically noncommittal word. In her international aid programmes, the Church has a great tradition of solidarity that can be developed even further.

➡ 103, 193–195, 449, 474–478, 580 ➡ 344 ➡ 332

266 Why does sustainability require "subsidiarity"?

Without the principle of subsidiarity, sustainable development would lack its organizational centrepiece: what can be accomplished by a smaller organization *should* be done by that organization. It does not have to be regulated and organized from above. Ecology is easily misused as a way of demanding more State action, more regulations, and more centralization, instead of promoting structures of freedom and adaptation to the socio-cultural and natural environments in each particular case.

➡ 186–188, 299, 449 ➡ 1883, 2241 ➡ 323

> Someone who wants to live in harmony with nature would actually have to fight over hunting grounds and either eat the weaker ones or drive them away. But do we really want to live that much in harmony with nature?

PAUL WATZLAWICK (1921–2007), Austrian-American psychologist and philosopher

> The thirst for power and possessions knows no limits. In this system, which tends to devour everything which stands in the way of increased profits, whatever is fragile, like the environment, is defenceless before the interests of a deified market, which become the only rule.

POPE FRANCIS, EG 56

> God our Father gave us the task of protecting the earth—not to money, but to us men and women. We have this task! Instead, men and women are sacrificed to the idols of profit and consumption: it is the "culture of waste".

POPE FRANCIS, 5th June 2013

267 *What can the faith contribute to discussions about "sustainability"?*

"Sustainability" can also become an ideology; only rarely then does it appear as something socially and technologically feasible, as a political plan that should be put into action forcefully. The Christian faith is critical of ideologies, for it does not believe in perfect solutions. It does mobilize all possible forces to achieve sustainable, just, and dignified human living conditions, but in the end, it lives by the hope that God will ultimately perfect what we human beings cannot achieve, even with the best intentions, namely, a paradise that actually works. Sustainability is a

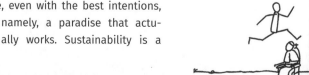
Any work that is aimed at the destruction of the living, those who come after us, our fellow creatures, and the earth itself cannot be reconciled with Christian faith.
DOROTHEE SÖLLE

"Would you tell me, please, which way I ought to go from here?" Alice asked. "That depends a good deal on where you want to get to," said the Cat.

LEWIS CARROLL (1832–1898), English author of *Alice in Wonderland*

 There are other weak and defenceless beings who are frequently at the mercy of economic interests or indiscriminate exploitation. I am speaking of creation as a whole. We human beings are not only the beneficiaries but also the stewards of other creatures. Thanks to our bodies, God has joined us so closely to the world around us that we can feel the desertification of the soil almost as a physical ailment and the extinction of a species as a painful disfigurement. Let us not leave in our wake a swath of destruction and death which will affect our own lives and those of future generations.

POPE FRANCIS, EG 215

concern about the future that is motivated, not by optimism about progress, but rather by a vision of life well lived within the limits of nature.

➡ 100 ➡ 285

268 *How can Christians live well within the limits of nature?*

Sustainability (as safeguarding the ecological, social, and economic stability of human environments) cannot simply mean ever faster speeds and more and more goods. Then the rich would only be living even more shamelessly at the expense of those who cannot keep up in the race. Prosperity that *uses resources sparingly and thoughtfully*—in other words, that does not keep gobbling up the earth's finite resources—is the only sort of prosperity that offers as many people as possible a chance to *share* in it. This is the only kind of prosperity that Christians can advocate, because it is just. This perspective lends new meaning to "doing without": do without things that you are taking away from others forever!

➡ **172, 359, 470** ➡ **339–340** ➡ **45**

269 *Where is "God" in the ecological crisis?*

The ecological crisis occurs, not at the desks of theologians and sociologists, but rather in the lived experiences of farmers who have suffered losses due to extreme climate and of poor migrant workers in the slums of cities with millions of inhabitants. Where is God in those situations? God is first of all in the people who systematically share, because in Jesus Christ a merciful God condescended to share personally in human misery. God is also there in various efforts to see the plundered earth as *creation* again and to make regenerative environments possible. The Christian view of man does not define the value of the human being by the quantity of goods that he or she produces and consumes, and thus it can foster moderate, just, and responsible dealings with them. The Church, moreover, is the oldest "global player" and therefore especially capable of worldwide responsibility. For only *responsibility* will turn the tide in the ecological crisis.

➡ **465, 470, 480** ➡ **2415–2418** ➡ **57, 427, 436**

God of love, show us our place in this world…
Enlighten those who possess power and money
that they may avoid the sin of indifference,
that they may love the common good, advance the weak,
and care for this world in which we live.
POPE FRANCIS, From the Prayer of LS

It is not merely a question of discovering technologies that prevent the damage, even though it is important to find alternative sources of energy, among other things. Yet, none of this will suffice unless we ourselves find a new way of living, a discipline of making sacrifices, a discipline of the recognition of others to whom creation belongs as much as it belongs to us.
POPE BENEDICT XVI,
11th May 2008

The wasting of creation begins when we no longer recognize any need superior to our own, but see only ourselves. It begins when there is no longer any concept of life beyond death, where in this life we must grab hold of everything and possess life as intensely as possible, where we must possess all that is possible to possess.
POPE BENEDICT XVI,
6th August 2008

❞ We must face the prospect of changing our basic ways of living. This change will either be made on our own initiative in a planned and rational way, or forced on us with chaos and suffering by the inexorable laws of nature.
JIMMY CARTER (b. 1924), former U.S. President, in a speech in 1976

From important Church documents

THE ENVIRONMENT

| Evangelium Vitae | |

Responsibility for Creation/the Environment

As one called to till and look after the garden of the world (cf. Gen 2:15), man has a specific responsibility towards the environment in which he lives, towards the creation which God has put at the service of his personal dignity, of his life, not only for the present but also for future generations. It is the ecological question—ranging from the preservation of the natural habitats of the different species of animals and of other forms of life to "human ecology" properly speaking—which finds in the Bible clear and strong ethical direction, leading to a solution which respects the great good of life, of every life. In fact, "the dominion granted to man by the Creator is not an absolute power, nor can one speak of a freedom to 'use and misuse', or to dispose of things as one pleases. The limitation imposed from the beginning by the Creator himself and expressed symbolically by the prohibition not to 'eat of the fruit of the tree' (cf. Gen 2:16–17) shows clearly enough that, when it comes to the natural world, we are subject not only to biological laws but also to moral ones, which cannot be violated with impunity."

Pope St John Paul II, Encyclical Evangelium Vitae (1995), 42

| World Day of Peace 2010 | |

Finding Common Strategies

To be sure, among the basic problems which the international community has to address is that of energy resources and the development of joint and sustainable strategies to satisfy the energy needs of the present and future generations. This means that technologically advanced societies must be prepared to encourage more sober life-styles, while reducing their energy consumption and improving its efficiency. At the same time there is a need to encourage research into, and utilization of, forms of energy with lower impact on the environment and "a worldwide redistribution of energy resources, so that countries lacking those resources can have access to them."

Pope Benedict XVI, Message for World Day of Peace 2010

| The United States Conference of Catholic Bishops | |

The Challenge of Climate Change

At its core, global climate change is not about economic theory or political platforms, nor about partisan advantage or interest group pressures. It is about the future of God's creation and the one human family. It is about protecting both "the human environment" and the natural environment. It is about our human stewardship of God's creation and our responsibility to those who come after us. With these reflections, we seek to offer a word of caution and a plea for genuine dialogue as the United States and other nations face decisions about how best to respond to the challenges of global climate change. The dialogue and our response to the challenge of climate change must be rooted in the virtue of prudence. While some uncertainty remains, most experts agree that something significant is happening to the atmosphere. Human behaviour and activity are, according to the most recent findings of the international scientific bodies charged with assessing climate change, contributing to a warming of the earth's climate. Although debate continues about the extent and impact of this warming, it could be quite serious … Consequently, it seems prudent not only to continue to research and monitor this phenomenon, but to take steps now to mitigate possible negative effects in the future.

USCCB statement, "Global Climate Change: A Plea for Dialogue, Prudence and the Common Good", 15th June 2001, from the Introduction

Pope Francis

Mankind Is Endangered

What does cultivating and preserving the earth mean? … The verb "cultivate" reminds me of the care a farmer takes to ensure that his land will be productive and that his produce will be shared. What great attention, enthusiasm, and dedication! Cultivating and caring for creation … means making the world increase with responsibility, transforming it so that it may be a garden, an inhabitable place for us all. … Instead we are often guided by the pride of dominating, possessing, manipulating, and exploiting; we do not "preserve" the earth, we do not respect it, we do not consider it as a freely given gift to look after. … However "cultivating and caring" do not only entail the relationship between us and the environment, between man and creation. They also concern human relations.

Pope Francis, General Audience, 5th June 2013

Evangelium Vitae

Co-operating with the Creator

The genealogy of the person is inscribed in the very biology of generation. In affirming that the spouses, as parents, co-operate with God the Creator in conceiving and giving birth to a new human being, we are not speaking merely with reference to the laws of biology. Instead, we wish to emphasize that God himself is present in human fatherhood and motherhood quite differently than he is present in all other instances of begetting "on earth". Indeed, God alone is the source of that "image and likeness" which is proper to the human being, as it was received at Creation. Begetting is the continuation of Creation.

Pope St John Paul II, Encyclical Evangelium Vitae (1995), 43

11

Living in Freedom from Violence

PEACE

Peace
I leave with you;
my peace I give to you;
not as the world gives
do I give
to you.

JN 14:27

Lord, make me an instrument of your peace. Where there is hatred, let me sow love; where there is injury, pardon; where there is doubt, faith; where there is despair, hope; where there is darkness, light; and where there is sadness, joy.

On a prayer card printed in 1913

 Peace to you.
LK 24:36
So the Risen Lord greeted the disciples.

270 **Why do we need God, if we want peace?**

Peace is first of all an *attribute of God* before it is a *task for us human beings*. Anyone who tries to bring about peace without God is forgetting that we no longer live in paradise but are sinners. Our lack of peace on earth is a sign that the unity between God and mankind has disintegrated. Human history is characterized by violence, divisions, and bloodshed. People yearn for the peace that they have lost through sin; in doing so, they are silently yearning for God as well.

➡ **488, 491–494** ➡ **374–379, 400, 410–412**
➡ **66, 70, 395**

271 *What does Jesus have to do with peace?*

Jesus Christ "is our peace" (Eph 2:14). The Old Testament prophets foretold that one day a mighty Messiah (Hebrew: Anointed = Greek: Christ) would come. And this Messiah/Christ would bring the long-awaited era of peace, a new world in which "the wolf shall dwell with the lamb, and the leopard shall lie down with the kid" (Is 11:6). The Messiah would be the "Prince of Peace" (Is 9:6). Christians believe that Jesus is this great sign and beginning of a new world. He is the most basic peacemaker—by freeing us human beings from slavery to sin, he struck at the root of all dissension. Through his death on the Cross, Jesus Christ reconciled mankind with God and also tore down the wall of hostility that divided peoples (cf. Eph 2:14–16).

→ 488–492 → 2305 → 395

272 *Why must Christians spread peace?*

Jesus Christ established peace between heaven and earth and opened all the doors to a life of reconciliation and inner joy. But his peace does not spread by itself. Human beings have the freedom to accept God's offer of reconciliation in faith or to reject it in disbelief. In order to make their decision, people must first hear that in God peace is possible, both in their personal lives and also between hostile groups and nations. They can learn about this if they encounter people who have been reconciled: people who do *not* hit back, do *not* take revenge, do *not* use violence. Sharing the Gospel of peace in word and deed creates the beginnings of more and more genuine peace.

→ 490–493 → 2304 → 332

273 *Do only Christians have a mission of peace?*

Peace is a value that all human beings recognize and a duty that applies to all. No one can be exempt

> When Jesus came into the world, "Peace on earth" came too. When He left the world, He left His peace.
>
> A Golden Treasury for the Young

 So we are ambassadors for Christ, God making his appeal through us. We beg you on behalf of Christ, be reconciled to God.
2 COR 5:20

In view of the risks which humanity is facing in our time, all Catholics in every part of the world have a duty to proclaim and embody ever more fully the "Gospel of Peace" and to show that acknowledgement of the full truth of God is the first, indispensable condition for consolidating the truth of peace.
POPE BENEDICT XVI, Message for the World Day of Peace 2006

> Peace is not absence of conflict, it is the ability to handle conflict by peaceful means.
>
> **RONALD REAGAN** (1911-2004) President of the United States

POVERTY
@SUCKS!

from the duty to seek peace. Moreover, peace is a good that is as fragile as it is valuable. Day by day, peace must be built up anew. Peace can last only if both Christians and non-Christians recognize that all are responsible for a common life of reconciliation, justice, and goodwill.

➡ **494–495** ➡ **2304–2305** ➡ **327, 395**

274 How does a Christian get started making peace?

Peace does not begin in trenches or around treaty tables. The peace that comes from above always begins in the heart of an individual human being; from there it spreads. A Christian finds peace in and with himself through prayer and listening to the Word of God. The sacraments are important, too, especially Confession, which is a real sacrament of peace. One attains inner peace also when one takes the first step and meets one's neighbour in real charity. In order to live with one another in peace, Christians know of no more effective method than a permanent willingness to forgive and to be reconciled. "To him who strikes you on the cheek, offer the other also" (Lk 6:29). Your own peace radiates: in the family, in your circle of friends, and in society as a whole.

➡ **95, 517–518** ➡ **1723** ➡ **279, 284, 311**

275 What is peace?

Many say that peace is the absence of war; others think that peace is a stable equilibrium between hostile powers. These definitions are inadequate, however. Peace is the tranquility of order and, more deeply, happiness in God's good order. This sort of peace is our goal. We find ourselves on the path of peace when we work in justice and love toward a world that is ordered as God intended. Moreover, we find ourselves alongside all people who honestly and

> Whenever you share love with others, you'll notice the peace that comes to you and to them.
> **ST TERESA OF CALCUTTA** (1910–1997)

> No peace in the world without peace among nations; no peace among nations without peace in the family; no peace in the family without peace in me; no peace in me without peace with God.
> Chinese Proverb

> Blessed are the peacemakers, for they shall be called sons of God.
> **MT 5:9**

> It is normal for husband and wife to argue: it's normal. It always happens. But my advice is this: never let the day end without having first made peace. Never!
> **POPE FRANCIS,** 14th September 2014, homily at Mass with Rite of Marriage

> Young people are the source of hope for the future. Your historic destiny is to build a civilization of love, of brotherhood and solidarity.
> **POPE ST JOHN PAUL II,** World Youth Day 1995 in Manila

Peace is not simply the absence of warfare, based on a precarious balance of power; it is fashioned by efforts directed day after day toward the establishment of the ordered universe willed by God, with a more perfect form of justice among men.

POPE PAUL VI, PP 76

 Since the way of peace passes in the last analysis through love and seeks to create the civilization of love, the Church fixes her eyes on him who is the love of the Father and the Son, and in spite of increasing dangers she does not cease to trust, she does not cease to invoke and to serve the peace of man on earth.

POPE ST JOHN PAUL II,
Dominum et vivificantem, Conclusion

 The Church has an unconditional obligation to the victims of any ordering of society, even if they do not belong to the Christian community.

DIETRICH BONHOEFFER
(1906–1945)

sincerely seek the truth, care for the well-being and safety of their fellow human beings in justice, and unselfishly give them their love. And at the same time we work for God's original cause when we promote the rights of all human beings and defend them in every way.

➡ **494** ➡ **2304–2305** ➡ **66, 395**

276 *Where does the Church begin in her commitment to peace?*

The Church's offer of peace is connected with the peace of Christ and is different from other strategies for resolving conflicts: "Peace I leave with you; my peace I give to you; *not as the world gives* do I give to you" (Jn 14:27). Christ's peace is the love that led him to the Cross. "By his wounds you have been healed" (1 Pet 2:24). The Church lives by this faith in the unconditional love that God has for every human being. From the liberating faith in this love of God emerges a new way of approaching others, whether it is an individual person or entire peoples or social groups. Wherever Christians are, there must be peace.

➡ **516** ➡ **2302–2307** ➡ **284**

Let not your hearts be troubled, neither let them be afraid. JN 14:27

277 *What is forgiveness?*

People can do terrible things to other people: deprive them of social influence, lie to them, and betray them. Instead of becoming bitter about something that we cannot eradicate, Christians have another option for making peace and achieving inner peace: forgiveness. Forgiveness does not make light of the evil that has occurred and does not undo what has happened. Forgiveness means bringing God into play, "who forgives all your iniquity, who heals all your diseases" (Ps 103:3). When backed by God, people have the strength to forgive and even to make new beginnings possible where they seem humanly impossible.

→ 517 → 2839–2840 → 524

278 *What does the Church do for peace?*

Before any outward activity, the Church *prays* for peace; Christians believe that prayer has the power to change the world. Moreover, prayer is an important source of strength in Christian efforts for peace. In her proclamation of the Good News, the Church unceasingly calls for peace and obliges the faithful to work for it. On 1st January, the Solemnity of Mary, the Holy Mother of God, each year, the Church celebrates the World Day of Peace, and she attempts to create an atmosphere of peace and love at the events that she sponsors (for instance, World Youth Days). The Church wishes to show thereby that she believes in a civilization of love and peace and that this civilization is not only theoretically plausible but also possible in practice. When Christians follow the Gospel, they are the greatest peace movement in the world.

→ 519–520 → 763–764 → 123, 282

279 *How does the Church work politically for peace?*

Especially in the approximately 180 countries in which the Church is diplomatically represented through the → HOLY SEE, she does all that she can to make peace and to contribute to the safeguarding of peace. The Church stands up for human rights (for instance, freedom of religion or the defence of human life), she calls for disarmament and encourages economic and social development, so as to

---

You have heard that it was said, 'You shall love your neighbour and hate your enemy.' But I say to you, Love your enemies and pray for those who persecute you, so that you may be sons of your Father who is in heaven; for he makes his sun rise on the evil and on the good, and sends rain on the just and the unjust.

MT 5:43–45

In the Church's Liturgy, in her prayer, in the living community of believers, we experience the love of God, we perceive his presence, and we thus learn to recognize that presence in our daily lives. He has loved us first, and he continues to do so; we too, then, can respond with love.

POPE BENEDICT XVI, DCE 17

The greatest prayer of man is not for victory but for peace.

DAG HAMMARSKJÖLD (1905–1961), second UN Secretary General, Nobel Peace Prize winner (posthumously)

In my experience, whenever people strive to live the Gospel as Jesus teaches us, everything begins to change: all aggressiveness, all fear and sadness then give way to peace and joy.

KING BAUDOUIN OF BELGIUM (1930–1993)

HOLY SEE
(from Latin *Sancta Sedes*): the title under which the Catholic Church, which in the person of the Pope and the Curia is a sovereign, non-State subject in international law, acts politically. It maintains diplomatic relations and is represented in non-State organizations.

The Catholic Church, because of her universal nature, is always directly engaged in the great causes for which the men and women of our age struggle and hope. In her presence and her concern for the future of men and women everywhere, the Holy See knows that it can count on Your Excellencies to offer an important service, since it is precisely the mission of diplomats to transcend borders and to bring peoples and governments together in the desire to co-operate harmoniously.

POPE ST JOHN PAUL II, Address to the Diplomatic Corps, 10th January 2005

No peace treaty may be deemed valid that contains within its provisions the seeds of another war.

IMMANUEL KANT (1724–1804), *Perpetual Peace* (1795)

create the basis for peaceful coexistence in society. The Holy See also sends mediators to regions in crisis or advises and mediates behind the scenes in crisis situations, for example, the mediation of Pope St John XXIII between U.S. President John F. Kennedy and the leader of the U.S.S.R. and its Communist Party, Nikita Khrushchev, during the 1961 Cuban Missile Crisis, or of the Saint Egidio Community, which played a leading role in the signing of the 1992 peace treaty for Mozambique that was able to end sixteen years of raging civil war.

 444, 445

280 *What contact does the Holy See have with international organizations?*

The Holy See is a permanent observer in various international organizations, for example at the United Nations (UN, since 1964), at the Food and Agriculture Organization of the UN (FAO, since 1948), at UNESCO (since 1951), at the World Trade Organization (WTO), and at the European Council. With the reform of the United Nations in 2004, the member States granted the Holy See more rights in the UN Plenary Assembly. It can participate in the debate at the annual Plenary Assembly and also has the right to speak, insofar as the interests of the Holy See are concerned.

 444, 445

281 *Why is the Holy See merely an "observer" at the United Nations and not a full member?*

The Holy See considers itself committed to unconditional political neutrality. Full membership would involve it directly in political, military, and economic matters. In many political votes, for example concerning problematic decisions about engaging in war, the Holy See would have to abstain; moreover, full membership would make it more difficult for the Holy See to be available for diplomatic "good offices" (e.g., mediation).

→ **444, 445**

 282   *Are there other organization in which the Holy See is a full member?*

Yes. Examples of organizations to which the Holy See belongs as a full member are the International Atomic Energy Organization (IAEO), the Organization for Security and Co-operation in Europe (OSCE), the Organization for the Prevention of Chemical Weapons (OPCW), the International Telecommunications Union, and the Office of the United Nations High Commissioner for Refugees (UNHCR).

→ **444**

 283   *What is the Church's position on the United Nations and its Charter?*

The Catholic Church stands behind the Charter of the United Nations. This organization was formed after the experiences of World War II and was supposed to prevent future wars. The UN Charter forbids in principle the resolution of conflicts between States by force, with two exceptions: legitimate self-defence in the case of an attack, and measures taken by the UN Security Council within the framework of its responsibility for maintaining peace.

→ **501** → **1930–1931** → **329**

 284   *How do war and violence come about?*

 Through the United Nations, States have established universal objectives which, even if they do not coincide with the total common good of the human family, undoubtedly represent a fundamental part of that good. The founding principles of the Organization—the desire for peace, the quest for justice, respect for the dignity of the person, humanitarian co-operation and assistance—express the just aspirations of the human spirit and constitute the ideals which should underpin international relations.
POPE BENEDICT XVI, Address to the United Nations, 18th April 2008

 May the God of peace create in all an authentic desire for dialogue and reconciliation. Violence is not conquered with violence. Violence is conquered with peace!
POPE FRANCIS, 20th July 2014

Many wars come about because of long-standing hatred between peoples, because of ideologies, or because of the desire of

> War is a massacre of people who are unacquainted with each other, for the benefit of people who are acquainted but do not massacre each other.
>
> **PAUL VALÉRY** (1871–1945), French poet

> Every word that comes from Hitler's mouth is a lie: when he says peace, he means war, and when he in the most blasphemous way takes the name of the Almighty, he means the power of the Evil One, the fallen angel Satan.
>
> Flyer #4 of the Munich resistance group "White Rose" (July 1942)

individual men or groups for power and wealth. People also resort to war and violence, though, out of despair, for instance when they have no political voice or when they are suffering from hunger, poverty, oppression, or other injustices. When a few rich people live at the expense of many poor people, this inequity often leads to outbreaks of violence.

→ 494 → 2302–2303 → 396

285 *How does the Church regard war?*

War is the worst and most momentous failure of peace. Therefore, the Church again and again condemns the "savagery of war" (cf. Vatican Council II, GS 77, and also CCC 2307–2317). "Because of the evils and injustices that all war brings with it, we must do

> Anyone who preaches war is the devil's army chaplain. Proverb

> Whatever decision the Christian makes, whether for the path of the soldier or for the path of the conscientious objector, the individual must not claim for himself a higher quality of Christian discipleship or deny that someone else is a Christian because he takes another position.
>
> Declaration of the Council of the Evangelical [Lutheran] Church in Germany, 1989

everything reasonably possible to avoid it" (CCC 2327). However, "as long as the danger of war persists and there is no international authority with the necessary competence and power, governments cannot be denied the right of lawful self-defence once all peace efforts have failed" (GS 79, CCC 2308). War is always a "defeat for humanity" (John Paul II, Address to the Diplomatic Corps, 13th January 2003).

→ 497 → 2307–2309 → 398–399

286 *What preventive strategies are there for avoiding war and violence?*

The fight for peace can never consist solely in disarmament or the violent suppression of conflicts. Violence is often caused by lies and usually by injustice. Unjust structures lead again and again to exploitation and misery. Lack of participation and curtailed freedom express themselves in violent resistance. That is why war can be avoided long-term only when free societies are formed, in which just conditions prevail and all human beings have prospects for development. Sensible developmental aid also helps to avoid war.

→ 498 → 2317 → 397

 Development is the new name for peace.
POPE PAUL VI, PP 76

 The "structures of sin" and the sins which they produce are likewise radically opposed to peace and development, for development, in the familiar expression [from] Pope Paul's Encyclical, is "the new name for peace". In this way, the solidarity which we propose is the path to peace and at the same time to development.
POPE ST JOHN PAUL II, SRS 39

287 *What has to be done if political actors cannot maintain peace by themselves?*

Of course Catholic social teaching is aware that States often no longer have suitable means of defending themselves effectively and of maintaining peace. Besides developmental aid, the Church counts on the work of regional and international organizations to promote peace and to establish trust between nations. Often it has proved to be very fortunate that the Catholic Church has an international structure and cannot be co-opted nationally. Thus she has the

God, give me a good sword and no opportunity to use it.
Proverb

Mankind must put an end to war before war puts an end to mankind.
JOHN F. KENNEDY (1917–1963)

freedom to make independent judgements and to encourage Christians living under unjust regimes.

➡ 498, 499 ➡ 2308 ➡ 398

288 *What sort of sanctions should there be in the case of a conflict or when there is danger of war?*

Sanctions of the international community are significant measures that can be taken against States that oppress parts of their own populace or endanger the peaceful coexistence of nations. The goals of these measures must be formulated clearly. The sanctions must be reviewed regularly by the competent organs of the international community to evaluate objectively the actual consequences thereof for the civilian population. Their real purpose is to pave the way for negotiations and talks; sanctions must, however, never be used to punish an entire population directly. Thus, for example, a trade embargo should be for a

limited time and may not be justified if it becomes clear that everyone without distinction is affected by its consequences.

→ 507

289 *What should happen if war begins, despite everything?*

Wars of conquest and aggression are immoral in themselves. When a war breaks out, the responsible authorities in the State being attacked have the right and the duty to organize a defence, even by force of arms. This is why States can have armed forces and possess weapons, so as to protect their population from external attacks. Likewise, Christians, too, can be soldiers, inasmuch as the military forces serve to defend the security and freedom of a country and have peacekeeping functions. Enlisting children and youths as soldiers is a crime. Their deployment

If the Arabs put down their weapons, there will be no more war. But if Israel puts down its weapons, there will be no more Israel.

ARNO LUSTIGER (b. 1936), German songwriter

in armed forces of any sort whatsoever must be stopped, and the former "child soldiers" must be re-integrated back into society.

→ 500, 502–503, 512 → 2308 → 398

290 *What are the conditions for a "defensive war"?*

Defence by force of arms is justified only under a few conditions that are to be applied narrowly. Whether these conditions are fulfilled must be decided by those institutions which are "in charge of preserving the common good". Four criteria are considered especially important:

There is nothing that war has ever achieved that we could not better achieve without it.

MAX FRISCH (1911–1991), Swiss writer

1. The damage by the aggressor must be "lasting, grave, and certain".

2. There are no other means left of preventing or putting an end to the damage inflicted. All available peaceful ways of resolving the conflict must be exhausted.

The great Carthage waged three wars. After the first it was still powerful. After the second it was still habitable. After the third it was no longer to be found.

BERTOLT BRECHT (1898–1956), German playwright

3. The consequences of the defensive use of arms must not be worse than the damage inflicted by the aggressor. Here the devastating consequences of the use of weapons of mass destruction must especially be taken into consideration.

4. The defence must have a realistic chance of success.

→ 500 → 2309 → 399

291 ***Are there limits to the use of force in the case of a defensive war as well?***

Even when self-defence by force of arms is justified, not all means may be employed to strike back at the aggressor. In all circumstances, the "traditional limits of necessity and proportionality" must be observed. This means that in a defence against an unjust attack, only as much force may be used as is absolutely necessary to achieve the purpose of self-defence.

➡ 501 ➡ 2313–2314 ➡ 398

> War is bad, in that it makes more wicked men than it takes away.
>
> **IMMANUEL KANT** (1724–1804), *Perpetual Peace* (1795)

> If the machine of government is of such a nature that it requires you to be the agent of injustice to another, then, I say, break the law.
>
> **HENRY DAVID THOREAU** (1817–1862), American writer

> Never act against your conscience, even if the state demands it.
>
> **HEINRICH HEINE** (1797–1856), German poet

 292 ***What should soldiers bear in mind while at war?***

Soldiers are obliged not to obey orders that violate international law. For example, a soldier may never participate in the mass shooting of civilians or prisoners of war, even if his superiors order him to do so. In such a case, he cannot rely on the excuse that he was only following orders. He is responsible for his actions.

➡ 503 ➡ 2312 ➡ 380

293 ***What about the victims of war?***

Innocent victims who could not defend themselves against an attack must be protected in all circumstances. This protection applies to the civilian population in general. The parties waging war are also responsible for refugees and national, ethnic, religious, or language minorities. The attempt to wipe out entire population groups through genocide

Victims of war
The statistic annual report of the UNHCR, Global Trend, notes in late 2013 that more than 51.2 million people were refugees—that is six million more than the year before. The total number of refugees breaks down into three groups: 16.7 million people had to leave their homeland, 33.3 million were in transit within their country, and 1.2 million people were seeking asylum somewhere in the world. Every other refugee was a child.

> The goal of eliminating the use of force in international politics can, even in the future, come up against man's obligation to protect himself from foreign arbitrariness and power....For both individual states and society as a whole lack the means that would, in such limit cases, make defensive action superfluous.
>
> **THE GERMAN BISHOPS,** *A Just Peace,* (2000) 150.

or "ethnic cleansing" is a crime against God and against humanity.

→ **504–506** → **2314** → **379**

294 *What must be done when there is a threat of genocide?*

The international community has the moral obligation to intervene in favour of groups whose survival is endangered or whose fundamental rights are being violated massively. In such an intervention, international law must be observed strictly and the principle of the equality of States must be observed.

In this connection, the Church has spoken favourably of the International Criminal Court, which is supposed to prosecute those who are responsible for especially serious acts: genocide, crimes against humanity, war crimes, the crime of a war of aggression.

 506 → **2317**

295 *Should the arms trade be forbidden?*

The Church is committed to the goal of a "general, balanced, and controlled disarmament" (John Paul II, 14th October 1985), since the enormous worldwide increase of weapons presents a considerable threat to stability and freedom. The principle of sufficiency—every State may possess only the means required for its legitimate defence—must be kept in mind both by the States that buy weapons and also by those that manufacture or deliver weapons. Any excessive accumulation of weapons and universal trade in them are morally unjustifiable. Trade in so-called light weapons must also be strictly controlled by the States.

 508, 511 → **2315–2316**

296 *When are weapons of mass destruction permitted?*

The use of any weapon that causes more than individual and proportionate harm to civilians is immoral. By definition, then, the use of weapons of "mass destruction" is forbidden. The Church expressly rejects the so-called "logic of deterrence". The indiscriminate destruction of cities, countries, and populations

It is necessary before all else to provide Peace with other weapons—weapons different from those destined to kill and exterminate mankind. What is needed above all are moral weapons, those which give strength and prestige to international law—the weapon, in the first place, of the observance of pacts.

POPE PAUL VI (1897-1978), Message for the World Day of Peace 1976

But experience has shown that wars are no longer local. All modern wars become world wars eventually. And none of the big nations at least can stay out. If we cannot stay out of wars, our only hope is to prevent wars.

ROBERT H. JACKSON (1892–1954), Chief Prosecutor in the 1945-46 Nuremberg Trials

In a nuclear war there would be no victors, only victims.

POPE BENEDICT XVI, Message for the World Day of Peace 2006

With disregard for the clearly expressed will of governments and peoples to put a final end to the use of such an insidious weapon, mines are still being laid even in places which had already been cleared. Seeds of war are also being spread by the massive and uncontrolled proliferation of small arms and light weapons, which it seems are passing freely from one area of conflict to another, increasing violence along the way. Governments must adopt appropriate measures for controlling the production, sale, importation, and exportation of these instruments of death.

POPE ST JOHN PAUL II (1920–2005), Message for the World Day of Peace 1999

through biological, chemical, or nuclear weapons of mass destruction is a serious crime against God and humanity.

➡ **508–509** ➡ **2314**

297 *Are there any weapons that must not be used under any circumstances?*

The Church demands the prohibition of weapons that inflict excessively traumatic injury and indiscriminately strike anyone, for example anti-personnel land mines, which cannot be limited to military targets and do damage even long after the end of hostilities. The international community must make efforts to clear mines.

➡ **510** ➡ **2316**

298 *Is there a right to terrorism as a last resort?*

Terrorism must be severely condemned. It often strikes innocent, arbitrarily selected victims. Terrorists display total, cynical contempt for human life;

 There exists ... a right to defend oneself against terrorism.

POPE ST JOHN PAUL II, (1920–2005), Message for the World Day of Peace 2002

Violence does not build up the kingdom of God, the kingdom of humanity. On the contrary, it is a favourite instrument of the Antichrist, however idealistic its religious motivation may be. It serves, not humanity, but inhumanity.

JOSEPH RATZINGER/POPE BENEDICT XVI, from his book *Jesus of Nazareth: Holy Week*

nothing can justify their actions. Terrorism sows hatred, bloodshed, death, and the desire for retaliation and revenge. The targets of terroristic attacks are generally scenes of everyday life and not military targets, as in the framework of a declared war.

➡ **513** ➡ **2297** ➡ **392**

299 *What are we to think about religious-motivated terrorism?*

No religion should tolerate terrorism, much less preach it. To declare oneself a terrorist in God's name and to murder innocent people in his name is a grave blasphemy. Similarly, no one who dies while committing a terrorist act can be described as a "martyr". The Christian martyr (= witness) confirms the truth of his faith by his willingness to die for it, if necessary, but in doing so he never destroys the lives of other human beings. The Catholic Church calls upon all religious groups and communities likewise to distance themselves unequivocally from all religiously motivated terrorism, and at the same time she asks all religions to eliminate together the causes of terrorism and to make friendship among peoples possible.

➡ 515 ➡ 2297–2298 ➡ 392

 To try to impose on others by violent means what we consider to be the truth is an offense against human dignity and ultimately an offense against God, whose image that person bears.

POPE ST JOHN PAUL II (1920–2005), Message for World Day of Peace 2002

 This is a point which must be clearly reaffirmed: war in God's name is never acceptable! When a certain notion of God is at the origin of criminal acts, it is a sign that that notion has already become an ideology.

POPE BENEDICT XVI, Message for World Day of Peace 2007

300 *How can terrorism be fought effectively?*

The fight against terrorism begins by fighting the possible causes of terrorism. Even international

co-operation, however, cannot limit itself to punitive measures. We must therefore create conditions in which uncontrollable aggression does not build up in the first place or else cannot be manifested. At the same time, the right of self-defence against terrorism cannot be exercised in a moral and legal vacuum.

➡ 513, 514 ➡ 2297 ➡ 392

❞ I believe terrorism cannot be won over by military action. Improving the lives of poor people is a better strategy than spending it on guns.

MUHAMMAD YUNUS (b. 1940), Bangladeshi social entrepreneur, winner of the Nobel Peace Prize

DIGRESSION

 The Church has no wish to hold back the marvellous progress of science. On the contrary, she rejoices and even delights in acknowledging the enormous potential that God has given to the human mind. At times some scientists have exceeded the limits of their scientific competence by making certain statements or claims. But here the problem is not with reason itself, but with the promotion of a particular ideology which blocks the path to authentic, serene, and productive dialogue.

POPE FRANCIS, EG 243

 301 *What ethical principles are generally recognized in the natural sciences today?*

There are four principles that are accepted world-wide: 1. *Universality:* the effort to achieve generalizability through verifiable, standardized argumentation; 2. *Communalism:* the right of all to share in the results of science; 3. *Disinterestedness:* the setting aside of the researcher's private interests; 4. *Scepticism:* the willingness to have one's own findings called into question.

302 *Can scientific findings be misused?*

Yes. Since the time of the atom bomb, at the latest, we have known that science does not take place in an ethics-free environment. Today this topic is discussed above all in the field of "biosecurity". How should we deal with the research that might contribute to medical progress or other socially important goals but that at the same time could also be misused by bio-terrorists or other criminals? For in fact many research findings in the life sciences can not only be applied for the benefit of individuals and of society but also misused with the intention to harm.

→ 509 → 2293–2294

303 What is meant by DURC?

Dual Use Research of Concern (abbreviated DURC) includes studies relevant to biosecurity that are expected to produce knowledge, products, or technologies that can be misused immediately by third parties to harm the life or health of people, the environment, or other legally protected goods and interests.

304 What can be done to prevent terrorists from spreading, for example, synthetic pathogens as weapons?

First, we must create an awareness worldwide that "freedom of science" requires a background of valid legal systems. The scientists themselves also need an ethical code of research; it is not enough for them to be concerned only about the technical side of their work. Furthermore, regulations and controls are needed at the international level. Research can no longer be limited to a single nation. It is irresponsible today not to provide an appropriate risk-prevention strategy.

 Scientific research leads to the knowledge of ever new truths about man and about the cosmos, as we see it. The true good of humanity, accessible in faith, unfolds the horizons within which the process of its discovery must move. Consequently research, for example, at the service of life and which aims to eliminate disease, should be encouraged. Also important are investigations that aim to discover the secrets of our planet and of the universe, in the awareness that the human being is not in charge of creation to exploit it foolishly but to preserve it and make it inhabitable. Thus faith, lived truly, does not come into conflict with science but, rather, co-operates with it, offering the basic criteria to promote the good of all and asking it to give up only those endeavours which—in opposition to God's original plan—produce effects that are detrimental to the human being. For this reason too it is reasonable to believe: if science is a precious ally of faith for understanding God's plan for the universe, faith, remaining faithful to this very plan, permits scientific progress always to be achieved for the good and truth of man.
POPE BENEDICT XVI,
21st November 2012

From important Church documents

PEACE

Pacem in Terris

Thinking of Peace in Terms of Human Nature

Many people think that the laws which govern man's relations with the State are the same as those which regulate the blind, elemental forces of the universe. But it is not so; the laws which govern men are quite different. The Father of the universe has inscribed them in man's nature, and that is where we must look for them; there and nowhere else.

Pope St John XXIII, Encyclical Pacem in Terris (1963), 4

Pacem in Terris

The Obligation to Disarm

There is a common belief that under modern conditions peace cannot be assured except on the basis of an equal balance of armaments and that this factor is the probable cause of this stockpiling of armaments. Thus, if one country increases its military strength, others are immediately roused by a competitive spirit to augment their own supply of armaments. And if one country is equipped with atomic weapons, others consider themselves justified in producing such weapons themselves, equal in destructive force. ... [E]ven though the monstrous power of modern weapons does indeed act as a deterrent, there is reason to fear that the very testing of nuclear devices for war purposes can, if continued, lead to serious danger for various forms of life on earth. Hence justice, right reason, and the recognition of man's dignity cry out insistently for a cessation to the arms race. The stock-piles of armaments which have been built up in various countries must be reduced all round and simultaneously by the parties concerned. Nuclear weapons must be banned. A general agreement must be reached on a suitable disarmament programme, with an effective system of mutual control. ... Everyone, however, must realize that, unless this process of disarmament be thoroughgoing and complete, and reach men's very souls, it is impossible to stop the arms race, or to reduce armaments, or—and this is the main thing—ultimately to abolish them entirely. Everyone must sincerely co-operate in the effort to banish fear and the anxious expectation of war from men's minds.

Pope St John XXIII, Encyclical Pacem in Terris (1963), 59–61

Pacem in Terris

Nations Have the Right to Self-Determination

No country has the right to take any action that would constitute an unjust oppression of other countries or an unwarranted interference in their affairs. On the contrary, all should help to develop in others an increasing awareness of their duties, an adventurous and enterprising spirit, and the resolution to take the initiative for their own advancement in every field of endeavour.

Pope St John XXIII, Encyclical Pacem in Terris (1963), 64

The Absurdity of the Arms Trade

Solicitudo Rei Socialis

If arms production is a serious disorder in the present world with regard to true human needs and the employment of the means capable of satisfying those needs, the arms trade is equally to blame. Indeed, with reference to the latter it must be added that the moral judgement is even more severe. As we all know, this is a trade without frontiers capable of crossing even the barriers of the blocs. It knows how to overcome the division between East and West, and above all the one between North and South, to the point—and this is more serious—of pushing its way into the different sections which make up the southern hemisphere. We are thus confronted with a strange phenomenon: while economic aid and development plans meet with the obstacle of insuperable ideological barriers, and with tariff and trade barriers, arms of whatever origin circulate with almost total freedom all over the world.

Pope St John Paul II, Encyclical Sollicitudo Rei socialis (1987), 24

No Peace without Justice

Evangelii Gaudium

Today in many places we hear a call for greater security. But until exclusion and inequality in society and between peoples are reversed, it will be impossible to eliminate violence. The poor and the poorer peoples are accused of violence, yet without equal opportunities the different forms of aggression and conflict will find a fertile terrain for growth and eventually explode. When a society—whether local, national, or global—is willing to leave a part of itself on the fringes, no political programmes or resources spent on law enforcement or surveillance systems can indefinitely guarantee tranquility. This is not the case simply because inequality provokes a violent reaction from those excluded from the system, but because the socioeconomic system is unjust at its root. Just as goodness tends to spread, the toleration of evil, which is injustice, tends to expand its baneful influence and quietly to undermine any political and social system, no matter how solid it may appear. If every action has its consequences, an evil embedded in the structures of a society has a constant potential for disintegration and death. It is evil crystallized in unjust social structures, which cannot be the basis of hope for a better future.

Pope Francis, Apostolic Exhortation Evangelii Gaudium (2013), 59

QUESTIONS
305–328

Personal
and Societal
Commitment

For I was hungry
and you gave me food,
I was thirsty
and you gave me drink,
I was a stranger and you welcomed me,
I was naked and you clothed me,
I was sick and you visited me,
I was in prison and
you came to me.

MT 25:35–36

You show that you are a letter from Christ … written not with ink but with the Spirit of the living God, not on tablets of stone but on tablets of human hearts.

2 COR 3:3

The seven gifts of the Holy Spirit: the gift of understanding, the gift of wisdom, the gift of counsel, the gift of knowledge, the gift of fortitude, the gift of fear of the Lord, the gift of piety.

Compiled from various passages of the Old and New Testament

305 *Is being Christian a private matter?*

No one can be a Christian merely for his own benefit. Coming to Jesus, seeking his friendship, and following him also means publicly professing faith in him, allowing him to speak to us and commission us. "You are the light of the world. A city set on a hill cannot be hidden. Nor do men light a lamp and put it under a bushel, but on a stand, and it gives light to all in the house" (Mt 5:14–15). *All of us* who have been baptized and confirmed—even when we have not been specially commissioned to do so as a priest, deacon, catechist, or religion teacher—are "messengers" and "witnesses" of the Gospel. "Go into all the world and preach the gospel to the whole creation" (Mk 16:15), and "make disciples of all nations, baptizing them in the name of the Father and of the Son and of the Holy

Spirit (Mt 28:19). So that we might proclaim the Kingdom of God (and not ourselves) in word and deed, God gives us the seven gifts of the Holy Spirit.

➡ 71 ➡ 763–769, 774–776, 780 ➡ 123

306 Why must a Christian become socially involved?

"God is love" (1 Jn 4:8), and "Charity is at the heart of the Church's social doctrine" (Pope Benedict, CiV 2). Being Christian, however, means more than adopting particular values and convictions. At its core, being a Christian is an encounter with the person of Christ. Seeking him also in the "least" of our brothers (Mt 25:40), following him, indeed, imitating him (Thomas à Kempis) is the most direct way of being a Christian. Jesus had respect for the freedom and dignity of sinners and the socially marginalized. Jesus himself is the social → AGENDA of the Church. Catholic social teaching is only the systematic development of what is already present in its fullness in Jesus Christ: the man who is rediscovered in his original dignity (personhood), who is freed from greed and sin and seeks to serve his neighbour (solidarity), who keeps the "welfare of the city" (Jer 29:7) in mind (common good), as well as a society in which groups and communities can develop freely in peace and justice (subsidiarity)—that is the grand vision.

➡ 555 ➡ 91 ➡ 11

307 How would Jesus act today? How are we supposed to know what to do?

With her social doctrine, the Church does not give us a quick-and-easy recipe book that specifies every last detail of how we can do God's will in our contemporary conflicts and societal upheavals. But by learning the principles of her social doctrine, deepening our sacramental life, and seeking in prayer God's will for

> Holiness: allowing God to live his life in us.
>
> **ST TERESA OF CALCUTTA**

> I cannot think of love without a pressing need for conformity, for likeness and, above all, for sharing all the pains and difficulties, all the hardships of life. To be rich, at ease, living comfortably off my possessions when you were poor, afflicted, and living painfully off a hard labour—no, I cannot, my God; I cannot love like that.
>
> **CHARLES DE FOUCAULD** (1858–1916)

AGENDA
from the Latin word for "things to be done"

The revolutions of history have changed political and economic systems, but none have really changed the human heart. True revolution, the revolution that radically transforms life, was brought about by Jesus Christ through his Resurrection. Moreover Benedict XVI said of this revolution that "it is the greatest mutation in the history of humanity". →

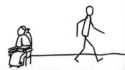

→ Let us think about this: it is the greatest mutation in humanity's history, it is a true revolution, we are revolutionaries and, what is more, revolutionaries of this revolution. For we have taken this road of the greatest metamorphosis in humanity's history. In this day and age unless Christians are revolutionaries they are not Christians.

POPE FRANCIS, 17th June 2013

You know that those who are supposed to rule over the Gentiles lord it over them, and their great men exercise authority over them. But it shall not be so among you; but whoever would be great among you must be your servant, and whoever would be first among you must be slave of all. For the Son of man also came not to be served but to serve, and to give his life as a ransom for many.

MK 10:42–45

O LORD, you have searched me and known me! You know when I sit down and when I rise up; you discern my thoughts from afar. You search out my path and my lying down, and are acquainted with all my ways.

PS 139:1–3

our concrete circumstances, we can be confident of God's guidance and support.

➡ **81–86** ➡ **1776–1779, 1783 ff.**
➡ **291, 295, 297, 397–398**

308 *What is the Christian way of living together?*

If "power" is central, then societies are structured according to the principle of "Might makes right." That, of course, is not Christian; life together in society then becomes a battle for self-preservation. If "work" is held up as the pinnacle of meaning in societal coexistence, then people soon feel that they are harnessed to a meaningless machine and enslaved. Nor does God want us to take "luck" or "comfort" as our highest good. Life would then resemble a lottery that often favours those who cheat; we would follow our instincts and drives and impose all sorts of constraints on ourselves in order to prevent the worst from happening. Catholic social doctrine says: God's master plan for human coexistence is *social charity*. When we live in the sight of a personal God who

willed us and has some *purpose* for us, then we are children of a common father, brothers and sisters to one another. Then gratitude, meaning, and responsibility determine our individual and common life. A culture of mutual respect comes about. Then trust, consolation, and joy in life make sense. Social charity overcomes the spirit of impersonality, creates emotional cohesion in society, and makes possible a social consciousness that even transcends denominational boundaries.

➡ **582–583** ➡ **1889, 2212** ➡ **321, 324**

 Even the longest journey begins with the first step.

Chinese proverb

309 *What is the first step toward faith-based social involvement?*

Nothing motivates more profoundly than *love*. Someone who loves can accomplish great works and go a long way. Therefore, the first step is always to build up an intensive personal relationship with Jesus ("What the Heart of Jesus wants, I will do", Charles de Foucauld), to develop an ever deeper love for the Church,

 Love is the greatest power for the transformation of reality because it pulls down the walls of selfishness and fills the ditches that keep us apart.

POPE FRANCIS, 17th June 2013

and to lead a socially committed life. This motivates a Christian not to overlook even the "least ones" whom Jesus took so much to heart. It motivates a Christian to witness to his faith even in a recognizably hostile environment. It motivates a Christian to lead an alternative life-style of hospitality, reconciliation, and peace. It motivates a Christian, if necessary, even to give his life, when the cause of truth and justice demands it.

Do you know what the best tool is for evangelizing the young? Another young person. Do not be afraid to go and to bring Christ into every area of life, to the fringes of society, even to those who seem farthest away, most indifferent.

POPE FRANCIS to young people at World Youth Day in Rio 2013

➡ 326–327 ➡ 1691–1698 ➡ 348, 454

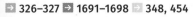

One thing Jesus asks of me: That I lean on him and only in him I put complete trust; that I surrender myself to him unreservedly. Even when all goes wrong and I feel as if I am a ship without a compass, I must give myself completely to him. I must not attempt to control God's action.

ST TERESA OF CALCUTTA (1910–1997)

310 *Why should I become involved in an explicitly "Christian" way?*

Many say: The main thing is to be a good person! What need is there to add anything "Christian" to that? History shows, however, that mere humanism of an atheistic sort has often left mankind in the lurch. Nowhere is "what is human" better promoted than with God. Only in the light of Christ can we properly understand what it means to be human (cf. GS 22). Someone who does the will of God represents the true interests of man, precisely in those areas where human beings are weak, dependent on help, and seemingly "useless". Even though a few Church leaders have sometimes

> ## Do as God did: become a man!
> **BISHOP FRANZ KAMPHAUS** (b. 1932), bishop emeritus of the German diocese of Limburg

falsified and betrayed the will of God, God has made the Church the place where human beings can reach true fulfillment with his help. Christ did not live for himself, but "for us"; he even went to a horrible death for every individual human being. And he did so for the most social of all motives: out of love. That is why, ultimately, a follower of Christ cannot act asocially without being a Christian in name only.

> The people who keep on asking if they can't lead a decent life without Christ, don't know what life is about.
>
> **C. S. LEWIS** (1868–1963)

➡ **6–7, 327** ➡ **1816, 2044–2046** ➡ **307**

311 *What support will I have if I become involved?*

> He who did not spare his own Son but gave him up for us all, will he not also give us all things with him?
>
> **ROM 8:32**

Christians have a home in the Church, brothers and sisters who are animated by the same hope. Their strength is also limited, but they draw from God's reservoir. The *sacraments* make them strong and steadfast. The *Word of God* lends them insight and gives them wings. We can rely on the Word of God and be assured of this because of the testimonies of the first Christians, many of whom went to their deaths for their profession of faith. If the evangelists had merely made up the Resurrection of Jesus, they certainly would not have been willing to be insulted for it or to die for it. The occasionally differing accounts in the Gospels go to show that they are credible testimonies. If the evangelists had in fact wanted to bring an invented ideology into the world, they could have ironed out the discrepancies.

→ 1, 18–19, 60 → 168, 748–750 → 24, 121–126

312 *Welfare states organize comprehensive social transfers. What need is there for involvement by the Church?*

Money alone does not create a humane society as the Gospel understands it. Visiting the sick, welcoming the stranger, caring for the imprisoned—these things cannot be delegated exclusively to public institutions and professional specialists. State-organized assistance programmes are important, but often they are also an excuse not to have to do anything more for the needy ourselves. The Church's programmes, such as charitable institutions, social services, soup kitchens, clothing drives, etc., are remarkable above all because in them the needy and those who are helping meet personally and do so with the appreciative awareness that we are all loved by God. This spirit makes the difference!

→ 571–572 → 1889, 1892–1896 → 446–447

313 *Why should I become involved specifically in the Church?*

Outside the Church there are many excellent, worthwhile organizations in which Christians can become involved. Pope Francis challenges the Church not to remain in herself but to go "to the peripheries... to the limits of human existence" and poverty. But this must not lead the Church to overextend herself socially and lose her power to change society, just

And the angel of the LORD came again a second time and touched him [Elijah], and said, "Arise and eat, else the journey will be too great for you." And he arose, and ate and drank, and walked in the strength of that food forty days and forty nights to Horeb, the mount of God.

1 KINGS 19:7–8

I would prefer even the worst possible Christian world over the best pagan world, because in a Christian world there is room for things that no pagan world ever made room for: cripples and sick people, the old and the weak, and there was more than just room for them: love for those who seemed and still seem useless to the godless world. I believe in Christ, and I believe that 800 million Christians on this earth can change the face of the earth. And I leave it to the reflection and imagination of my contemporaries to picture a world in which there had been no Christ.

HEINRICH BÖLL (1917–1985), winner of the Nobel Prize for Literature

 You are the salt of the earth; but if salt has lost its taste, how shall its saltiness be restored?

MT 5:13

because many Christians prefer to become involved outside the Church instead of doing so together with their brothers and sisters. The past sins of Catholics and individual bad experiences are no reason to withdraw from the charitable and social works of the Church. Strictly speaking, there is no such thing as "the Church", if that is understood as an organization that consists of (active) officials and (passive) beneficiaries. The Church is a place of God's presence

Those who are well have no need of a physician, but those who are sick; I came not to call the righteous, but sinners.

MK 2:17

" You and I!

ST TERESA OF CALCUTTA (1910–1997), in answer to the question, what in the Church most needs to change

in the world, a *body* that consists of all the baptized, a *people* made up of sinners and saints. We are all "the Church". Then, too, the Church is always what we make of her as her members. That is why every Catholic must be involved in the Church and for the Church and find his own way of shaping society along with her in the spirit of the Gospel. One Christian is no Christian! Together we are supposed to be the *salt of the earth* and *the light of the world*.

→ 575–576 → 770–773, 781–782, 787–790, 823–829 → 121–128

314 Why do socially committed Christians need pastoral ministers?

It is a good thing that already in the Gospel Jesus thought of "shepherds" who lovingly care for those who are entrusted to them and, if necessary, go after them when they wander off and go astray (Mt 18:12–13). Socially committed laymen need to listen to spiritual directors and their encouragement, guidance, and consolation, but even more they need to receive the Blessed Sacrament regularly, if possible even daily. Giving them the gift of the sacraments, especially the Eucharist and Reconciliation, but also assisting them in crisis situations and in life-changing decisions is one of the most urgent tasks of a true spiritual director. Another apostolic service to the people of God is networking and strengthening mutually supportive core groups of believers through theological and spiritual input. Moreover, young people and those who are thinking about joining the Catholic Church need substantial catechesis so that they can learn about their faith—an authentic mission for bishops, priests, and other pastoral ministers.

➡ 3, 577, 580 ➡ 874, 896 ➡ 248–259

315 What special things do Christians have to offer their fellowmen?

Not special things, but *Someone special:* Jesus Christ. Christians who fight for a more humane world in the midst of poverty and misery do not necessarily have better social programmes or better

The priest is not a mere office-holder, like those which every society needs in order to carry out certain functions. Instead, he does something which no human being can do of his own power: in Christ's name he speaks the words which absolve us of our sins, and in this way he changes, starting with God, our entire life. Over the offerings of bread and wine he speaks Christ's words of thanksgiving, which are words of transubstantiation—words which make Christ himself present, the Risen One, his Body and Blood—words which thus transform the elements of the world, which open the world to God and unite it to him. The priesthood, then, is not simply "office" but sacrament: God makes use of us poor men in order to be, through us, present to all men and women, and to act on their behalf. This audacity of God who entrusts himself to human beings—who, conscious of our weaknesses, nonetheless considers men capable of acting and being present in his stead—this audacity of God is the true grandeur concealed in the word "priesthood".

POPE BENEDICT XVI, Homily at the conclusion of the Year for Priests, 2010

In 1973, we decided to have adoration one hour every day. We have much work to do. Our homes for the sick and dying destitute are full everywhere. And from the time we started having adoration every day, our love for Jesus became more intimate, our love for each other more understanding, our love for the poor more compassionate, and we have double the number of vocations.

ST TERESA OF CALCUTTA (1910–1997)

> Through [Christ our Lord] the holy exchange that restores our life has shone forth today in splendour: when our frailty is assumed by your Word not only does human mortality receive unending honour but by this wondrous union we, too, are made eternal.

Preface III of the Nativity of the Lord

> If our religion is really the truth, if the Gospel is truly God's word, then we ought to believe it and live accordingly, even if we did so all alone.

CHARLES DE FOUCAULD
(1858–1916)

financial policies; often they do not even have greater idealism in their backpacks. Ultimately they have only one thing to communicate: a God who became man. No philosophy and no other religion knows so much about the Almighty. The God of Jesus Christ knows and understands us in our humanity. Many people today are lonely and feel abandoned in an anonymous society. Not even the Internet with all sorts of social networks can replace personal interaction. There is still a yearning to be accepted personally as we are, with our strengths and weaknesses. Our Christian proclamation says: Every individual is loved quite personally by God, and every individual can encounter this love through a relationship with Jesus Christ. That is a great message, particularly for people who are going through crises and asking themselves questions about the meaning of life and the future.

➡ 577 ➡ 871–873, 898–913 ➡ 138–139, 440

> Only live fish can swim against the current.
Unknown

> There is much suffering in the world—very much. And the material suffering is suffering from hunger, suffering from homelessness, from all kinds of disease, but I still think that the greatest suffering is being lonely, feeling unloved, just having no one. I have come more and more to realize that it is being unwanted that is the worst disease that any human being can ever experience.

ST TERESA OF CALCUTTA
(1915-2005)

316 *What can I do so as not to be alone in my social commitment?*

In many countries, someone who decides to live *with Jesus* and *in the Church* runs the risk of walking a lonely, misunderstood path. The lies of materialism and hedonism flatter the world and mislead many people into a life of illusion and superficial pleasures. This is why we need the "Church in miniature": core groups, domestic churches, prayer meetings,

small cells, Bible discussion groups, religious communities, study groups, etc. In a small, friendly community, young Christians can strengthen one another in the faith. Together they can pray, seek God's will, form groups of people interested in learning more about

> Where two or three are gathered in my name, there am I in the midst of them.
> **MT 18:20**

their faith, become acquainted with Church teaching, and even spend their free time with each other. Where such groups do not yet exist, they should be founded, even if they have only two or three members at first. The important thing is that these groups be integrated into the specific local parish community, for example, by regularly celebrating the Holy Eucharist together with it.

> You are going to laugh: the Bible!
> **BERTOLT BRECHT,** a non-Christian playwright, when asked what his favourite book was

→ 576 → 1877–1882 → 122, 211, 321

> Do not be disturbed by the Scriptures which you do not yet understand, nor be puffed up by what you do understand; but wait with submission for what you do not understand, and hold fast with charity to what you do understand.

ST AUGUSTINE (354–430)

Study this Catechism with passion and perseverance. Make a sacrifice of your time for it! Study it in the quiet of your room; read it with a friend; form study groups and networks; share with each other on the Internet. By all means continue to talk with each other about your faith. You need to know what you believe. You need to know your faith with that same precision with which an IT specialist knows the inner workings of a computer.

POPE BENEDICT XVI,
Foreword to YOUCAT

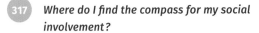

317 *Where do I find the compass for my social involvement?*

No book is more important for Christians than SACRED SCRIPTURE. "To read Sacred Scripture", St Francis of Assisi says, "is to take advice from Christ." Besides Scripture, the Catholic Church lives by sacred Tradition, the living faith of the Church enkindled by the fire of the Holy Spirit. In the CATECHISM OF THE CATHOLIC CHURCH, this faith, which has grown and become deeper over the course of two millennia, has found its contemporary expression. Everything that a Christian should know about the contents and the necessary form of his faith is collected in this volume. Someone who is socially committed and involved finds the central teachings of the Church in the social encyclicals from Pope Leo XIII on. They are concisely summarized in the COMPENDIUM OF THE SOCIAL DOCTRINE OF THE CHURCH. Then there is YOUCAT, to give young people easier access to the Catechism. DOCAT was composed in order to circulate the Church's social teaching widely among young people.

→ 580–583 → 2419–2425 → 438–440

318   Can the Church change her doctrine and adapt to the spirit of the times?

The truths of the faith are not up for grabs. They do not depend on majorities, and they exist independently of the percentage of the population that currently agrees with them. The Church will never rewrite her CREED; she cannot change the number or the content of the SACRAMENTS or decide that there will be more than TEN COMMANDMENTS or fewer. Nor will she ever modify the original form of her LITURGY and PRAYER. Nevertheless, the Church would sin against the Holy Spirit if she did not put out all her feelers for the "signs of the time" in which God is speaking to us today, too. The insights gained from that process can lead to a deepening and elaboration of the Church's teaching; they will never replace, however, the sure, hard-won knowledge of the Church (DOGMAS). Precisely in her social teaching, the Church is expected to keep applying her excellent set of tools better to the challenges of societal, political, and economic change.

→ 72–75 → 185–197, 1084–1098, 2052–2074
→ 13, 25–28, 143, 344–349

> The joys and the hopes, the griefs and the anxieties of the men of this age, especially those who are poor or in any way afflicted, these are the joys and hopes, the griefs and anxieties of the followers of Christ. To carry out such a task, the Church has always had the duty of scrutinizing the signs of the times and of interpreting them in the light of the Gospel. Thus, in language intelligible to each generation, she can respond to the perennial questions which men ask about this present life and the life to come, and about the relationship of the one to the other.

Vatican Council II, GS introduction

The Church's mission cannot manage without the laity, who, drawing strength from the Word of God, from the sacraments, and from prayer, must live the faith at the heart of the family, school, work, popular movements, unions, political parties, and the government, by bearing witness to the joy of the Gospel.
POPE FRANCIS,
19th May 2014

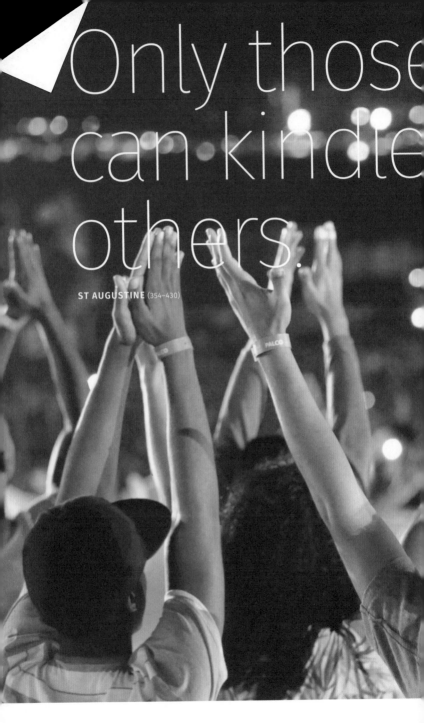

Only those
can kindle
others.

ST AUGUSTINE (354–430)

who burn
a fire in

I am a consistent critic of "party-parliamentarism". I am for non-partisan elections of true people's representatives who are accountable to their districts, and who in case of unsatisfactory work can be recalled. I do understand and respect the formation of groups on economical, co-operative, territorial, educational, professional and industrial principles, but I see nothing organic in political parties.

ALEKSANDR SOLZHENIT-SYN (1918–2008), winner of the Nobel Peace Prize

We help, we lead others to Jesus with our words and our lives, with our witness. I like to recall what St Francis of Assisi used to say to his friars: "Preach the Gospel at all times; if necessary, use words." Words come … but witness comes first: people should see the Gospel, read the Gospel, in our lives.

POPE FRANCIS, 27th September 2013

319 Can I become active in a political party even if its positions do not always agree with those of Christian doctrine?

Yes. As Catholics we have the mission of transforming society into a "civilization of love". When we become active in political parties, we take in hand the means with which to prove our solidarity with the weak. We serve the common good by emphasizing the primacy of the human person in party work and by being mindful of subsidiary societal structures. Political parties devise platforms for themselves, and they need majorities in order to implement them. Since a Christian platform is often connected with inconvenient positions, there will scarcely be any parties in which Christian doctrine is reflected 100 percent. That makes it all the more important for Catholics to collaborate responsibly so as to strengthen the right positions and make them capable of winning a majority. The prerequisite for responsible involvement is a fundamental recognition by the party of inviolable human dignity, of human rights, personhood, and the defence of innocent human life at all stages of its development and in all conditions of dependence, of marriage as a union of a man and a woman, and also of the Church's legal status in our society, as is codified in various national constitutions. Catholic Christians have no place in political parties in which violence against human life or dignity is glorified or approved or that have a platform that includes social hatred, demagoguery, racism, or class warfare.

→ 573–574 → 2442 → 440

320 Should I become active in non-Christian unions, associations, and organizations?

Yes. Christians must not retreat into a ghetto of like-minded people. A good, humanly trustworthy soccer player who admits to his team that he is a Catholic

Christian gives just as splendid a testimony as a member of a trade union who is generally known to be fighting for justice out of Christian motives. There are of course three prerequisites for such involvement: I must not collaborate in anything that contradicts the dignity of my Christian vocation (excessive consumption of alcohol, harmful rituals, sexual libertinism, etc.). My involvement must not hinder me in the expression of my faith. And my involvement must not be misused ideologically. Caution is called for when nice-sounding social goals are only the extension of ideological interests that remain completely silent about the Christian component. For then well-meaning Christians quickly become harnessed to the carriages of non-Christian powers.

➡ 71–72, 83–84, 327, 571–574 ➡ 2442 ➡ 440

321   *Are there professions or particular sorts of social involvement that are incompatible with our faith?*

Yes, there are fields of activity and professions that clearly contradict Christian anthropology and the Church's minimum ethical standards. In following Christ, Christians must be willing to accept occupational disadvantages as part of the bargain, even when they are under great economic pressure. It is impossible to be a Christian and at the same time to work in an abortion or euthanasia facility. Prostitution, pimping, the production and distribution of pornography are just as definitely forbidden as indirect or direct participation in the drug trade, human trafficking, and other harmful, oppressive, and degrading practices. In banks and in the finance sector, Christians are pressured more and more often to sell bad products to their customers. Journalists must decide in conscience how far they can go along with certain practices in the popular media without

Those who follow this evil path in life, such as members of the mafia, are not in communion with God: they are excommunicated. When adoration of money is substituted for adoration of the Lord, this pathway leads to sin, to personal interest and exploitation.
POPE FRANCIS, Calabria, 21st June 2014

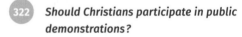

Have courage, go forward, and make noise. Where there are young people so should there be noise. Go ahead! In life there will always be people who suggest that you slow down, blocking your path. No! Go against the tide of this civilization that is harming itself. Do you understand this? Go against the current; and this means making noise, go ahead but with the values of beauty, goodness, and truth. I wanted to tell you this. Be joyful young people!

POPE FRANCIS,
28th August 2013

,, Nothing is more difficult and nothing demands more character than to be publicly opposed to the times and to say No loud and clear.

KURT TUCHOLSKY (1880–1935), German author

losing their identity as Christians. Belonging to Jesus means: no professional, financial, economic, or political collaboration with criminal organizations (Mafia, 'Ndrangheta, etc.), governmental systems of injustice, or businesses that destroy the environment, violate human dignity (sub-living wages, sickening workplace conditions, child labour), harass and persecute the Church, manufacture weapons of mass destruction, or ruthlessly pursue profits with no care about social consequences.

➡ 193, 332 ➡ 1939–1942 ➡ 440

322 *Should Christians participate in public demonstrations?*

It goes without saying that Christians should go out into the streets more frequently than in the past and not just when their own concerns are at stake. Wherever the powerful suppress justice, Christians must be in the first row of protestors. Pope Francis says: "Young people in the streets. ... Please, don't leave it to others to be the protagonists of change. You are the ones who hold the future!" (Pope Francis on 27th July 2013, at World Youth Day in Rio de Janeiro) Christians must demonstrate (with others) to protest

hatred and violence, degrading workplace conditions, the withholding of just wages, the destruction of livelihoods, or the oppression of minorities. Often Christians want to be good citizens and therefore are less skilled in the methods of public protest than left-leaning political groups, for example. They must learn that in order to create political awareness, they too must go out into the streets to defend human life from conception to natural death. Because Christianity worldwide is the most persecuted religion, Christians should also protest for the rights of disadvantaged and oppressed Christians, for the observance of Sunday as a work-free day, and against defamation of the Church.

I know that you want to be good soil, true Christians, authentic Christians, not part-time Christians: "starchy", aloof, and Christian in "appearance only". I know that you don't want to be duped by a false freedom, always at the beck and call of momentary fashions and fads. I know that you are aiming high, at long-lasting decisions which are meaningful. Is that true, or am I wrong? Am I right?

POPE FRANCIS, at World Youth Day in Rio, 2013

➡️ 71–72, 284–286 ➡️ 1932, 2185–2188 ➡️ 332, 365–366

323 *What is the significance of national and international meetings of young Christians?*

Pilgrimages, youth camps, prayer festivals, and the World Youth Days bring young Catholic Christians together at regular intervals. In many countries, these events are powerful proclamations of a Christian youth culture. In other countries, they provide inspiring and

Since Baptism is a true entry into the holiness of God through incorporation into Christ and the indwelling of his Spirit, it would be a contradiction to settle for a life of mediocrity, marked by a minimalist ethic and a shallow religiosity.

POPE ST JOHN PAUL II,
Apostolic Letter *Novo Millennio Ineunte* 31

consoling experiences for young Catholics who feel isolated and alone in everyday life because of their faith. The international World Youth Days in particular have led to the growth of a "Catholic feeling", a pride in belonging to this *new people of God* that has grown up among all the peoples of the earth since the times of the apostles. It is not uncommon for young Catholics to relate that a particular World Youth Day or a prayer festival was the initial spark for a radical, life-changing decision: From now on my life belongs to God! Of course, not everyone who has

> The Church is an old woman with wrinkles and creases. But she is my mother. And no one strikes my mother.

KARL RAHNER (1904–1984),
German theologian

I dream of a "missionary option", that is, a missionary impulse capable of transforming everything, so that the Church's customs, ways of doing things, times and schedules, language and structures can be suitably channelled for the evangelization of today's world rather than for her self-preservation.

POPE FRANCIS, EG 27

participated in a World Youth Day instantly becomes a believing Catholic. Nor is every one of those potential Catholics evangelized on

that occasion. But just to experience the Eucharistic community intensified many times over, with such a great number of believers or seekers, can be the beginning of a great life story *with God*.

→ 97–99, 285, 423, 520 → 2178–2179

324 *May a Catholic criticize the Church in public?*

A criticism that arises from an attitude of love and seeks to help the Church in her process of conversion, can be justified. Catherine of Siena, Francis of Assisi, Bernard of Clairvaux, and Popes Benedict XVI and Francis have done so. The more deeply one identifies with the Church, the more unconditionally one follows Jesus, the more pointedly one may remind the Church and her officials about the Gospel. Someone who criticizes priests and bishops must always keep in mind that they are the heirs to a special promise made by Jesus: "He who hears you hears me" (Lk 10:16). At the same time, another Scripture verse applies to them: "Woe to the shepherds who destroy and scatter the sheep of my pasture!" (Jer 23:1). Catholics are not free to reject authoritative Church teaching. A believing Catholic who accepts the basic principles of the Church and her authoritative teachers can nevertheless discuss individual positions critically. Constructive arguments are welcome, when there is an objective basis for them and they are consistent with the fundamental values and principles of Catholic teaching.

→ 117 → 790–796 → 127

325 *When does involvement in the Church betray its own foundations?*

It happens again and again that Church groups, communities, and institutions abandon unity with the Universal Church because they think that they have to act or decide differently in a specific matter.

> By divine institution, Bishops succeed the Apostles through the Holy Spirit who is given to them. They are constituted Pastors in the Church, to be the teachers of doctrine, the priests of sacred worship and the ministers of governance.
>
> Codex Iuris Canonici (Code of Canon Law)

> The trouble with most of us is that we would rather be ruined by praise than saved by criticism.
>
> **NORMAN VINCENT PEALE** (1898–1993), Methodist minister and inspirational author

Beloved, do not believe every spirit, but test the spirits to see whether they are of God; for many false prophets have gone out into the world. By this you know the Spirit of God: every spirit which confesses that Jesus Christ has come in the flesh is of God.

1 JN 4:1–2

99 This is the thrilling romance of Orthodoxy. People have fallen into a foolish habit of speaking of orthodoxy as something heavy, humdrum, and safe. There was never anything so perilous or so exciting as orthodoxy. It was sanity; and to be sane is more dramatic than to be mad. It was the equilibrium of a man behind madly rushing horses...she swerved to the left and right, so exactly as to avoid enormous obstacles...The orthodox church never took the tame course or accepted the conventions: the orthodox church was never respectable. It would have been easier to have accepted the earthly power of the Arians. It would have been easy, in the Calvinist seventeenth century, to fall into the bottomless pit of predestination. It is easy to be a madman; it is easy to be a heretic....To have fallen into any one of the fads from Gnosticism to Christian Science would indeed have been obvious and tame. But to have avoided them all has been one whirling adventure; and in my vision the heavenly chariot flies thundering through the ages, the dull heresies sprawling and prostrate, the wild truth reeling but erect.

G.K. CHESTERTON
(1874–1936) English writer

Very often the reason given for the separation is the need for an anticipated prophetic act—whether taking up weapons against unjust civil regimes, opposition to the precepts of the Church, or the illicit celebration of the Holy Eucharist with Christians from other denominations. The Church does in fact need prophets who will help bring about changes for the better within the Church. Without them, the Church would never have awakened to the problems of workers and would have missed completely the breakthrough of freedom of the press. So it is always important to test carefully whether "prophetic courage" is really serving the Church or whether it originates in willfulness and smugness and results in disobedience and division.

→ 460 → 166, 176–184, 168

326 *How can involvement in social issues be reinforced ecumenically?*

Social life is precisely the area that offers many opportunities for ecumenical collaboration. Making common cause for democracy, protection of the unborn, defence of marriage, peace, and social justice can help lay the foundations for and strengthen the trust between Christians that is required in order to overcome what divides them in other areas and to find the way back to unity in the truth of the Gospel.

→ 159, 135 → 820–822 → 131

327 *How can inter-religious co-operation reinforce involvement in social issues?*

It is obvious that believers of different religions should join forces for the good of mankind and should stand up for justice and peace as well as for environmental protection. Pope Francis describes the spirit in which that should happen: "We do not impose anything, we do not employ any subtle strategies for attracting believers; rather, we bear witness to what we believe and who we are with joy and simplicity. In fact, an encounter wherein each party sets aside his beliefs, pretending to renounce what he holds most dear, would certainly not be an authentic relationship" (28th November 2013). Inter-religious cooperation is therefore possible. Christians must approach those of other faiths with love and trust, but they must also make sure that their own profession of faith remains clear, because occasionally the same words may be used to express completely different concepts of God. There is a real danger of mixing religions (syncretism). Making common cause with radical groups that fight against the Church and try to set up a theocracy with Sharia law is unthinkable.

→ 12 → 817–822, 841–848 → 130, 136

328 *How can Christians and Muslims coexist peacefully?*

In many countries today, Christians are being perse-cuted by radical Muslims. Some Christians run the risk of demonizing the whole Muslim faith community, marginalizing it, and withdrawing all co-operation from it. They forget that many of Muslims condemn vi-olence, and also one of Jesus's central demands: love of neighbour. Where Christians and Muslims live to-gether, they should do everything to promote a good, neighbourly atmosphere and personal relationships. Christians should also distinguish themselves by tak-ing the first step and showing unexpected signs of hospitality and trust.

→ 515–517, 537 → 841 → 136

There is much that we can do to ben-efit the poor, the needy, and those who suffer and to favour justice, promote reconciliation, and build peace. But before all else we need to keep alive in our world the thirst for the absolute and to counter the dominance of a one-dimensional vision of the human person, a vision which reduces hu-man beings to what they produce and to what they consume: this is one of the most insidious temp-tations of our time.
POPE FRANCIS,
20th March 2013

In necessary mat-ters, unity; in du-bious matters, freedom; in all things, love.

ST AUGUSTINE (354–430)

Today is the first day of the rest of your life.

Unknown

From important Church documents

LOVE IN ACTION

The Danger of Exclusion
Centesimus Annus

Those who fail to keep up with the times can easily be marginalized, as can the elderly, the young people who are incapable of finding their place in the life of society, and, in general, those who are weakest or part of the so-called Fourth World. The situation of women too is far from easy in these conditions.

Pope St John Paul II, Encyclical Centesimus Annus (1991), 33

The Language of Works
Centesimus Annus

Today more than ever, the Church is aware that her social message will gain credibility more immediately from the *witness of actions* than as a result of its internal logic and consistency. This awareness is also a source of her preferential option for the poor, which is never exclusive or discriminatory towards other groups. This option is not limited to material poverty, since it is well known that there are many other forms of poverty, especially in modern society—not only economic but cultural and spiritual poverty as well. The Church's love for the poor, which is essential for her and a part of her constant tradition, impels her to give attention to a world in which poverty is threatening to assume massive proportions in spite of technological and economic progress.

Pope St John Paul II, Encyclical Centesimus Annus (1991), 57

Making Room for New Life
Evangelium Vitae

There are still many married couples who, with a generous sense of responsibility, are ready to accept children as "the supreme gift of marriage". Nor is there a lack of families which, over and above their everyday service to life, are willing to accept abandoned children, boys and girls and teenagers in difficulty, handicapped persons, elderly men and women who have been left alone. Many centres in support of life, or similar institutions, are sponsored by individuals and groups which, with admirable dedication and sacrifice, offer moral and material support to mothers who are in difficulty and are tempted to have recourse to abortion. Increasingly, there are appearing in many places groups of volunteers prepared to offer hospitality to persons without a family, who find themselves in conditions of particular distress or who need a supportive environment to help them to overcome destructive habits and discover anew the meaning of life.

Pope St John Paul II, Encyclical Evangelium Vitae (1995), 26

Love and Truth

`Caritas in Veritate`

In the present social and cultural context, where there is a widespread tendency to relativize truth, practicing charity in truth helps people to understand that adhering to the values of Christianity is not merely useful but essential for building a good society and for true integral human development. A Christianity of charity without truth would be more or less interchangeable with a pool of good sentiments, helpful for social cohesion, but of little relevance. In other words, there would no longer be any real place for God in the world. Without truth, charity is confined to a narrow field devoid of relations. It is excluded from the plans and processes of promoting human development of universal range, in dialogue between knowledge and praxis.

Pope Benedict XVI, Encyclical Caritas in Veritate (2009), 4

What Is Charity

`Caritas in Veritate`

Charity is love received and given. … As the objects of God's love, men and women become subjects of charity, they are called to make themselves instruments of grace, so as to pour forth God's charity and to weave networks of charity. This dynamic of charity received and given is what gives rise to the Church's social teaching, which is *caritas in veritate in re sociali:* the proclamation of the truth of Christ's love in society. This doctrine is a service to charity, but its locus is truth. Truth preserves and expresses charity's power to liberate in the ever-changing events of history. It is at the same time the truth of faith and of reason, both in the distinction and also in the convergence of those two cognitive fields. Development, social well-being, the search for a satisfactory solution to the grave socio-economic problems besetting humanity, all need this truth. What they need even more is that this truth should be loved and demonstrated. Without truth, without trust and love for what is true, there is no social conscience and responsibility, and social action ends up serving private interests and the logic of power, resulting in social fragmentation, especially in a globalized society at difficult times like the present.

Pope Benedict XVI, Encyclical Caritas in Veritate (2009), 5

Love Forms Community

`Caritas in Veritate`

Because it is a gift received by everyone, charity in truth is a force that builds community, it brings all people together without imposing barriers or limits. The human community that we build by ourselves can never, purely by its own strength, be a fully fraternal community, nor can it overcome every division and become a truly universal community. The unity of the human race, a fraternal communion transcending every barrier, is called into being by the word of God-who-is-Love. In addressing this key question, we must make it clear, on the one hand, that the logic of gift does not exclude justice, nor does it merely sit alongside it as a second element added from without; on the other hand, economic, social, and political development, if it is to be authentically human, needs to make room for the *principle of gratuitousness* as an expression of fraternity.

Pope Benedict XVI, Encyclical Caritas in Veritate (2009), 34

All Are Required

Evangelii Gaudium

In virtue of their baptism, all the members of the People of God have become missionary disciples (cf. Mt 28:19). All the baptized, whatever their position in the Church or their level of instruction in the faith, are agents of evangelization, and it would be insufficient to envisage a plan of evangelization to be carried out by professionals while the rest of the faithful would simply be passive recipients. The new evangelization calls for personal involvement on the part of each of the baptized. Every Christian is challenged, here and now, to be actively engaged in evangelization; indeed, anyone who has truly experienced God's saving love does not need much time or lengthy training to go out and proclaim that love. Every Christian is a missionary to the extent that he or she has encountered the love of God in Christ Jesus: we no longer say that we are "disciples" and "missionaries", but rather that we are always "missionary disciples".

Pope Francis, Apostolic Exhortation Evangelii Gaudium (2013), 120

Share What You Have Received

Evangelii Gaudium

Of course, all of us are called to mature in our work as evangelizers. We want to have better training, a deepening love, and a clearer witness to the Gospel. In this sense, we ought to let others be constantly evangelizing us. But this does not mean that we should postpone the evangelizing mission; rather, each of us should find ways to communicate Jesus wherever we are. All of us are called to offer others an explicit witness to the saving love of the Lord, who despite our imperfections offers us his closeness, his word, and his strength and gives meaning to our lives. In your heart you know that it is not the same to live without him; what you have come to realize, what has helped you to live and given you hope, is what you also need to communicate to others.

Pope Francis, Apostolic Exhortation Evangelii Gaudium (2013), 121

Being a Disciple

Evangelii Gaudium

Being a disciple means being constantly ready to bring the love of Jesus to others, and this can happen unexpectedly and in any place: on the street, in a city square, during work, on a journey.

Pope Francis, Apostolic Exhortation Evangelii Gaudium (2013), 127

Becoming More Missionary

Evangelii Gaudium

An evangelizing community gets involved by word and deed in people's daily lives; it bridges distances, it is willing to abase itself if necessary, and it embraces human life, touching the suffering flesh of Christ in others. Evangelizers thus take on the "smell of the sheep", and the sheep are willing to hear their voice. An evangelizing community is also supportive, standing by people at every step of the way, no matter how difficult or lengthy this may prove to be. It is familiar with patient expectation and apostolic endurance. Evangelization consists mostly of patience and disregard for constraints of time. Faithful to the Lord's gift, it also bears fruit. An evange-lizing community is always concerned with fruit, because the Lord wants her to be fruitful. It cares for the grain and does not grow impatient at the weeds. The sower, when he sees weeds sprouting among the grain, does not grumble or overreact. He or she finds a way to let the word take flesh in a particular situation and bear fruits of new life, however imperfect or incomplete these may appear. The disciple is ready to put his or her whole life on the line, even to accepting martyrdom, in bearing witness to Jesus Christ, yet the goal is not to make enemies but to see God's word accepted and its capacity for liberation and renewal revealed. Finally, an evangelizing community is filled with joy; it knows how to rejoice always. It celebrates every small victory, every step for-ward in the work of evangelization. ... I dream of a "missionary option", that is, a missionary impulse capable of transforming everything, so that the Church's customs, ways of doing things, times and schedules, language and structures can be suitably channeled for the evangelization of today's world rather than for her self-preservation. The renewal of structures demanded by pastoral conversion can only be understood in this light: as part of an effort to make them more mission-oriented, to make ordinary pastoral activity on every level more inclusive and open, to inspire in pastoral workers a constant desire to go forth and in this way to elicit a positive response from all those whom Jesus summons to friendship with himself.

Pope Francis, Apostolic Exhortation Evangelii Gaudium (2013), 24 and 27

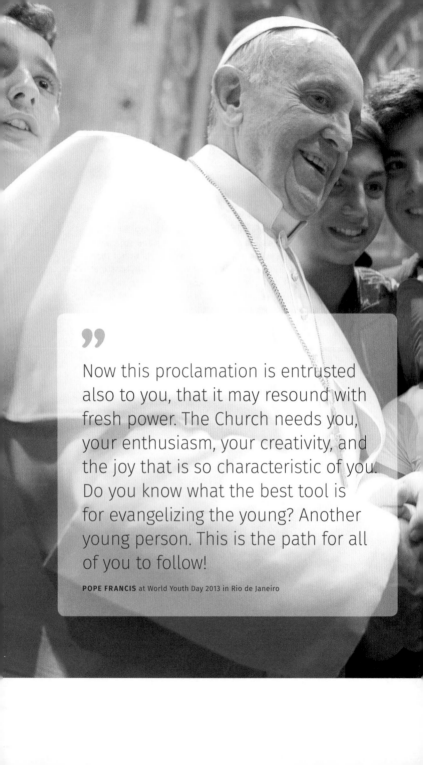

99

Now this proclamation is entrusted also to you, that it may resound with fresh power. The Church needs you, your enthusiasm, your creativity, and the joy that is so characteristic of you. Do you know what the best tool is for evangelizing the young? Another young person. This is the path for all of you to follow!

POPE FRANCIS at World Youth Day 2013 in Rio de Janeiro

Index of Names

Scripture Index

Index of Subjects

Abbreviations

CA	*Centesimus Annus,* Encyclical of Pope John Paul II (1991)	
CiV	*Caritas in Veritate,* Encyclical of Pope Benedict XVI (2009)	
EG	*Evangelii Gaudium,* Apostolic Exhortation of Pope Francis (2013)	
EV	*Evangelium Vitae,* Encyclical of Pope John Paul II (1995)	
GS	*Gaudium et Spes,* Pastoral Constitution of the 2nd Vatican Council on the Church in the Modern World (1965)	
CCC	Catechism of the Catholic Church	
CS	Compendium of the Social Doctrine of the Church	
LE	*Laborem Exercens,* Encyclical of Pope John Paul II (1981)	
LG	*Lumen Gentium,* Dogmatic Constitution of the 2nd Vatican Council on the Church (1964)	
LS	*Laudato Si',* Encyclical of Pope Francis (2015)	
MM	*Mater et Magistra,* Encyclical of Pope John XXIII (1961)	
OA	*Octogesima Adveniens,* Apostolic Exhortation of Pope Paul VI (1971)	
PP	*Populorum Progressio,* Encyclical of Pope Paul VI (1967)	
PT	*Pacem in Terris,* Encyclical of Pope John XXIII (1963)	
QA	*Quadragesimo Anno,* Encyclical of Pope Pius XI (1931)	
RH	*Redemptor Hominis,* Encyclical of Pope John Paul II (1979)	
RN	*Rerum Novarum,* Encyclical of Pope Leo XIII (1891)	
SRS	*Solicitudo Rei Socialis,* Encyclical of Pope John Paul II (1987)	

Acknowledgements

The YOUCAT Foundation thanks not only the various authors and editors who contributed their special competence and their efforts to the project.

It also thanks the Union of Catholics in Economics and Management and its president Bernd-M. Wehner, who gave encouragement for the DOCAT and made possible the financial support that brought young people together to discuss the text of DOCAT.

Likewise the YOUCAT Foundation thanks the Central Office of Catholic Social Sciences in Mönchengladbach which was helpful in so many ways in creating the DOCAT.

We are thankful for all the young photographers who participated in the worldwide photo contest and can now be proud of 'their' photo in DOCAT.

Special thanks to our young critical readers: Laurin Büld, Paul Cremer, Lorena Helfrich, Nathalie Keifler, Judith Klaiber, Benno Klee, Daniel Lui, Stephan Peiffer, Lars Schäfers, Jan Schiefelbein, Maria Schipp, Marcel Urban (under the direction of Barbara Müller, Nils Baer, Marco Bonacker, Alexander von Lengerke, Bernhard Meuser). Wonderful that you have helped us—as representatives of all the young people around the world who are now following the call of Pope Francis to learn the Church's social teaching.

Picture Index

Photographers: 1000 Words /Shutterstock 72-73; Cynthia Abou Zeid 61, 75, 143; altanaka /Shutterstock 120; Jörg Anders/bpk 140; Sarymsakov Andrey /Shutterstock 130; Leonid Andronov /Shutterstock 201; Asia Images /Shutterstock 143; Zvonimir Atletic /Shutterstock 108; Felipe Belloni 17; Martine Boutros 23, 205; Richard Bruneau 188-189, 221; calvio/Thinkstock 151; Diego Cervo /Shutterstock 83; Charles Constantine 178, 246; CoolKengzz/Shutterstock 134; Carmo Cordovil 236, 259; D&S Photographic/Shutterstock.com 232; Dream Perfection /Shutterstock 64; Erzbistum Köln 97; Francisco Eugênio 14; Stefan Fitzek 222; forestpath /Shutterstock 171; Miriam Fricke 105; Yulia Grigoryeva /Shutterstock 37; Gumpanat /Shutterstock 212-213; Jorg Hackemann /Shutterstock 224; Florian Hernschier 114; Historisches Archiv des Erzbistums Köln bzw. AEK, Bildsammlung 97; hxdbzxy /Shutterstock 81; Chris Jenner /Shutterstock 107; David Jesus FSC 232; Marina Jorge 125; Jesus My Joy 64; KAMONRAT /Shutterstock 149; Jorisvo/Shutterstock.com 191; Jorisvo/Shutterstock.com; 242-243 Martin Karski (www.martinkarski.de) 139; kenny1 /Shutterstock 188; Denis Kuvaev /Shutterstock 61; Richard Lagos 90, 134, 212-213; Jeronimo Lauricio 58, 69, 245, 250, 285; Emilie Leclerc 98, 147; Stefan Leimer 203; Alexander von Lengerke 37, 49, 130, 138, 160-161, 291; Christian Lermer 118, 120-121; lotsostock / Shutterstock 125; LWL Westfalen 36; Rob Marmion /Shutterstock 118; Frank May/picture-alliance 270; Riccardo Mayer/Shutterstock 217; Alex Lima Mazullo 101, 103, 208, 242-243, 262-263, 282, 292-293; Meunierd /Shutterstock 147; Mylu 274; Giulio Napolitano/Shutterstock 10; Noble Nooruparayil 46, 74; Vanessa Nossol 274; Kerstin Otto 288-289; Lica Pires 32, 81; Dario Pizzano 76; QQ7 /Shutterstock 160; Radiokafka /Shutterstock 138; Jorge O. Ramírez Carreón 35; Rawpixel.com /Shutterstock 101;176; Rawpixel.com 101; Rawpixel.com 178; Stefano Rellandini/Reuters 10; Sandra Ribeiro Neto 42-43; Gino Santa Maria 184; Angelica Rocha, World Youth Day 208, 288-289; Rido 90; Fabio Santoro / WYD Brasil 50; Lukas Schlichtebrede 126; Benjamin Scofield 250; Hari Seldon 156; Luc Serafin 50, 83, 107, 149, 176, 177, 191, 215; Patrick Sfeir 228-229; Francesco Sforza/Osservatore romano 302-303; lzf /Shutterstock 105; Chris Singshinsuk /Shutterstock 262; Olha Soroka 95; Leandro Carlos Souza Santos 108; Syda Production 245; Thinkstock 192; Timof/Shutterstock 74; Travel Stock /Shutterstock 63; SP-Photo /Shutterstock 16; Stocktrek images/Thinkstock 266; Swapan Photography /Shutterstock 95; Tutti Frutti /Shutterstock 13; Marcel Urban 224; ver0nicka /Shutterstock 250; Mykola Vepryk 72-73, 184;VGstockstudio /Shutterstock 4; Brit Werner 138-139, 294; World Youth Day website 285; Akl Yazbeck 18-19.

Free Sources: Creative Common-Linzenz by-sa-2.0 (http://creativecommons.org/licenses/by-sa/2.0) blu-news.org 171, Trocaire from Ireland (Kibera17) 217, Christian Wolf (www.c-w-design.de) 201; Creative Common-Lizenz by-sa-3.0 (http://creativecommons.org/licenses/by-sa/3.0): 4028mdk09 167; National Archief, Den Haag, Rijksfotoarchief: Fotocollectie Algemeen Nederlands Fotopersbureau (ANEFO), 1945 1989 - negatiefstroken zwart/wit, nummer toegang 2.24.01.05, bestanddeelnummer 922-2301 253; Public Domain: Staff Sgt. Marc Lane (https://www.dvidshub.net/image/190261) 63.